KT-171-325

Kodak

CELEBRATING THE BRAND
CREATIVE CORPORATE SCENOGRAPHY

FOREWORD
VORWORT

Trade shows are markets. Modern trade shows function as mirrors of the economy. But their significance is much greater than a concentrated gathering of competitive businesses. Trade shows reveal much more than the conventional supply and demand. Such events cannot really be invented. They evolve because visionary individuals with clear business objectives enter into partnerships with creative staging experts who produce strategically attractive visual interpretations of the themes. To achieve these objectives, communication structures have to be devised that must not only be rational, but strongly emotional as well, in order to create an ambiance that is best described as the magnetism of the event. Only when these fundamental prerequisites are satisfied can a trade show become a world event. photokina has achieved that status as the World's Fair of Imaging. Global trading was practiced there even before that concept became commonplace. photokina is world-friendly and vibrant, because international brands favor it. But favoring it also means being able to use it efficiently. In that general context, KODAK has set exemplary standards, to the point of developing its own trade show culture. This book documents the fascinating process as it evolves from the inspiration to the execution. »Celebrating the Brand« is meant to be a salute to all those who create trade show stands.

Messen sind Märkte. Diese modernen Tradeshows funktionieren wie Spiegelbilder der Wirtschaft. Ihr Stellenwert ist jedoch weit höher anzusetzen als das konzentrierte Zusammentreffen von wirtschaftlichem Wettbewerb. Messen machen viel mehr sichtbar als die übliche Transparenz von Angebot und Nachfrage. Solche Ereignisse können nicht wirklich erfunden werden. Sie entwickeln sich, weil weitsichtige Menschen mit klarem wirtschaftlichem Kalkül sich partnerschaftlich verbünden mit kreativen Inszenierungsexperten, die den Themen Gesichter geben. Zum Erreichen dieses Zieles müssen kommunikative Strukturen kreiert werden, die sowohl rational wie in besonderem Maße emotional jenes Klima erzeugen, das als Magnetismus des Ereignisses definiert werden kann. Nur wenn diese Grundvoraussetzungen gegeben sind, kann eine Messe ein Weltereignis sein. Die photokina als Weltmesse des Bildes hat diesen Rang. Hier wird bereits »global« gehandelt, als es diesen Begriff noch gar nicht gibt. Die photokina ist deshalb weltoffen und spannend, weil internationale Marken diesen Marktplatz wollen. Mit diesem Wollen verbindet sich zugleich auch der Anspruch des Könnens. KODAK hat in diesem Sinne absolut vorbildliche Maßstäbe gesetzt und so etwas wie eine eigene Messe-Kultur entwickelt. Dieses Buch dokumentiert den spannenden Prozess von der Inspiration bis zur Realisation. »Celebrating the Brand« ist als Appell zu verstehen an alle, die Messen machen.
[Klaus Tiedge]

»The scenographic space is a closed system, a world of its own that has the objective of drawing the greatest possible attention of the visitor to the specific subject, to the message that is being conveyed. Der szenographische Raum ist ein abgeschlossenes System, eine eigene Welt mit dem Ziel, die größtmögliche Konzentration des Besuchers auf das behandelte Thema, auf die zu transportierende Message zu lenken.«
[UWE R. BRÜCKNER]

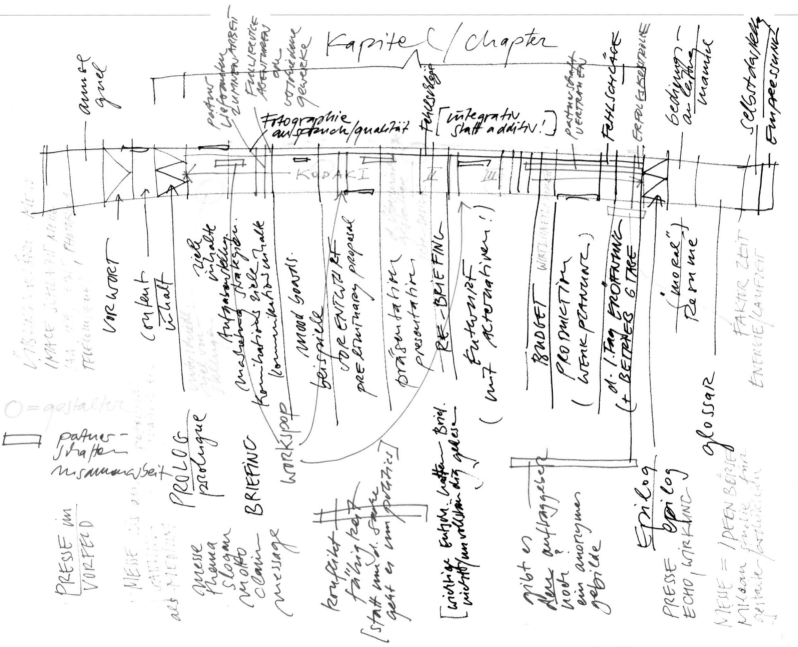

09. 01. 2005:
First conceptual draft for book's
structure

THREE PROJECTS – ONE STRUCTURE

DREI PROJEKTE – EINE STRUKTUR

3 successful trade show stands at 2-year intervals

2 different locations

3 different messages

3 self-standing presentations

All three projects have a common language with a high recognition factor that proves the enormous potential of corporate architecture.

3 erfolgreiche Messestände, im Abstand von je 2 Jahren.

2 verschiedene Locationen

3 unterschiedliche Botschaften

3 eigenständige Auftritte

Alle drei Projekte haben eine gemeinsame Handschrift mit hoher Identifikationskraft und zeigen das enorme Potential von Corporate Architecture

photokina 2000 [KODAK I]

The theme: KODAK The Universal Language

The message: Pictures, analog and digital – Best of both worlds

The location: Hall 8, 5.500 m^2

photokina 2002 [KODAK II]

The theme: KODAK Share Moments. Share life.

The message: Clear focus on output

The location: Hall 4, 8.500 m^2

photokina 2004 [KODAK III]

The theme: KODAK Anytime. Anywhere.

The message: The new digital world of KODAK

The location: Hall 4, 8.500 m^2

THE BRIEF

THE COMPETITION

THE PROPOSAL

WORKSHO

Content, Product, Message Inhalt, Produkt, Botschaft
The first steps in the creative process: analyzing, interpreting and evaluating.
Die ersten Schritte im Kreativprozess, Analysieren, Interpretieren und Bewerten.

Strategy and risk Strategie und Risiko
The creation of concepts and a structured path to completion requires the dedicated application of creative techniques and design methodologies that make an effective planning process possible in the first place. Creative talents, organizational skills and willingness to take risks are needed. The task was made the subject of an invitational competition. Das Gestalten von Konzepten und das strukturierte Umsetzen in die Realität erfordert den gezielten Einsatz von Kreativtechniken und Entwurfsmethodiken, die einen effektiven Gestaltungsprozess erst möglich machen. Konzipieren, Arrangieren und Riskieren ist gefragt. Die Aufgabe war als einstufiger Einladungswettbewerb ausgeschrieben.

The pool of ideas Das Ideenkonzentrat
Conceptual ideas are the result of design- and creative phases that are necessary for presenting the idea, the story and the message in a convincing manner. In a manner of speaking, the pool of ideas and the lifeblood of the designer. Die Konzeptideen sind das Resultat von Entwurfs- und Gestaltungsphasen, die notwendig sind, um die Idee, Story und die Botschaft überzeugend darzustellen. Sozusagen das Ideenkonzentrat und Herzblut der Gestalter.

The first test Die erste Bewährungsprobe
Searching for a common language Auf der Suche nach einer gemeinsamen Sprache.

| AUGUST | SEPTEMBER | OCTOBER | NOVEMBER | DECEMBER | JAN |

Searching, finding, and inventing Das Suchen, Finden und Erfinden

RESET

THE DISCOVERY

The black hole Das Schwarze Loch
The trials and tribulations of a project – doubting, failing, lamenting are the result. Die Irrungen und Wirrungen eines Projekts, Zweifeln, Scheitern und Wehklagen sind die Folge.

Ideas evolve into a concept Ideen werden

THE CONCEPT

Konzept
The concept describes the essential elements such as location, space, object, the interplay of form and content, appearance and significance, taking into consideration the use of such media as light, sound, projection, and additional digital media. Das Konzept beschreibt die wesentlichen Elemente wie Ort, Raum, Objekt, das Zusammenspiel von Form und Inhalt, Abbild und Bedeutung unter Berücksichtigung von medialem Einsatz von Licht, Ton, Projektion und weiterer digitaler Medien.

Conviction, enthusiasm, and confidence. Überzeugung, Begeisterung und Vertrauen
Well prepared and ready to persuade with good ideas. Gut vorbereitet, überzeugen mit guten Ideen.

THE PRESENTATION

The grand gesture and lasting impression Die große Geste, der nachhaltige Eindruck
The independent, surprising, and fascinating creative element that impresses and that is remembered. Das eigenständige, überraschende und faszinierende Gestaltungselement, das prägt und hängenbleibt.

THE KEY TAKE-AWAY

The importance of the overall appearance Die Bedeutung des Gesamterscheinungsbildes
From the first contact to the lasting message Vom ersten Kontakt zur nachhaltigen Botschaft

THE COMMUNICATION CONCEPT

The power of pictures Faszination Fotografie – Die Magie der Bilder
At KODAK, images are not only an important part of staging, they also represent product and are purveyors of significant additional messages. From product shots to emotional pictures. Bei KODAK sind Bilder nicht nur Teil der Inszenierung, sie sind gleichzeitig Produkt, Qualitätsbeweis und wesentliche additive Botschaften. Von der Produktabbildung bis zum emotionalen Stimmungsbild.

THE POTENTIAL OF PHOTOGRAPHY

The magic date Das magische Datum
Feared, yet eagerly anticipated. Stress turns to euphoria. The fascination of the result delights everyone. Gefürchtet und herbeigesehnt. Stress schlägt um in Euphorie. Die Faszination des Ergebnisses macht alle glücklich.

Was the great effort worthwhile? Hat sich der ganze Aufwand gelohnt?
The effect outside and inside the company. Die Wirkung nach außen und nach innen.

THE GRAPHIC CONCEPT

Information, orientation, legibility. Information, Orientierung, Lesbarkeit
A coherent appearance. Everything consistently designed, using color codes for visitor-friendly orientation. Ein durchgängiges Erscheinungsbild. Alles konsequent durchgestaltet mit Farbcodes zur besseren Orientierung. Auf die Dosierung kommt es an.

PLANNING AND PRODUCTION

The significance of details for the overall project. Die Bedeutung der Details für das Ganze
Precision and flexibility are a necessity. The better the planning, the fewer the unpleasant surprises. Good planning requires experience and the courage to try new approaches. Präzision und Flexibilität sind gefragt. Je besser eine Planung, umso weniger unliebsame Überraschungen. Gute Planung braucht Erfahrung und den Mut, Neues ausprobieren zu wollen.

THE OPENING

PRESS

The resonance Die Resonanz
Good care of journalists and ample press material ensure success. It is a known proverb that success has many fathers. Gute Journalistenbetreuung und umfangreiches Pressematerial sichern den Erfolg. Der Erfolg hat bekanntlich viele Väter.

THE RÉSUMÉ

FEBRUARY	MARCH	APRIL	MAY	JUNE	JULY	AUGUST	SEPTEMBER	OCTOBER	NOVEMBER

PHOTOKINA 2000: 20.09. – 29.09.
PHOTOKINA 2002: 25.09. – 30.09.
PHOTOKINA 2004: 28.09. – 03.10.

Legend (right column):

- THE BRIEF
- THE COMPETITION
- THE PROPOSAL
- THE WORKSHOP
- RESET
- THE DISCOVERY
- THE CONCEPT
- THE PRESENTATION
- THE KEY TAKE-AWAY
- THE COMMUNICATION CONCEPT
- POTENTIAL OF PHOTOGRAPHY
- THE GRAPHIC CONCEPT
- PLANNING AND PRODUCTION
- THE OPENING
- PRESS AND EVALUATION
- THE RÉSUMÉ

CONTENT

chapter number / Kapitelnummer

content links
Verweise auf Seiten mit inhaltlichen Zusammenhängen

chapter **I. 1 HEADLINE CHAPTER**

USER MANUAL
LESEANLEITUNG

headline content
Überschrift Inhalt

pages and links Verweise

II S.123
III S.234

The essence for fast readers
Wissenswertes für Schnellleser

Generating a concept begins with the question: »What can this accomplish?«, followed by a vague intuition and finishing with a clear understanding of what it should accomplish. Die Konzeption beginnt immer mit der Frage: Was kann das? Gefolgt von einer vagen Intuition und mündet in einer klaren Vorstellung von dem, was es können sollte.

key learning

This field contains important comments and information for the process of creating a concept. Dieses Feld beinhaltet wichtige Kommentare und Informationen für den konzeptionellen Gestaltungsprozess.

Field for comments
Kommentarbereich

»… not another picture book as an ego trip, but a behind-the-scenes look at a process, with all its ups and downs, confusions and alternatives, misunderstandings, necessary compromises, and ultimately the rewarding applause …«
[URB]

chapter register / Register

»... kein weiteres Bilderbuch als Nabelschau, sondern ein Blick hinter die Kulissen eines Prozesses mit all seinen Höhen und Tiefen, Verwirrungen und Alternativen, Missverständnissen, den notwendigen Kompromissen und dem erlösenden Applaus ...«
[URB]

pagina right page / Pagina rechte Seite
... and left page / ... und linke Seite

BRAND LEADERSHIP WITH LONG TRADITION
MARKENFÜHRUNG HAT TRADITION

George Eastman 1890

As far back as 1888, George Eastman, founder of the Eastman KODAK Company, already recognized the significance of a strong brand name. His idea was that his product and his company should be identified by a single, self-standing and unmistakable brand name. When George Eastman applied to the British Patent Office to register the name KODAK as a trademark, he submitted the following claim: KODAK is not a word from a foreign language, it is a word that I composed myself that has all the advantages of a successful trademark. First of all, it is short. Second, it is easy to pronounce in any language. Third, there is nothing that can be associated in any form with the name KODAK. It was George Eastman's ingenious idea to assemble complicated photographic processes and to combine them to create uncomplicated and easy-to-use products. It was this user-friendly product idea that first made photography accessible to broad segments of the population. He introduced the slogan »You press the button, we do the rest« to promote his first successful multiple-use camera, which he named »The KODAK«.

The price of this camera was $25 and it came loaded with enough film for 100 round exposures. The entire camera had to be returned to KODAK for processing. The cost of processing and returning the reloaded camera and the 100 mounted prints to the owner was $10. The introduction of this simple photographic system started George Eastman on the road to success in the twentieth century. Beginning in 1890, the KODAK brand was presented worldwide. KODAK established subsidiaries and shops in the best locations of the world's major capitals, and this caused the Brand name KODAK quickly to become known across all borders, so that an efficient network of sales and processing could be created. George Eastman recognized the importance of brand design at a very early stage. He gave British arts and crafts architect George W. Wolton the assignment of devising a sales and motivational campaign for his products. The stores were to be luxurious and unconventional and they were also to convey quality, security and confidence. In the year 1935, the corporate identity of KODAK was further refined by incorporating specific KODAK yellow and KODAK red colors as integral components of its corporate design. The powerful KODAK brand and its unmistakable color code strengthen the company's identity and to this day they facilitate the instant recognition of the KODAK brand. George Eastman thought from the inside to the outside, he provided an adequate form for the content, he was a pioneer of modern marketing strategy and very early on he recognized the importance of a strong brand name. To this day, corporate design, corporate architecture and corporate communications are primary components of brand management that characterize the image of the top megabrand KODAK around the world.

1898

1900

1901

1902

Bereits 1888 erkannte George Eastman, der Firmengründer der KODAK Eastman Company, die Bedeutung der Marke. Seine Idee war es, dass die Identität seines Produktes und seines Unternehmens allein über eine klare, eigenständige und unverwechselbare Marke identifiziert werden sollte. George Eastman schrieb an das Britische Patentamt, als er den Namen KODAK als Warenzeichen eintragen ließ, folgende Begründung: KODAK ist kein Fremdwort oder ein Wort aus einer Fremdsprache, ich habe es selbst konstruiert und es beinhaltet alle Vorteile einer erfolgreichen Trademark. Erstens: Es ist kurz. Zweitens: Es kann in allen Sprachen leicht ausgesprochen werden. Drittens: Es existiert nichts, was mit dem Namen KODAK in irgendeiner Form in Verbindung gebracht werden kann. George Eastmans geniale Idee war es, existierende, komplizierte fotografische Vorgänge und Prozesse zusammenzuführen und daraus einfache und problemlose Produkte zu entwickeln. Erst seine »easy to use« Produkt-Ideen machten die Fotografie für breite Bevölkerungsschichten zugänglich. Mit dem Slogan »You press the button we do the rest« warb er für seine erste (Mehrweg-) Kamera, der er den Namen »The KODAK« gab. Diese Kamera kostete $25 und war mit einem Film für 100 Aufnahmen geladen. Die Kamera und der belichtete Film wurden zurückgegeben, und man erhielt die runden Bilder und eine neu geladene Kamera für $10 zurück. Mit der Entwicklung dieses einfachen fotografischen Systems ermöglichte George Eastman den Siegeszug

der Fotografie im zwanzigsten Jahrhundert. Ab 1890 präsentierte sich die Marke KODAK weltweit. KODAK eröffnete Niederlassungen und Geschäfte in den besten Lagen in den großen Hauptstädten der Welt, was zur Folge hatte, dass der Name KODAK schnell bekannt wurde und über alle Grenzen hinweg ein gut funktionierendes Verkaufs- und Labornetz aufgebaut werden konnte. Die Bedeutung von Brand-Design erkannte Eastman sehr früh. Er gab dem britischen Arts-and-Crafts-Architekten George W. Wolton den Auftrag, eine Einkaufs- und Erlebniswelt für seine Produkte zu gestalten. Die Geschäfte sollten luxuriös und außergewöhnlich sein, aber auch Qualität, Sicherheit und Vertrauen vermitteln. Im Jahr 1935 wurde die Corporate Identity von KODAK weiterentwickelt, das KODAK Gelb und KODAK Rot war von da an ein weiterer Bestandteil des Corporate Design. Die einprägsame Marke KODAK mit ihrem unverwechselbaren Farbcode gibt dem Unternehmen zusätzlich Identität und trägt bis heute zur schnellen Identifizierung der Marke KODAK bei. George Eastman dachte von innen nach außen, schloss vom Inhalt auf die adäquate Form, er gilt als einer der Vordenker der modernen Markenführung und erkannte schon sehr früh die Bedeutung des Markenwertes. Corporate Design, Corporate Architecture und Corporate Communication sind bis heute wesentliche Bestandteile der Markenführung und prägen das Image des Top-Megabrands KODAK auf der ganzen Welt.

The deluxe and smartly laid-out interiors of company stores.

Billboard
KODAK Girl
1920

catalogue
1937

BRAND LEADERSHIP FACE TO FACE
MARKENFÜHRUNG AUF AUGENHÖHE

Trade shows are indubitably among the oldest and most important marketing tools. Today, there are new trends that influence trade show activities, such as the increasing globalization of business activities, the digitalization of business procedures by means of new media and growing consumer interest in ancillary emotional benefits and experiential consumerism caused by the saturation of markets. Companies generally no longer pursue mainly operational sales targets with their trade show activities, tailoring them instead to strategic objectives of customer information and communication. Trade shows can promote an up-to-date image and awareness of a company, while also serving as a means for showcasing a product or a brand. Because they offer an opportunity for direct, live introductions and company presentations, they can use powerful imagery to very effectively communicate technical details, benefits and advantages, easy operation, as well as an emotional assurance of the performance of their products and their services. Today's trade show stands are no longer mere showcases, they are communication platforms and working spaces for the exhibitors. The latter expect their trade show participation to produce as many qualified contacts as possible, potential new customers, firm orders and new business opportunities, in an ideal setting for information, communication and customer care. Trade show visitors seek complete solutions and rapid profitability.

Today the need for information before making the decision to buy is extremely high. Offers, products and services are compared and evaluated more critically than ever, based on the most diverse criteria. This is where a trade show stand must provide a dramatically effective setting. A clear and direct approach is preferable. A prerequisite for effectively conveying information and communication is a logical arrangement of the presentations and themes. It must also be taken into account that customers have a limited amount of time, so that it is imperative that visitors be welcomed by qualified and well-trained staff members. The presence of a company or a brand has to be impressive, convincing and memorable. Only when every one of these prerequisites is met do the unique strengths of this medium achieve their maximal effectiveness, namely the direct personal contact and communication at eyelevel. Successful trade show management strives for new creative ways of seeing and scenographically staged theme spaces and action areas, and they are increasingly incorporating top events into the trade fair concepts. Stands at trade shows are communication spaces, and they have become more varied, more colorful, more informative, more communicative and interactive. The advantages of trade fairs have to be weighed against a significant economic disadvantage: trade show participation is cost-intensive. The expenses include the direct costs of the rent of the stand area, the trade show infrastructure, stand construction and stand personal, as well as advertising and mass media communication and follow-up

work after the show. The trend for ever larger and more attractive stands and the integration of events into the stand concepts naturally entails increases in costs. That in turn has triggered discussions about the efficiency of the participation in trade shows. Trade show stands compete for budget allocations with other marketing tools. Trade shows in the investment goods sector enjoy a very large budget share, whereas in the sector of consumer goods and services more consideration is now being given to the distribution of budget allocations to other communication instruments that address similar marketing objectives. Event marketing is currently in great favor. Yet, in spite of all the reservations being raised by marketing strategists, there is nothing more effective than personal contact and direct communication in an emotional environment.

Messen gehören zweifellos zu den ältesten, aber auch zu den wichtigsten Marketinginstrumenten. Aktuelle Trends wie die zunehmende Globalisierung wirtschaftlicher Aktivitäten, die Digitalisierung von Geschäftsprozessen durch den Einsatz neuer Medien sowie die angesichts gesättigter Märkte feststellbare Hinwendung der Konsumenten zum emotionalen Zusatznutzen und Erlebniskonsum beeinflussen die Messeaktivitäten. In der Regel verfolgen Unternehmen mit ihrem Messenengagement nicht mehr vordergründig operative Verkaufsziele, sondern vor allem strategische Ziele der Information und Kommunikation mit dem Kunden. So tragen Messen zur Aktualität und Bekanntheit von Unternehmen bei und bieten eine Identifikationsmöglichkeit für Produkt oder Marke. Durch die Möglichkeit einer ganzheitlichen, direkt erlebbaren Angebots- und Firmenpräsentation können sowohl technische Details, Nutzen und Vorteile, die einfache Bedienung als auch ein emotionales Leistungsversprechen von Produkten und Dienstleistungen imagewirksam vermittelt werden. Messestände sind heute nicht nur Schaufenster,

Trade show stand photokina 1998

sondern immer mehr Kommunikationsplattform und »Workingspace« der Aussteller. Erwartet der Aussteller für das Feedback eines Messeauftritts möglichst viele qualifizierte Kontakte, neue Interessenten und Kunden, konkrete Aufträge und Geschäftsanbahnungen sowie ein ideales Umfeld für Information, Kommunikation und Kundenpflege, so suchen die Messebesucher ganzheitliche Lösungen mit schneller Rentabilität. Der Informationsbedarf vor der konkreten Kaufentscheidung ist heute extrem hoch. Angebote, Produkte und Dienstleistungen werden kritischer denn je nach den unterschiedlichsten Kriterien verglichen und geprüft. Hier muss der Messestand den dramaturgisch adäquat inszenierten Rahmen bieten. Der klare und schnelle Weg wird bevorzugt. Voraussetzung für das Informations- und Kommunikationsgeschehen ist eine konsequente Gliederung der Angebote und Themen auf dem Messestand. Dabei ist zu beachten, dass die Kunden nur ein kleines Zeitfenster zu Verfügung haben, deshalb muss dem Besucher ein qualifiziertes und gut geschultes Personal gegenübergestellt werden. Der Messeauftritt von Unternehmen oder Marken muss eindrucksvoll, überzeugend und nachhaltig wirken. Erst wenn alle diese Voraussetzungen geschaffen sind, kommen die konkurrenzlosen Stärken des Mediums optimal zur Geltung, nämlich der direkte persönliche Kontakt

und die Kommunikation auf gleicher Augenhöhe. Erfolgreiches Messemanagement setzt auf neue kreative Sichtweisen und szenographisch inszenierte Themenräume, Erlebnisbereiche und bezieht immer häufiger Topevents in seine Messekonzepte mit ein. Der Kommunikationsraum Messestand ist vielfältiger, bunter, informativer, kommunikativer und erlebnisorientierter geworden. Den Vorzügen von Messen steht ein entscheidender wirtschaftlicher Nachteil gegenüber: Messebeteiligung ist kostenintensiv. Das betrifft sowohl die direkten Kosten für die Miete von Standflächen und Messeinfrastruktur, den Standbau und das Standpersonal als auch den Aufwand für Werbeträger und massenmediale Kommunikation sowie die Nachbearbeitung.

Tendenziell ist davon auszugehen, dass die Messekosten aufgrund des Strebens nach immer größeren und attraktiveren Ständen und die Integration von Events in den Messeauftritt weiter ansteigen werden. Deshalb wird in letzter Zeit immer häufiger über die Effizienz von Messebeteiligungen diskutiert. Messen stehen im Wettbewerb um Budgetanteile mit anderen Marketinginstrumenten. Während in der Investitionsgüterbranche Messen traditionell einen sehr hohen Budgetanteil aufweisen, wird im Konsumgüter- und Dienstleistungsbereich über die Umverteilung von Budgets zugunsten anderer Kommunikationsinstrumente nachgedacht, die vergleichbare Marketingziele unterstützen. Eventmarketing erhält zur Zeit den größten Zuspruch. Trotz aller Bedenken der Marketingstrategen ist der persönliche Kontakt und die Kommunikation auf gleicher Augenhöhe, im emotionalen Umfeld, durch nichts zu ersetzen.

THE INTRAVENOUS EFFECT ON THE PRODUCT AND THE BRAND

DER INTRAVENÖSE EINFLUSS AUF PRODUKT UND MARKE

WHAT ARE THE BENEFITS OF CORPORATE ARCHITECTURE?

For several years now, the so-called »Bilbao Effect« has been celebrated in architecture as a synonym for structural identification with an institution (like the Guggenheim Museum) or for identification with an entire region (Bilbao and the Basque region). The success of other examples, such as the automobile city of Wolfsburg (Volkswagen), the Vitra building in Weil on the Rhine, or the flagship stores of Prada seem to justify the sometimes enormous costs. Traditionally, corporate design guidelines in architecture have been applied mainly to headings, colors and Corportate Identity materials in order to safeguard a certain uniformity of appearance. The possibilities of architectural design in support of a brand were hardly used at all, or they were guided by objectives that were defined in very general terms, such as »high-grade«, »representative«, or »futuristic«. Furthermore, architecture was regarded as a medium to be incorporated into corporate design, along with a variety of other means of communication and assorted advertising measures.

The image-strengthening potential of spatial and architectural creativity that has recently been rediscovered has been applied successfully, in part, to stand design for decades. Trade show stands require an immediate, quickly effective access to the product, to the message, and thus to the brand.

This intravenous effect does not necessarily mean a trite, poster-like presentation. A more lasting impression is an associative access, a clever, ingenious and surprising detour that leads the visitor through an association of presentation and brand, of slogan, message, and product that leaves a satisfying and memorable impression.

Beyond that, formally interesting and unmistakable stands offer the opportunity for diversity, for an at least temporary identification with product and brand, because the differences of today's products are only marginal in terms of components and manufacturing and often in design as well.

Trade show participation undoubtedly always involves somewhat deliberately exaggerated versions of redundant messages and of visually overcharged impressions. Neither a »more is more« nor a »less is less« approach is effective in the long run, as compared to integrative and creative conceptualization. Minimalism or highly aesthetic styles do not necessarily lead to better results, because excessively formal design often sacrifices the communication of messages, which must subsequently be added by means of necessary and costly explanatory measures. Not only is there an enormous potential of concepts derived from contents and messages in the design of museum displays, but also in the staging of commercial exhibits, with which qualitatively complex or very large contents can be reduced to manageable amounts. The self-explanatory deciphering of this code by means of memorable staging facilitates the perception and the legibility of the messages for the visitor.

Compared to movies or theatre shows, in which the action gradually comes to the point, or unlike exhibitions, in which information is presented at different levels of intensity, a trade show stand should have an immediate intravenous effect. Ideally it should be a solid message that produces an immediate connection to the product and brand world, both on an informative as well as an emotional level.

The staging of this psychological manner of conveying an advertising message thus resembles a kind of very carefully managed moment. The staged environment creates a powerful attraction effect that the visitor hopefully cannot resist.

To create such a composite condition for the purpose of generating a retentive perception of the product potential and the brand message, it is imperative to establish a smooth interplay of all the creative elements, such as graphics, light, projection and digital media. In this process, the desired identification with the stand presentation is generated by an attention-drawing tension between product (desirability), message (value potential) and the trade show visitor (customer). The credibility of a modern, likely-to-be successful brand presentation rests with a logical overall starting concept aimed at being an »overall work of art«.

CORPORATE ARCHITECTURE. WAS KANN DAS?

In der Architektur wird seit einigen Jahren der sogenannte »Bilbao Effekt« gefeiert, als Synonym für die gebaute Identifikation mit einem Unternehmen (Guggenheim Museum) oder Identifizierung einer ganzen Region (Bilbao und das Baskenland). Der Erfolg anderer Beispiele, wie die Autostadt in Wolfsburg, die Vitragebäude in Weil am Rhein oder die Flagshipstores von Prada, scheint den manchmal enormen Aufwand zu rechtfertigen.

Klassischerweise wurden Corporate-Design-Richtlinien in der Architektur hauptsächlich auf Beschriftungen, Farben und CI-konforme Materialien angewandt, um eine gewisse Einheitlichkeit im Erscheinungsbild zu gewährleisten. Die Möglichkeiten architektonischer Gestaltung zur Beeinflussung eines Markenimages wurden kaum genutzt oder waren durch sehr allgemeine Zielvorstellungen wie »hochwertig«, »repräsentativ« oder »zukunftsweisend« geprägt. Architektur wurde als weiteres additiv in das Corporate Design zu integrierendes Medium betrachtet, neben einer Vielzahl anderer Kommunikationsmittel und werbewirksamen Maßnahmen.

Das in der Architektur nun (wieder)entdeckte, imageprägende Potential räumlicher Gestaltung wird im Messedesign zum Teil seit Jahrzehnten erfolgreich genutzt. Messestände verlangen einen unmittelbaren, schnell wirkenden Zugang zum Produkt, zur Botschaft und damit zur Marke.

Diese intravenöse Wirkung bedeutet nicht notwendigerweise eine banale, plakative Präsentation. Nachhaltiger funktioniert ein assoziativer Zugang, ein schlauer, listiger und überraschender Umweg, der von den Besuchern eine Kontextualisierung von Auftritt und Marke, von Slogan (Motto), Botschaft und Produkt verlangt und nach dieser kombinatorischen Leistung ein erinnerungswürdiges Erfolgserlebnis auslöst.

Darüber hinaus bieten formal interessante unverwechselbare Auftritte die Chance zu Diversität, zur wenigstens temporären Identifikation mit Produkt und Marke, denn die Produkte unterscheiden sich in ihren Komponenten, der Herstellung und oft auch im Design nur marginal.

Zweifelsohne bedeuten Messeauftritte immer eine Art einkalkulierte Überforderung an redundanter Botschaft, an möglichst spektakulären Architekturen und visuell überfrachteten Eindrücken. Weder ein »more is more« noch ein »less is less« funktionieren hier dauerhaft als Zauberformeln, sondern ein eher integratives Konzipieren und Gestalten. Auch die totale Reduktion oder starke Ästhetisierung führt nicht zwangsweise zu besseren Ergebnissen, weil zu Gunsten formaler Designdominanz häufig die Vermittlung von Botschaften auf der Strecke bleibt, die dann durch kostspielige, im Nachhinein notwendige Erklärungsmaßnahmen hinzuaddiert werden müssen. Nicht nur in der Museumsgestaltung, sondern auch in der kommerziellen Szenographie liegt ein riesiges Potential an aus Inhalten und Botschaften entwickelten Konzepten, die mittels formaler Abstraktion und inszenatorischer Übersetzung qualitativ komplexe oder quantitativ üppige Inhalte auf ein gustierbares Maß reduzieren. Die selbsterläuternde Dechiffrierung dieser Codes mittels erinnerungswürdiger Inszenierungen erleichtert die Orientierung und die Lesbarkeit der Botschaften für den Besucher. Im Vergleich zu Kino und zu Theater, wo sich die Narration allmählich auf eine Pointe hinentwickelt, oder im Unterschied zu Ausstellungen, in denen Informationen auf verschiedenen Vertiefungsebenen angeboten werden, sollte ein Messestand unmittelbar intravenös wirken, im besten Fall eine gebaute Botschaft sein, die sowohl auf der informativen wie auf der emotionalen Ebene eine unmittelbare Verbindung zur Produkt- und Markenwelt herstellt.

Die Inszenierung einer solchen physisch erlebbaren Werbebotschaft ähnelt deshalb einer »Art Dressur des Augenblicks«. Das gestaltete Umfeld entwickelt eine Sogwirkung, der sich der Besucher möglichst nicht entziehen kann.

Um einen derartigen Aggregatzustand zu erzeugen, ist das integrative Zusammenspiel aller Gestaltungselemente wie Grafik, Licht, Projektion und digitale Medien zur nachhaltigen Wahrnehmung von Produktpotential und Markenbotschaft notwendig. Dabei geht die gewünschte Identifikation mit dem Messeauftritt von einem attraktivierenden Spannungsfeld zwischen Produkt (Begehrlichkeit), Botschaft (Wert, Potential) und Messebesucher (Kunde) aus. Die Glaubwürdigkeit eines zeitgemäßen erfolgversprechenden Markenauftritts liegt im konsequenten gesamtkonzeptionellen Ansatz mit dem Anspruch eines »Gesamtkunstwerkes«.

Titanic Exhibition Atelier Brückner 1997

THE TEAM IS THE STAR
DIE MANNSCHAFT IST DER STAR

I wish to thank Uwe R. Brückner [URB], who had the original idea for this book and whose well-organized archive made this documentation possible. The cooperation with Uwe Brückner [URB], Birgit Koelz [BK] and Helmut Kirsten [HK] was very pleasant. In reliving the three projects, I was able look at everything in a much more relaxed manner and at a necessary distance, which made working on this book an enduring experience.

On behalf of all the many colleagues who worked on these projects, I would like to applaud several contractors and their teams who played major roles in the success of the three events. I also wish to thank KODAK and the sponsors who have supported the creation of this book.

Bedanken möchte ich mich bei Uwe R. Brückner [URB], der die Idee zu diesem Buch hatte und mit seinem gut organisierten Archiv diese Dokumentation erst möglich machte. Die Zusammenarbeit mit Uwe Brückner [URB], Birgit Koelz [BK] und Helmut Kirsten [HK] hat mir sehr viel Spaß gemacht. In der Nachbearbeitung der drei Projekte kann ich alles viel entspannter und mit dem nötigen Abstand betrachten, was die Arbeit für dieses Buch zum nachhaltigen Erlebnis macht.

Stellvertretend für alle Mitwirkenden möchte ich mich bei einigen »Mitstreitern« und ihren Teams bedanken, die maßgeblich an den drei Projekten beteiligt waren. Mein Dank geht auch an KODAK und die Sponsoren, die dieses Buch unterstützt haben.

Friedrich O. Müller [FOM]

Without the courage to take risks, perseverance beyond the call of duty and the determination of transforming impossible challenges into successful solutions such complex and ambitious projects could not become reality. I thank everyone who cooperated to make this intention come true.

Ohne die Risikobereitschaft und das Engagement jenseits der Belastungsgrenze und die Überzeugung, das Unmögliche erfolgreich umsetzen zu können, sind derartig komplexe und ambitionierte Projekte nicht zu realisieren. Danke allen, die mitgeholfen haben, diese Intention Realität werden zu lassen.

Uwe R. Brückner [URB]

»The wonderful aspect of creative professionals is the fact that they get paid for the risk, the craziness, and the fun of experimenting. Das Schöne an dem Beruf der Kreativen ist, dass sie für das Risiko, die Verrücktheiten und den Spaß am Experiment auch noch bezahlt werden.«
[ROLF DERRER, LICHTDESIGNER]

ACKNOWLEDGEMENTS

PARTICIPATING INDIVIDUALS BETEILIGTE PERSONEN

THE PEOPLE FROM KODAK STUTTGART

Friedrich O. Müller **[FOM]**	photokina Manager
Gunter Plapp **[GP]**	worldwide photokina Coordinator
Rainer Sahlberger **[RS]**	Facility Management
Detlef Gerke **[DG]**	Product Planning / Installation
Ines Sahlfrank	Photography / Graphics / Displays
Sandra Jirsch **[SJ]**	Photography / Graphics / Displays
Waltraud Hüttl	Photography / Production
Heide Talmon	Team Coordinator
Holger Zeising	Team Assistant
Renate Mühlberger	Staff Planning
Sabine James	Staff Planning
Annegret Rolph	Budget
Kai-Uwe Kappich	Telecommunication
Hans Thalhofer	Travel / Hotel Bookings
Gerd Böhm	Press Services

REALISATION

Construction

Ralf Banse **[RB]**	Zeissig Messebau, Springe
	bluepool AG, Springe
	Design Production, Hannover

Display

Kai Malzacher **[KM]**	Heinze & Malzacher, Stuttgart
Martin Vöhringer **[MV]**	

Labs

Werner Maly **[WM]**	Labor Grieger, Stuttgart
Nicole Röckle **[NR]**	

Staff and Catering

Theo Hellmann	Intercris, Laatzen

Furniture rental

Dirk Deuerling	Klingenberg Hannover

Carpeting

Hans-Peter Hummel, Filderstadt	Expomobil

THE ATB TEAM

Uwe R. Brückner **[URB]**
Shirin Frangoul-Brückner **[SFB]**

KODAK I, II

Dominik Hegemann **[DH]**	Project Manager
Britta Nagel **[BN]**	Concept and Design
Birgit Koelz **[BK]**	Graphic Design

KODAK III

Harry Vetter **[HV]**	Project Manager
Juliane Herdfeld **[JH]**	Concept and Design
Irene Voth	Concept and Design
Helmut Kirsten **[HK]**	Graphic Design

CHAPTER OVERVIEW KAPITELÜBERSICHT

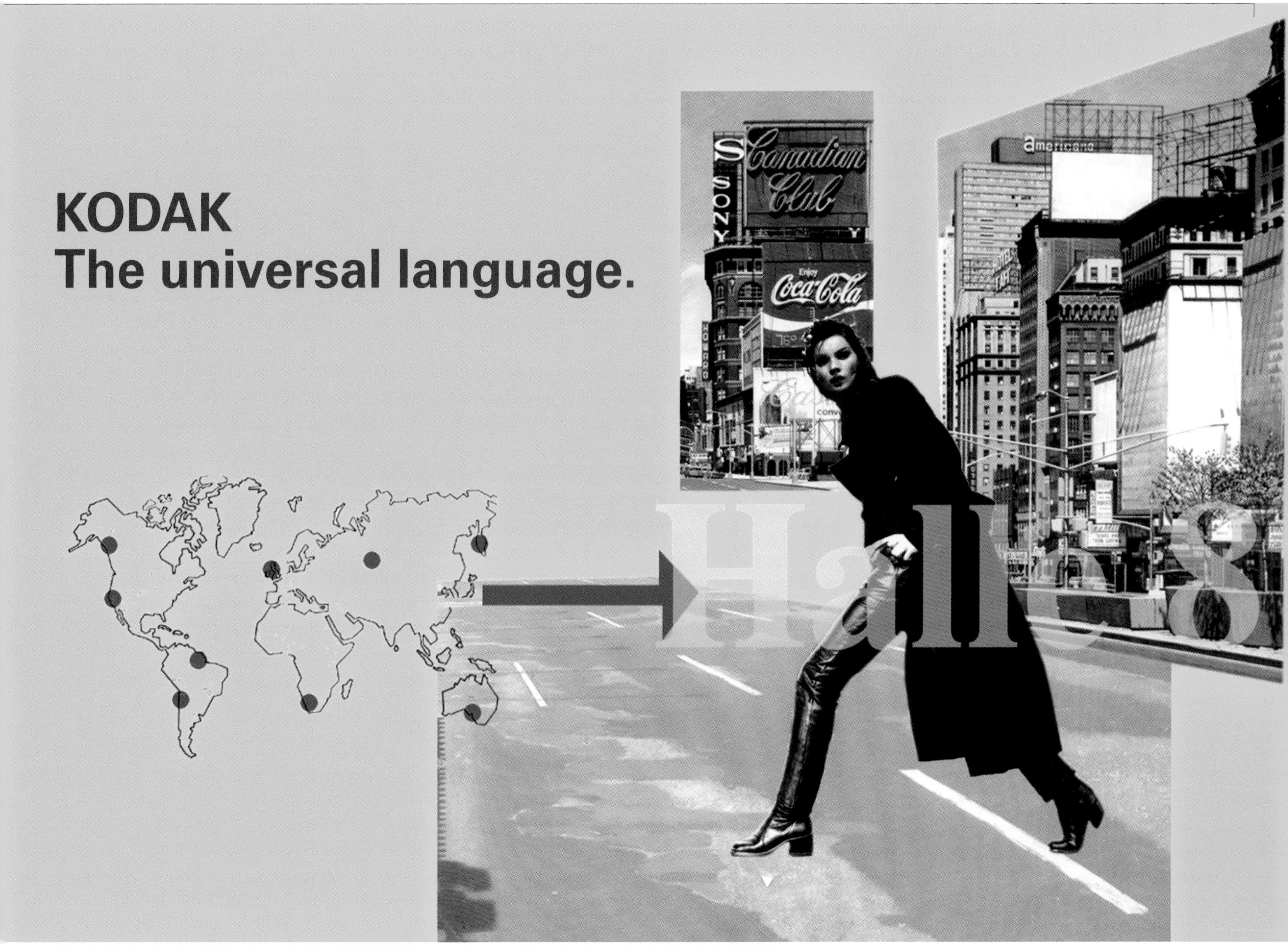

KODAK
The universal language.
Canadian Club
SONY
Coca-Cola
Halle 8

»The sky a picture, the façade a photograph, the street an image, the human being a snapshot. Der Himmel ein Bild, die Fassade ein Foto, die Straße ein Abbild, der Mensch ein Schnappschuss.«

[BN]

THE BRIEF FOR COMPETITIVE BIDS
DIE AUSSCHREIBUNG ZUM WETTBEWERB

pages and links Verweise
II. 94 – 99
III. 162 – 169

THE ROLE OF EXHIBITIONS

KODAK is the worldwide market leader and traditionally the largest exhibitor at the photokina, for many years presenting itself on the upper floor of Hall 8. KODAK stands for photography in all its aspects, serving both professional as well as amateur photographers. This is to be underscored by means of large, high-quality pictures with eye-catching contents. The stand design must take that into account, i.e. the theme of pictures is to be considered as an umbrella guideline.

Photography is communication, encounters and documentation – it has become a firm component of our daily lives.

«Everyday Picture- Taking» and KODAK pictures in all their variations constitute our message, and the design of the stand must express this message vigorously.

KODAK masters the universal language of photography perfectly.

Therefore our claim at this trade show is «KODAK – The universal language».

The emphasis in all product presentations is always the picture.

DESIGN PARAMETERS

The overall area that is available for the KODAK stand covers 5.500 m^2 (59.200 ft^2) including aisles. A two-story design is possible.

As in the past, the appearance of the stand should reflect the claim of the market leader: outstanding, leading, trendsetting. The building is a transit building. It is located between Building 6 and Building 10, so that it has to be taken into account that both sides serve as entrances as well as exits. The function of the stand is to attract the visitor into the building, to stimulate the visitor's curiosity, to provide competent information and then to foster a sales discussion. The objective is to design the stand in such a way as to make it easy for the visitor to orientate himself and to gain an overview of the complete line of products, so that he can quickly and easily find the way to his particular point of interest and to the respective product specialist. Easy orientation is a must. To achieve the objective, the hall must be kept open, which means that the architecture and the shape of the building and its peculiarities have to be incorporated in the stand design. For example: The view of the greenery to the north of the building should be preserved, daylight illumination of the stand is desirable, but the southern row of windows presents a problem because of the direct incidence of very bright daylight, and this requires a solution.

OTHER CONSIDERATIONS

KODAK is present at photokina with three lines of business: Consumer Imaging, Digital & Applied Imaging, and Professional Imaging. Solutions are offered for the most diverse types of customers: Products and services for photofans, offers for dealers, products for professional photographers, products for image-manipulation studios and professional labs, business applications. An environment appropriate for this target group and that projects an image of leadership has to be created for this product presentation. The objective of the KODAK presence at the trade show is to impress upon the visitor that KODAK means innovation, performance capability and competence. The presentation is also designed to generate confidence in the line of products and to emphasize to the dealer that KODAK products are well received.

In addition, it must be taken into account that dealers from all over the world come to the KODAK stand for the purpose of conducting their business discussions. To accommodate this aspect of the trade show, appropriate discussion facilities and logistics such as space and catering have to be incorporated in the stand layout. These areas are to be reserved a «controlled areas». The discussion areas for customers require approximately 40% of the overall stand space.

»Do we have any chance of competing with the current court architect at KODAK, or are we just sparring partners? Haben wir da überhaupt eine Chance, gegen die derzeitigen Haus- und Hofarchitekten von KODAK anzutreten, oder sind wir nur Sparringspartner …?«
[URB]

ENCOUNTER

COMMUNICATION

LANGUAGE

DAILY LIFE

INFORMATION

INFORMATION

CONTACT

MOVEMENT

CULTURES

»We will definitely participate!
Da machen wir auf jeden Fall mit!«

[SB]

DESIGNED AS AN EVENTS HALL, USED AS A TRADE SHOW PAVILION.
ALS VERANSTALTUNGSHALLE KONZIPIERT, ALS MESSEHALLE GENUTZT.

pages and links Verweise

II. 96 – 97

Hall 8: View from east to west

Hall 8: South-West View

»A hall with an area the size of a soccer pitch, heterogeneous light conditions, floor-to-ceiling glass windows along two sides, black box conditions in the center, an obtrusive ceiling structure that blocks the stand design, the charm of an automobile ferry, burdened with all sorts of constraining functional conditions – all of which demands respect. Fußballfeldgroße Halle, heterogene Lichtverhältnisse, Tageslicht durch geschosshohe Verglasung am Rand, Blackboxverhältnisse in der Mitte, aufdringliche, inszenierungsfeindliche Kassettendecke und der Charme einer Autofähre, belastet mit allerlei einschränkender Bedingungen funktionaler Art – das nötigt Respekt ab.«
[URB]

KODAK has had a stand on the upper floor of Hall 8 for 40 years, at first occupying only a part of that floor and then, in 1978, becoming the sole exhibitor covering the entire floor space of 5.500 m² (59.200 ft²). Hall 8 is located directly at the overpass from the historical Rhine fairgrounds complex to the new exhibit halls to the east. For decades, this was the strategically ideal location for the market leader. All trade show visitors who wish to visit all the halls always had to traverse the KODAK stand. Hall 8 was planned in the fifties as an events building but in later years it no longer met the needs of an optimal trade show building. The structure cannot overcome the obvious look of the fifties, in spite of many embellishments and renovations implemented by the Cologne Fairs Organization at the behest of KODAK. Unavoidable disadvantages had to be taken into consideration: An inadequate power supply that required supplemental power lines and power generators. Two outdated freight elevators that were bottlenecks for setting up and taking down the exhibit properties. The limited load factor of the floor area that necessitated costly load distribution and that permits only a two-story design along the perimeter of the hall. The very large windows along the southern and northern sides of the building, which had to be covered completely in order to achieve a controlled illumination of the stand. In addition, the air conditioning capacity was insufficient, so that on hot days, the atmosphere on the stand became almost unbearable. But none of this counts. What makes an area so valuable? It is location, location and once again location! Visitors become used to the KODAK stand, it becomes fully accepted, turning into the meeting point for the entire photographic industry.

Seit 40 Jahren präsentiert sich KODAK auf der photokina in der Halle 8, ganz am Anfang mit Teilbelegungen und seit 1978 als alleiniger Aussteller auf 5.500 m².
Die Halle 8 befindet sich direkt am Übergang vom historischen Rheinhallen-Komplex zum neuen Messebereich der Osthallen. Das wird über Jahrzehnte der strategisch ideale Platz für den Marktführer. Alle Messebesucher, die alle Hallen besuchen, müssen zwangsläufig immer bei KODAK vorbei. Die Halle 8 wird in den 1950er Jahren als Veranstaltungshalle geplant und erfüllt später längst nicht mehr die Anforderungen eines optimalen Messebaus. Das Gebäude kann den 1950er-Jahre-Look nicht verbergen, trotz vieler Kaschierungs- und Renovierungsmaßnahmen, die als Forderung von KODAK von der Kölnmesse durchgeführt werden. Die unveränderbaren Nachteile werden dennoch in Kauf genommen: Eine zu geringe Stromversorgung, die zusätzliche Leitungen und Stromgeneratoren erforderlich macht. Zwei veraltete Aufzüge, die ein Nadelöhr für Auf- und Abbau sind. Die geringe Bodenbelastung, die aufwändige Lastverteilungen nötig macht und dadurch eine zweigeschossige Bauweise nur im Randbereich der Halle zulässt. Die großen Fensterfronten an der Süd- und Nordseite, die nur durch totale Abdunklung eine kontrollierte Ausleuchtung des Standes ermöglichen. Eine schwach dimensionierte Klimaanlage lässt dazu an heißen Tagen den Aufenthalt unerträglich werden. Dies zählt alles nicht. Was macht einen Platz so wertvoll? Die Lage, Lage und nochmals die Lage. Die KODAK Halle wird »gelernt«, voll akzeptiert und deshalb zum Treffpunkt der gesamten Branche.

IDEA AND CONCEPT - CITY PICTURES - PICTURE CITY

IDEE UND KONZEPT – STADTBILDER – BILDERSTADT

Wenn ich die Geschichte in Worten erzählen könnte, brauchte ich keine Kamera herumzuschleppen.

Lewis W. Hine

THE GLOBAL LANGUAGE

Interactive visions. Direct intervention and changing of the city by the visitor might constitute an event. The dream vision of the visitors projected live on the constantly changing cityscape.

Interaktive Visionen. Ein besonderes Ereignis könnte das direkte Eingreifen und Verändern der Stadt durch den Besucher sein. Das Traumbild der Besucher als Live-Projektion auf die sich ständig verwandelnde Stadtkulisse.

THE COMPETITION

»With what could one possibly surprise KODAK nowadays? They have already viewed more concepts during the past 30 years than we could possibly imagine! Mit was kann man KODAK heute überhaupt noch überraschen? Die haben in den letzten 30 Jahren schon mehr Konzepte gesehen, als wir uns vorstellen könnnen!«

[URB]

THE CHANGEABLE CITY
DIE VERWANDELBARE STADT

»Nothing is more important than the brightness of everyday life, of the familiar, of the banal, of the small things in life. Nichts ist wichtiger als die Heiligkeit des alltäglichen Lebens, des Gewöhnlichen, des Banalen, der kleinen Dinge im Leben.«

[FRANK PERRY]

The KODAK city can change itself at regular time intervals and transform itself in fascinating ways all the way into the absurd. Farcical pictures capture the attention of the visitor, intrigue him for a moment, leading him into a different world – unexpectedly – before everyday routines set in again. Daydreams that occur while walking through the city become reality. The »contrived structure«, the city background, dissolves into an unfamiliar picture, an unfamiliar situation. The place is suddenly bathed in yellow color, sunflowers sway in the streets and strange animals rush by. Curiosity is aroused not only visually, but acoustically as well. The change from reality to dream is produced by means of projections, light and color, and also by two-layered spatial elements.

Die KODAK City kann sich in regelmäßigen zeitlichen Abständen verwandeln und auf fasziniernde Weise bis ins Absurde verkehren. Skurrile Bilder fangen den Blick des Besuchers ein, irritieren für einen kurzen Augenblick, entführen in eine andere Welt – unerwartet –, bevor sich das Alltägliche wieder einstellt. Tagträume beim Gang durch die Stadt werden wahr. Die »gebaute Struktur«, der Stadthintergrund löst sich auf in ein fremdes Bild, eine fremde Situation. Der Platz wird plötzlich in gelbe Farbe getaucht, auf der Straße wiegen sich Sonnenblumen, und seltsame Tiere huschen vorbei. Nicht nur visuell, auch akustisch werden Irritationen erzeugt. Der Wechsel von Wirklichkeit und Traum wird mit Hilfe von Projektionen, Licht und Farbe sowie zweischichtigen Raumelementen erzeugt.

abstract urban structures, the magic of city-hen as a homage to Jacques Tati

Concept Collage

»What if we fetch the wine from the KODAK cellar and the vegetables from your garden and use them to cobble up an entirely new menu? Was wäre, wenn wir den Wein aus dem Keller von KODAK und das Gemüse aus Ihrem Garten holen und ein komplett neues Menü daraus basteln?«

[URB]

THE STRUCTURE OF KODAK CITY
DIE STRUKTUR VON KODAK CITY

The most important areas accessible to the public are located along Main Street. This is where the entire spectrum of KODAK products is presented. The sections for professional photography, divided into »Social«, »Portrait« and »Commercial« line the southern side of Main Street. Along the northern side are the sections of »Consumer Imaging«. The presentations along Main Street evolve from analogue products to digital technologies, creating a progression from current analogue offerings to the digital future.

Alternating open and closed structures combine to form the city. In the »closed« areas that are only accessible to professional visitors, for example, dealers are welcomed in a world of pure color. The red room, the pink salon, the yellow hall, the blue room constitute effective accents of the concept.

A plaza for events and for picture-taking in the publicly accessible area expands Main Street. Photographers invited from all corners of the world take pictures on Main Street and on the plazas. They enliven these areas with photographic life at photokina 2000. Temporary barriers mark the areas of the activities.

Professional photography can be observed. This is also where the sports bar is located, featuring live broadcasts direct from the Olympic Games in Sydney.

Four small areas are provided as meeting points for both amateurs and professionals alike. Benches in appropriate locations serve for resting and for watching the lively goings-on. Different interest groups have different objectives in this city, where their paths often intersect each other.

Entlang der Hauptstraße sind die wichtigsten öffentlich zugänglichen Bereiche angesiedelt. Hier wird die ganze Bandbreite der Produktpalette von KODAK präsentiert. Auf der südlichen Seite der Hauptstraße befinden sich die Bereiche für die professionellen Gebiete, unterteilt in die Segmente »Social« und »Portrait« sowie »Commercial«.

Auf der nördlichen Seite befinden sich die Bereiche des sogenannten »Consumer Imaging«. In Richtung der Hauptstraße entwickelt sich die Präsentation von analogen Produkten hin zu digitalen Techniken. Eine Achse von analogen Angeboten zur digitalen Zukunft entsteht.

Ein Wechsel aus offenen und geschlossenen Baukörpern bildet den Städtebau. In den »geschlossenen« Bereichen, die nur den professionellen Besuchern zugänglich sind, werden beispielsweise die Händler in einer Welt aus purer Farbe empfangen. Das rote Zimmer, der rosa Salon, der gelbe Saal, der blaue Raum sind wirkungsvolle Akzente des Konzepts.

Ein Platz für Events, für Fotoshootings im öffentlich zugänglichen Raum erweitert die Hauptstraße. Eingeladene Fotografen aus allen Teilen der Welt fotografieren auf der Straße – auf den Plätzen. Sie erfüllen diese Spielräume mit fotografischem Leben auf der photokina 2000. Temporäre Absperrungen markieren die Orte des Geschehens.

Professionelle Fotografie kann beobachtet werden. Hier befindet sich auch die Sportsbar mit Live-Übertragungen direkt von der Olympiade in Sydney. Vier kleine Plätze sind Treffpunkt für Amateure und Professionelle zugleich. Bänke zum Ausruhen bieten die Möglichkeit zum Verweilen und Beobachten des bunten Treibens. Unterschiedliche Interessengruppen haben unterschiedliche Ziele in der Stadt, ihre Wege kreuzen sich.

Presentation areas
Conference areas

Product groups

Public areas
and aisles

Open and
closed areas

»Form follows content. Take advantage of existing resources. The most obvious and quintessential
resource of KODAK is the picture. The picture and its narrative potential as a global language. Form
follows content. Aus den vorhandenen Ressourcen schöpfen. Die offensichtlichste und ureigenste
Ressource von KODAK ist das Bild. Das Bild und sein narratives Potential, als globale Sprache.«
[URB]

SUCCESS AND EUPHORIA – CHAMPAGNE FOR EVERYONE
SIEG UND EUPHORIE – CHAMPAGNER FÜR ALLE

From the four proposals that were submitted, a jury of experts selected the concept entitled »KODAK City« entered by the Atelier Brückner [atb] of Stuttgart. It was a sobering realization that none of the four proposals that were presented completely satisfied the specifications. The jury nevertheless recommended additional development of the »KODAK City« concept, because it offered the best premise for further refinement to satisfy the requirements of the task that were set forth. That recommendation meant that the critical decision had been made - the starting shot had been fired. The euphoric mood of the participants: Champagne for everyone!

Eine Fachjury wählt für den photokina-Auftritt 2000 aus vier eingereichten Arbeiten das Konzept »KODAK City« vom Stuttgarter Atelier Brückner. Die nüchterne Erkenntnis: Keiner der vier Ansätze entspricht hundertprozentig den Anforderungen. Die Jury empfiehlt dennoch, das Konzept »KODAK City« weiterzuverfolgen, weil es für eine Weiterentwicklung im Sinne der Aufgabenstellung die besten Voraussetzungen bietet. Damit ist die überaus schwerwiegende Entscheidung getroffen, der Startschuss gefallen. Die euphorische Stimmungslage der Beteiligten: Champagner für alle …

»The competition had no clear winner, only the concept developed by atb had the potential for continued development in terms of the objectives set out by KODAK.Der Wettbewerb hatte keinen eindeutigen Sieger, aber nur das Konzept von atb versprach eine sinnvolle Weiterentwicklung im Sinne von KODAK.«

»New ideas and a new way of thinking – that is what KODAK needs. Neue Ideen und neues Denken – das braucht KODAK.«

»Steer away from pure architecture and aim for developing a concept. At KODAK, the products are already a part of the architecture Weg von der reinen Architektur hin zur Konzeptgestaltung. Bei KODAK sind die Produkte bereits Teil der Architektur.«

»Architecture and communication concept from the same source – up to now we were not accustomed to that. Architektur- und Kommunikationskonzept aus einer Hand, das kannten wir bis dahin nicht.«

»Stage designers and scenographers, that is what we need. Bühnenbildner und Szenographie, das ist es, was wir brauchen.«
[FOM]

»Scenography derived from facilitating contents provides a direct access to the message. Design becomes market identity. Eine aus den vermittelnden Inhalten generierte Szenographie eröffnet einen unmittelbaren Zugang zur Botschaft. Gestaltung wird zur Markenidentität.«
[URB]

»Well, if there is no first prize and we are still supposed to do it … ok, then they want a change. Also, wenn es keinen 1. Preis gibt und wir es trotzdem machen sollen … na ja, dann wollen die einen Wechsel.«
[SFB]

14 NOV 99

Kodak PHOTOKINA MESSEKONZEPT

THE WORKSHOP OR THE »YES, BUT …« MEETING
DER WORKSHOP ODER DAS »JA, ABER …«-MEETING

pages and links Verweise
II. 130 – 131
III. 198 – 199

»*Very good idea, it fits KODAK strategy of Take Pictures. Further. Everyday. Sehr gute Idee, und passt zu der Strategie von KODAK Take Pictures. Further. Everyday.*«

»*The trade show claim ›KODAK – The universal Language‹ is very well suited for underscoring the urban city concept. Great idea! Der Messe Claim ›KODAK – The Universal Language‹ ist bestens geeignet, das urbane Stadtkonzept zu unterstreichen. Tolle Idee.*«

»*To use the world language of photography and the multi-cultural life of a big city as the basic idea for the KODAK stand – simply great! Die Weltsprache Fotografie und das multikulturelle Leben einer Big-City als Basisidee für den KODAK Messestand zu verwenden. Einfach genial.*«
[FOM]

»Yes, but …« it means nothing other than a misunderstanding that the proposed solution does not correspond to the envisioned solution. This applies to the client's team, the designer team, and especially to the relationship between the two. »Ja, aber …«, das heißt nichts anderes als ein Missverständnis, dass die angebotene Lösung nicht der intendierten Vorstellung entspricht. Das gilt für das Auftraggeberteam, das Gestalterteam und besonders für das Verhältnis der beiden.

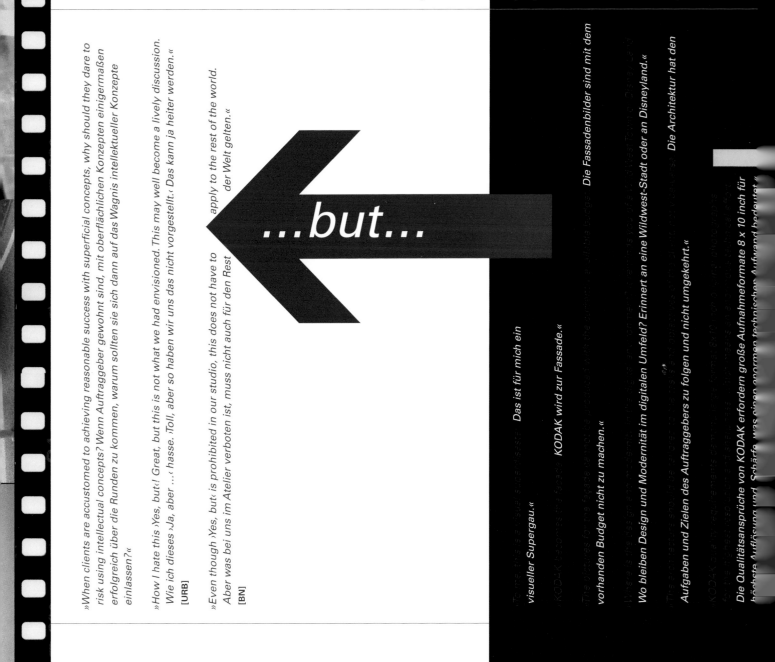

...but...

»When clients are accustomed to achieving reasonable success with superficial concepts, why should they dare to risk using intellectual concepts? Wenn Auftraggeber gewohnt sind, mit oberflächlichen Konzepten einigermaßen erfolgreich über die Runden zu kommen, warum sollten sie sich dann auf das Wagnis intellektueller Konzepte einlassen?«

»How I hate this ›Yes, but.‹ Great, but this is not what we had envisioned. This may well become a lively discussion. Wie ich dieses ›Ja, aber ...‹ hasse. Toll, aber so haben wir uns das nicht vorgestellt.‹ Das kann ja heiter werden.«
[URB]

»Even though ›Yes, but‹ is prohibited in our studio, this does not have to apply to the rest of the world. Aber was bei uns im Atelier verboten ist, muss nicht auch für den Rest der Welt gelten.«
[BN]

Das ist für mich ein visueller Supergau.«

KODAK wird zur Fassade.«

Die Fassadenbilder sind mit dem vorhanden Budget nicht zu machen.«

Wo bleiben Design und Modernität im digitalen Umfeld? Erinnert an eine Wildwest-Stadt oder an Disneyland.«

Die Architektur hat den Aufgaben und Zielen des Auftraggebers zu folgen und nicht umgekehrt.«

Die Qualitätsansprüche von KODAK erfordern große Aufnahmeformate 8 x 10 inch für

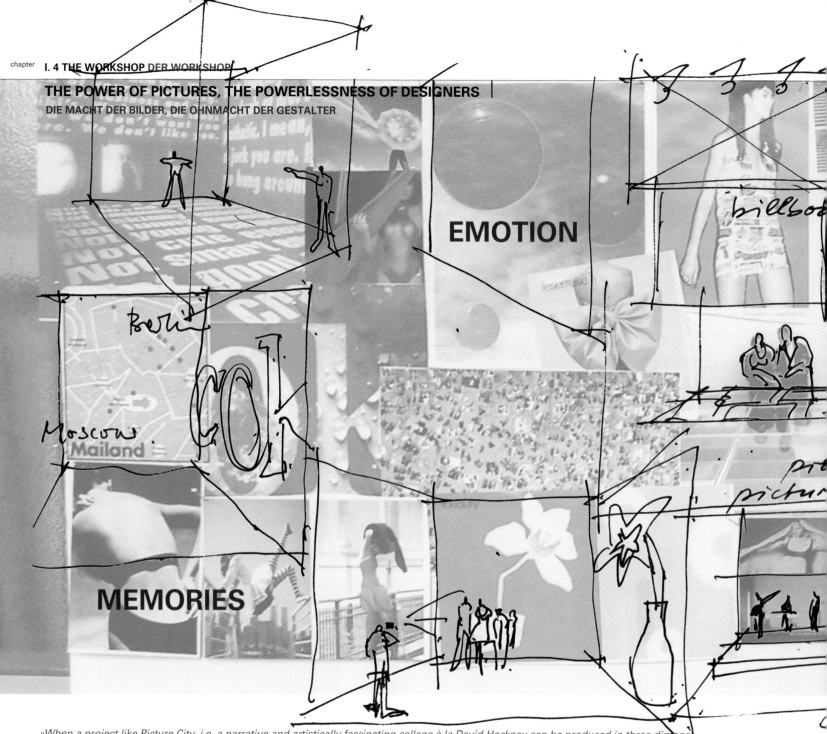

THE POWER OF PICTURES, THE POWERLESSNESS OF DESIGNERS
DIE MACHT DER BILDER, DIE OHNMACHT DER GESTALTER

EMOTION

MEMORIES

»When a project like Picture City, i.e. a narrative and artistically fascinating collage à la David Hockney can be produced in three dimensions, then why not for KODAK and its picture fetishism. With whom else? Wenn so etwas wie Picture City, also eine narrativ und
künstlerisch faszinierende Collage à la David Hockney, dreidimensional umsetzbar ist, dann doch mit KODAK und deren Bilderfetischis-
mus. Mit wem denn sonst?«
[URB]

DOCUMENTATION

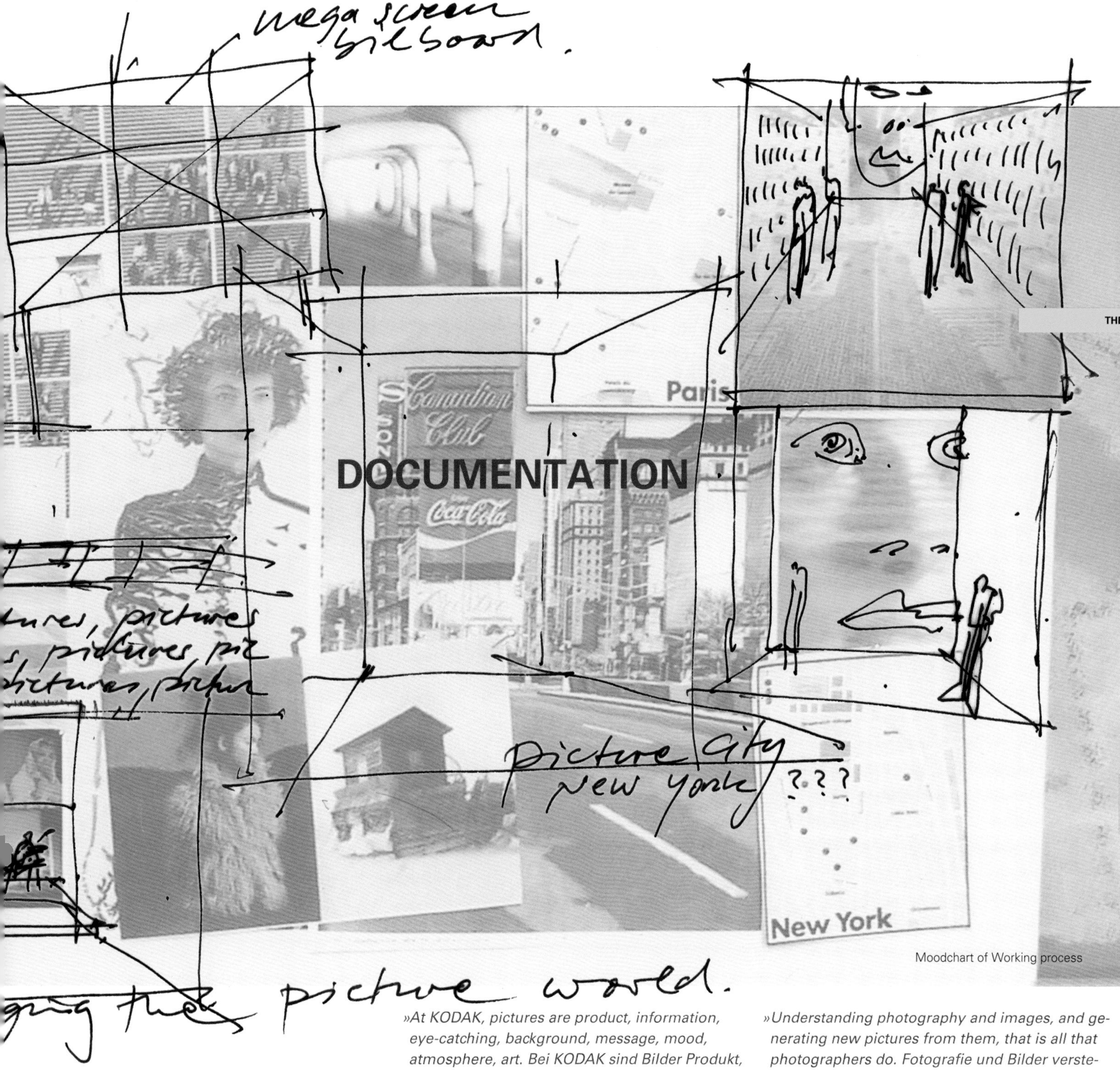

mega screen billboard.

pictures, pictures, pictures, pictures, pictures, pictures...

picture city new york ???

going there picture world.

Moodchart of Working process

»At KODAK, pictures are product, information, eye-catching, background, message, mood, atmosphere, art. Bei KODAK sind Bilder Produkt, Information, Eye-Catching, Hintergrund, Botschaft, Stimmung, Atmosphäre, Kunst.«
[FOM]

»Understanding photography and images, and generating new pictures from them, that is all that photographers do. Fotografie und Bilder verstehen und daraus neue Bilder generieren, das ist alles, was Fotografen machen.«
[FOM]

LOST IN PICTURE CITY – OR THE VISUAL WORST CASE SZENARIO
VERLOREN IN DER BILDERSTADT – ODER DER VISUELLE SUPERGAU

pages and links Verweise

II. 110 – 111

III. 178 – 179

Creative exuberance was followed by factual constraints.
Dialogue, juggling for position. Where is the consensus?
Dem kreativen Höhenflug folgt der Kontakt mit den
Sachzwängen. Dialog, Positionskampf. Wo ist der Konsens?

Picture City idea in danger

From Picture City to Metromap

»*We need a functioning orientation system. Wir brauchen ein
funktionierendes Orientierungssystem.*«

»*KODAK is present on a stand with several lines of business,
serving the most diverse customer segments. KODAK ist
mit mehreren Geschäftsbereichen auf einem Stand vertreten und bedient die unterschiedlichsten Kundensegmente,
deshalb ist ein funktionierendes Orientierungssystem ein
absolutes Muss.*«

»*An orientation system on the floor is not enough.
Das Leitsystem nur am Boden reicht nicht aus.*«

»*Overnight the grandiose success turned into a frustrating
aimlessness. The Picture City was in danger. Über Nacht
wurde aus einem grandiosen Sieg frustrierende Richtungslo-
sigkeit. Die Picture City war in Gefahr.*«

»*Three internal workshops produced no practical ideas. The
mantra of the client ›Orientation – we need orientation‹
got on our nerves. Drei interne Workshops brachten keine
brauchbaren Ideen, das Mantra der Auftraggeber ›Orientierung, wir brauchen Orientierung‹ ging uns auf die Nerven.*«
[URB]

»*The discussion areas must be clearly visible to all visitors at
a distance. Die Besprechungsbereiche müssen von weitem
für jeden Besucher leicht erkennbar sein.*«
[FOM]

Citymap as a guiding system

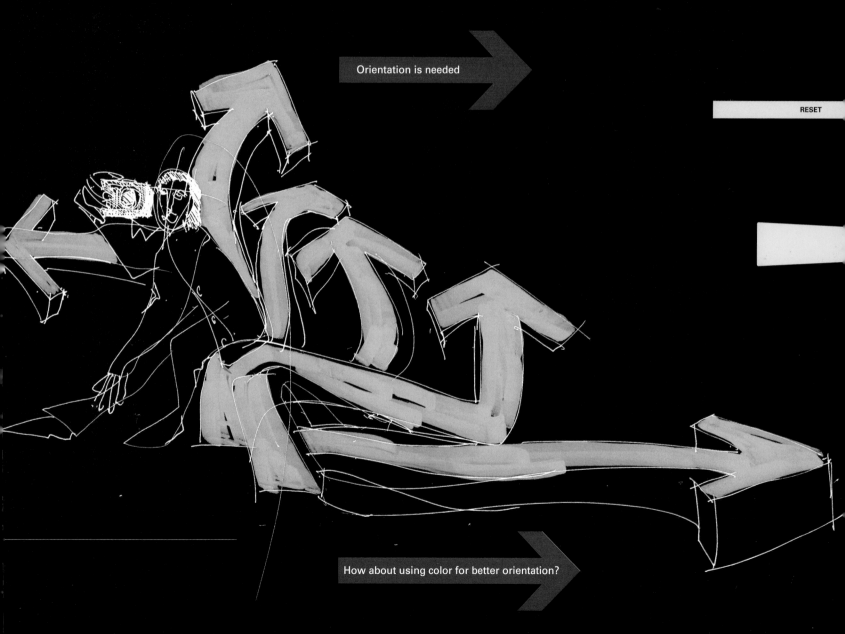

Orientation is needed

RESET

How about using color for better orientation?

chapter   **I. 6 THE DISCOVERY** DIE ENTDECKUNG

》 To draw from the resources. Aus den Ressourcen schöpfen.   **I.**

THE BEST IDEA WAS HANGING ON THE WALL
DIE BESTE IDEE HING AN DER WAND

The good idea is so close – often too close to be discerned in a wider context of significance.
Uwe Brückner happened to have the solution right in his hands and then before his eyes.
The so-called barcode on a carton of KODAK Ektachrome Film, which is normally used for opto-electronic product identification – small in size, yet incorporating all the visual qualities – becomes the object of creative focus. Aesthetics from a modern guiding system inspire the basis for a function- and marketing-oriented guiding scheme that is in keeping with the company's corporate identiy. Quite literally it is to remain in consideration, as proven later on. The expectation: To solve a basic problem. Stripes evolve into a refined highlight of trade show stand architecture. Das Gute liegt so nah – oft zu nah, um es in größerem Bedeutungszusammenhang zu sehen. Uwe Brückner hat die Lösung zufällig in der Hand, und dann auch vor Augen. Der sogenannte Barcode auf der KODAK Ektachrome Packung, normalerweise ein Hilfsmittel zur optoelektronischen Produkterfassung – winzig in den Dimensionen und dennoch mit allen visuellen Qualitäten – gerät in den kreativen Focus. Ästhetik aus einem modernen Leitsystem bietet die Basis für ein funktions- und markengerechtes Leitsystem in Einklang mit der Unternehmens-CI. Im wahrsten Sinne des Wortes will man damit auf dem Teppich bleiben, wie sich später zeigte. Die Erwartung: Damit soll ein Kernproblem gelöst werden. Streifen werden zum messearchitektonischen Highlight.

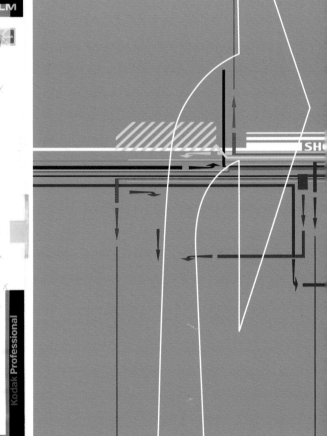

THE KEY POSITION

THE COLOR CODE EVOLVES - IN THE RIGHT DIRECTION

DER FARBCODE ENTWICKELT SICH – DIE RICHTUNG STIMMT

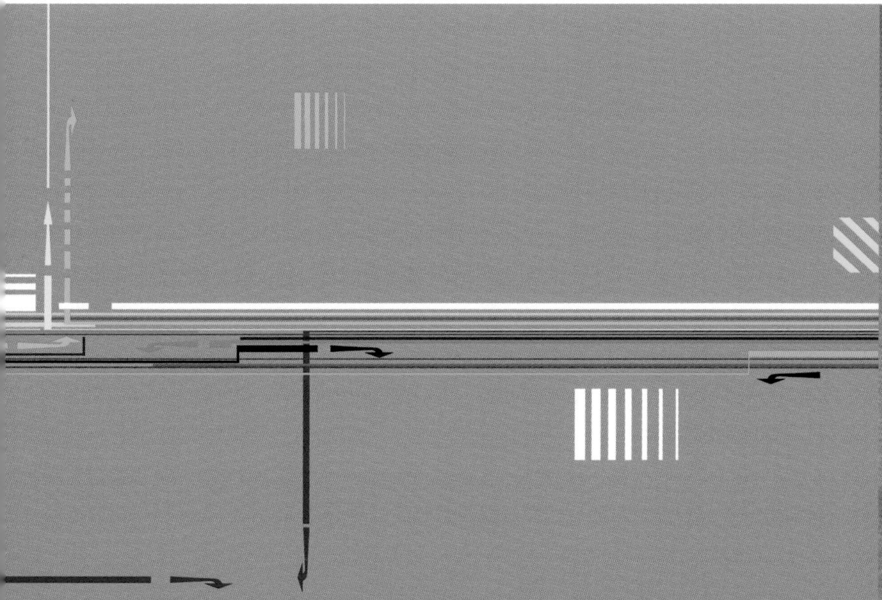

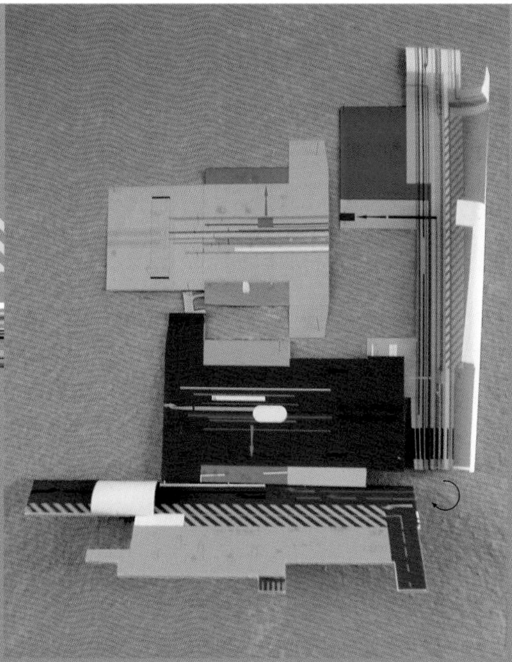

THE DISCOVERY

THE CONCEPT

»The color model«: By folding it appropriately, the 2-dimensional graphic design pinned on the board became a model for visualizing the planned orientation system. Birgit Koelz' congenial conversion of this idea into a color model was very convincing. »Das Faltmodell«: Die 2-dimensionale Grafik an der Pinnwand wurde durch Umklappen zum Anschauungsmodell des geplanten Orientierungssystems. Birgit Koelz´ kongeniale Umsetzung dieser Idee in ein Farbmodell war überzeugend.

Content-oriented design has much to do with analytical comprehension. To read with alert eyes – the answer often lies in a detail, in a fleeting moment. Inhaltsorientierte Gestaltung hat viel mit analytischem Verständnis zu tun. Lesen mit wachem Auge – oft steckt die Antwort im Detail, im flüchtigen Moment.

COLOR AS ORIENTATION
FARBE ALS ORIENTIERUNG

pages and links Verweise
I. 58 – 59, 68 – 69
II. 138 – 139
III. 226 – 227

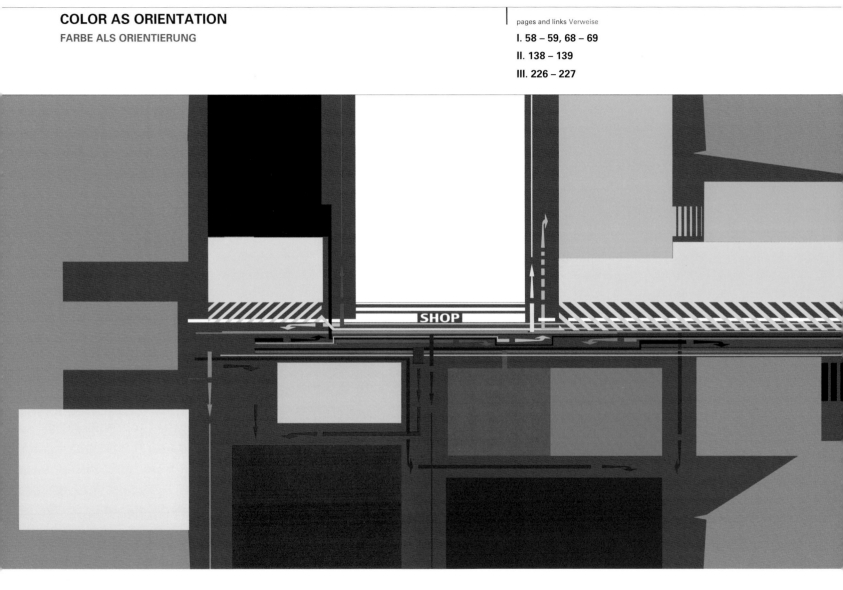

»*The color code made the markings possible. The identification and the finding of 24 different product sections became simple and problemfree. Mit dem Farbcode wurde die Markierung ermöglicht. Das Identifizieren und Auffinden der 24 unterschiedlichen Produktareas war dadurch einfach und problemlos.*«
[URB]

Every area is color-coded. Colored lines lead the visitor to the desired area. In addition, numbers are used in the city map as a supplemental aid to assist trade show visitors.

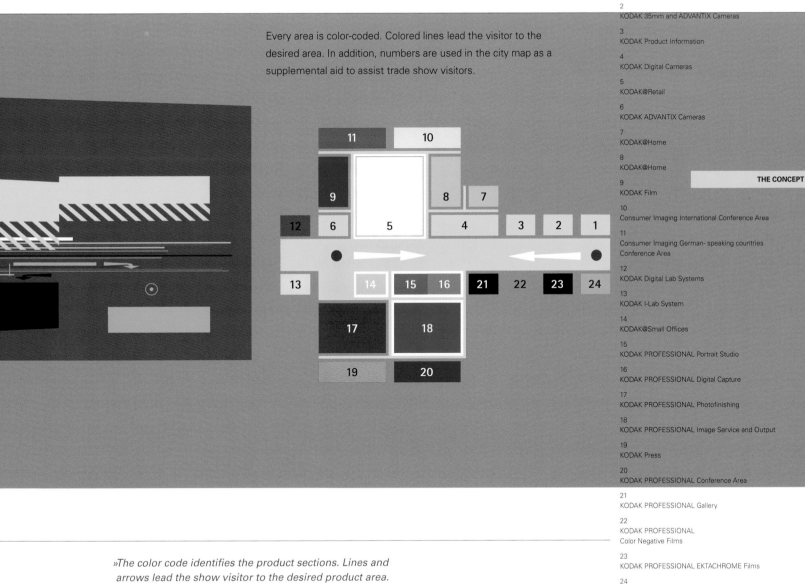

1
KODAK ULTRA Cameras

2
KODAK 35mm and ADVANTIX Cameras

3
KODAK Product Information

4
KODAK Digital Cameras

5
KODAK@Retail

6
KODAK ADVANTIX Cameras

7
KODAK@Home

8
KODAK@Home

THE CONCEPT

9
KODAK Film

10
Consumer Imaging International Conference Area

11
Consumer Imaging German- speaking countries Conference Area

12
KODAK Digital Lab Systems

13
KODAK I-Lab System

14
KODAK@Small Offices

15
KODAK PROFESSIONAL Portrait Studio

16
KODAK PROFESSIONAL Digital Capture

17
KODAK PROFESSIONAL Photofinishing

18
KODAK PROFESSIONAL Image Service and Output

19
KODAK Press

20
KODAK PROFESSIONAL Conference Area

21
KODAK PROFESSIONAL Gallery

22
KODAK PROFESSIONAL Color Negative Films

23
KODAK PROFESSIONAL EKTACHROME Films

24
KODAK at the Olympic Games

»The color code identifies the product sections. Lines and arrows lead the show visitor to the desired product area. Der Farbcode definiert die Produkträume. Linien und Pfeile führen den Besucher zu den entsprechenden Produktbereichen.«

[BK]

ROOM SKETCHES IN COLOR AND SHAPES
RAUMSKIZZEN IN FARBE UND FORM

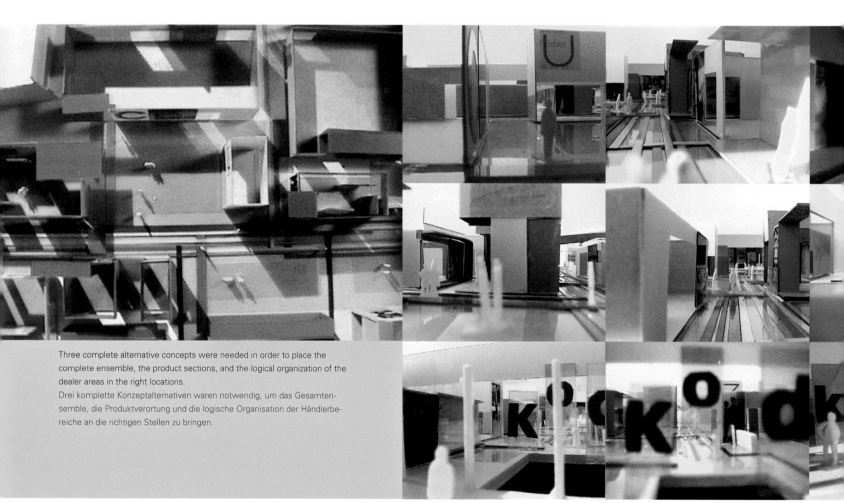

Three complete alternative concepts were needed in order to place the complete ensemble, the product sections, and the logical organization of the dealer areas in the right locations.

Drei komplette Konzeptalternativen waren notwendig, um das Gesamtensemble, die Produktverortung und die logische Organisation der Händlerbereiche an die richtigen Stellen zu bringen.

»... So many ideas, so much time and so much material makes me apprehensive. I ask myself, who is going to pay for this? This is not economically justifiable. Good Lord, if the company belonged to me?! URB's reply: ›... don't worry about it, this is our way of working. It distinguishes the special quality of the Brückner Studio ...‹ I experienced this philosophy, but only later did I understand it correctly ...

... So viele Ideen, so viel Zeit und so viel Material machen mich nachdenklich. Ich frage mich, wer soll das bezahlen. Wirtschaftlich vertretbar ist das nicht. Oh Gott, wenn mir das Unternehmen gehören würde?!
Antwort von URB: ›... machen Sie sich da mal keine Sorgen, dies ist unser Arbeitsstil. Das zeichnet die spezielle Qualität des Atelier Brückner aus ...‹ Diese Philosophie habe ich erlebt und erst später richtig verstanden ...«
[FOM]

THE CONCEPT

»The philosophy of the Brückner Studio: Alternatives instead of a single idea. I prefer to think in terms of alternatives, rather than tenaciously having to modify so-called ingenious ideas until they are unrecognizable. A lazy compromise costs just as much in the end, but the results are less effective. Die Philosophie von atb: Alternativen statt einer einzigen Idee. Es ist mir lieber, in Alternativen zu denken, als verkrampft sogenannte geniale Ideen bis zur Unkenntlichkeit verbiegen zu müssen. Ein fauler Kompromiss kostet am Ende gleich viel und bringt dennoch weniger ein.«
[URB]

RADIANT FACES – THE TOY TRAIN EFFECT WORKS!
STRAHLENDE GESICHTER – DER MÄRKLINEFFEKT WIRKT

pages and links Verweise
II. 122 – 129
III. 184 – 187

Experience has shown that many decision-makers do not possess a ready ability to envision a project in three dimensions. Complex Powerpoint presentations, graphic designs, illustrations and 3D animations cannot replace a conceptual three-dimensional model. The model is usually the center of attention. A scale model generates confidence in a concept, makes the feasibility seem realistic and it lets the viewer clearly envision how the project will look once it becomes reality. Accurately detailed concepts or design models enhance the client´s decision-making ability and with it the designer's probability of success.

Die Erfahrung hat gezeigt, dass viele Entscheidungsträger über kein ausgeprägtes räumliches Vorstellungsvermögen verfügen. Aufwändige Powerpoint-Präsentationen, Grafiken, Illustrationen und 3D-Animationen konnten kein konzeptionelles Modell ersetzen. Meistens steht das Modell im Mittelpunkt des Interesses. Erst ein maßstabgerechtes Modell erzeugt Vertrauen in ein Konzept, lässt die Machbarkeit realistisch erscheinen und gibt eine verlässliche Vorstellung von einer späteren Realisierung. Detailgetreue Konzept- oder Entwurfsmodelle erhöhen die Entscheidungsbereitschaft der Auftraggeber und damit auch die Erfolgsaussichten der Gestalter.

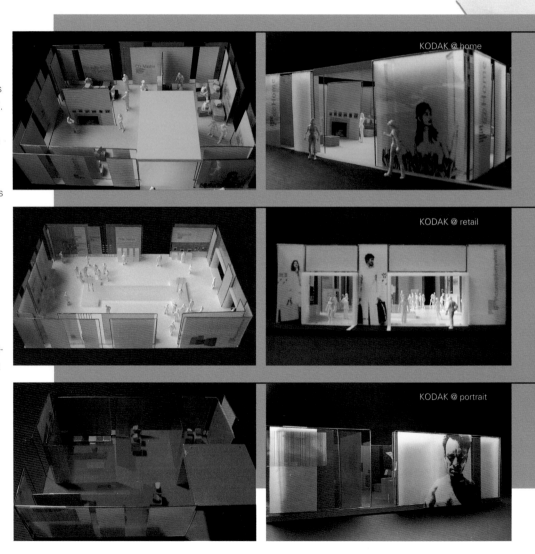

KODAK @ home

KODAK @ retail

KODAK @ portrait

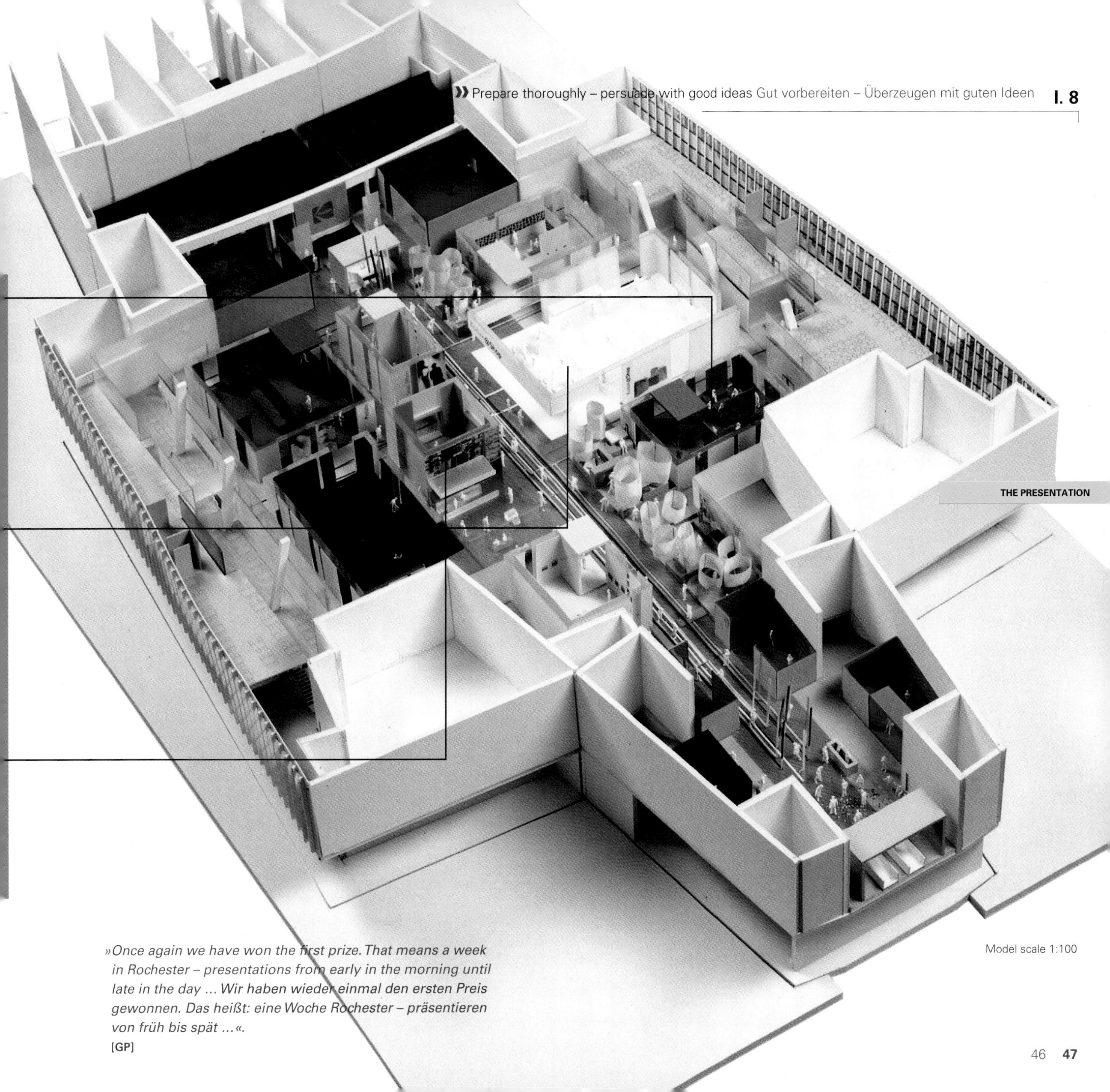

THE PRESENTATION

Model scale 1:100

»Once again we have won the first prize. That means a week
in Rochester – presentations from early in the morning until
late in the day ... Wir haben wieder einmal den ersten Preis
gewonnen. Das heißt: eine Woche Rochester – präsentieren
von früh bis spät ...«.
[GP]

WHAT IMPRESSES AND STICKS? WHAT DO PEOPLE TAKE AWAY?
WAS PRÄGT, WAS BLEIBT HÄNGEN, WAS NEHMEN DIE LEUTE MIT?

pages and links Verweise
II. 130 – 133
III. 188 – 201

DOWN TO EARTH

What we are searching for is the key take-away, the »Big Picture«, the bull's-eye shot, as Werner Kreober-Riel described it.
The purple cow, the classic example of a unique and unmistakable idea serves as an example and motivation.

Gesucht, wird das Key Take-Away, das »Big Picture«, der »Schuss in den Kopf«, wie Werner Kreober-Riel es nannte. Die Lila Kuh, das klassische Beispiel einer eigenständigen und unverwechselbaren Idee, muss als Vorbild und Ansporn herhalten.

»We need a key picture that impresses, that stays with you and that will make a lasting impression on visitors' minds.
Wir brauchen ein ›Schlüsselbild‹, das prägt, das hängen bleibt und sich nachhaltig in den Köpfen der Besucher verankert.«

[FOM]

»... what else does he [FOM] want now? A ›Key Take-Away‹ in the ›Touch-and-Feel Area‹, a kind of barbecue grill zone, perhaps? ... *was will er [FOM] denn jetzt noch? Ein ›Key Take-Away‹ in der Touch and Feel Area, eine Art Grillzone vielleicht?«*

[URB]

FROM THE »TOUCH-AND-FEEL« AREA TO THE »BARBECUE GRILL ZONE«.

About touching and trying out, having fun and communicating with friends.

Now the »creative« types can really let loose. Any number of sitting areas in different configurations – but where is the message? Where is the connection with our trade show claim »KODAK – The Universal Language«? What is the Key Take-Away? Many ideas but no solutions.

General dissatisfaction became widespread. Now it was a matter of saving what could be saved. Portions were taken from several drafts and used for developing new ideas, but this too, did not work. A salvage attempt by Uwe Brückner brought about the turn-around. The client meeting came to an end and no decision had been made when Uwe Brückner passed one of his famous sketches across the table, saying: But this is what KODAK is, language, typography, symbols, signs. The idea was born. The decision was made within a few minutes and all the participants were happy.

VON DER »TOUCH AND FEEL AREA« ZUR »GRILLZONE«.

Vom Anfassen und Ausprobieren, zum Spaß haben und Kommunizieren mit Freunden.

Jetzt legten die »Kreativen« richtig los. Jede Menge Sitzlandschaften in unterschiedlichen Designs, aber wo bleibt die Message? Wo ist die Verbindung zu unserem Messe-Claim »KODAK – The Universal Language«? Was ist der Key Take-Away?

Viele Ideen und keine Lösung.

Allgemeine Unzufriedenheit machte sich breit. Jetzt hieß es retten, was zu retten war. Aus verschiedenen Entwürfen wurden Teile entnommen und daraus neue Ideen entwickelt, auch dies funktionierte nicht. Ein Rettungsversuch von Uwe Brückner brachte die Wende. Das Kunden-Meeting ging zu Ende, und keine Entscheidung war gefallen, als Uwe Brückner eine seiner berühmten Skizzen über den Tisch schob, mit den Worten: Das ist doch KODAK, Sprache, Schrift, Symbole, Zeichen.

Die Idee war geboren. Die Entscheidung war in wenigen Minuten getroffen, und alle Beteiligten waren glücklich.

Fashion Advertising Awards 2000 © Tim Oeyen & Sanny Winters

THE KEY-TAKEAWAY

THE SOLUTION

Three-dimensional letters become texts, oversized, to be walked upon. Product features become presentation tables, seating furniture and showcase shelves. The barbecue grill zone becomes the key take-away.

DIE LÖSUNG

Dreidimensionale Buchstaben werden zu Texten, übergroß, begehbar. Produkteigenschaften werden zu Präsentationstischen, Sitzmöbeln und Vitrinenregalen. Die Grillzone wird zum fotogenen Key Take-Away.

NIGHTMARE TOUCH AND FEEL
ALPTRAUM GRILLZONE

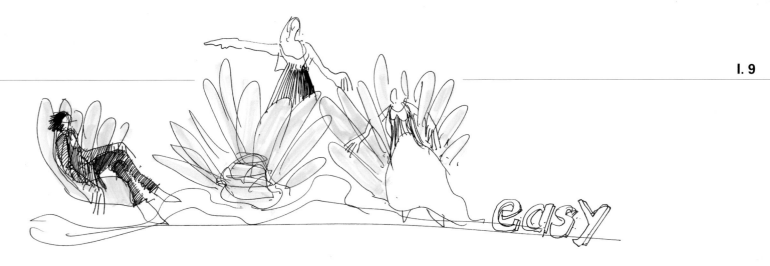

Even though the color orientation system was so well received, it was not yet time for applause. None of the many proposals for harmonizing the product presentations and the so-called »touch-and-feel-area« with the slogans of the product areas while also turning this »barbecue grill zone« into a photogenic key take-away met with the necessary acceptance.

Trotz des überzeugenden Farbleitsystems war die Kuh noch nicht vom Eis. Keiner der vielen Vorschläge, die Produktpräsentation und die sogenannte »Touch and Feel Area« mit den Slogans der Produktareas zusammenzubringen und diese »Grillzone« auch noch gleichzeitig zum fotogenen Key Take-Away zu gestalten, fand die notwendige Zustimmung.

THE KEY-TAKEAWAY

TOUCH AND FEEL. TRIAL AND ERROR

DIE GRILLZONE ALS SPIELWIESE

Several stand models were needed before products, slogans, and color concept harmonized. Etliche Modellalternativen waren nötig, damit Produkte, Slogans und Farbkonzept harmonierten.

A world of impressions is conjured up by the models: scenographic spaces as a miniature trade show cosmos. Im Modell wächst eine Erlebniswelt: szenographische Räume als Makromessekosmos.

To design for contents and messages means to convey reasons and intentions, because then the design can contextualize, and establish the relationship between environment and products. Aus den Inhalten und Botschaften heraus zu gestalten heißt, Sinn und Absicht zu vermitteln, dann kann Gestaltung kontextualisieren, den Zusammenhang zwischen Environment und Produkt herstellen.

WISHES AND REALITY – OR THE LIMITS OF ASSIGNMENT PHOTOGRAPHY
WUNSCH UND WIRKLICHKEIT – ODER DIE GRENZEN DER AUFTRAGSFOTOGRAFIE

pages and links Verweise
III. 204 – 225

To KODAK, exhibiting pictures means displaying photography of the very highest level. Abiding by this credo means that every shoot is a fresh challenge in creativity and technique aimed at presenting the client and the critical target audience of photographers with outstanding photographic performances. There are several possibilities for achieving such peak performances. One can commission an internationally recognized photographer who is fully respected by his colleagues, or one can invite a striving young photodesigner, for whom KODAK would provide an opportunity to launch his professional future. But caution is the better part of wisdom: neither assignment photographs made to exact specifications, nor freelance work performed on assignment automatically guarantee outstanding photographs.

A renowned photographer receives an assignment for a series of 5 photographs on a given theme. There is a briefing, a pre-production meeting, the selection of models, the styling, and the location – everything is clear. The expectations run high. The result: one photograph exceeds our expectations, it is simply world-class. A second photograph meets our expectations completely and we are satisfied. A third photograph meets our expectations, except for minor weaknesses, we can still accept it. The fourth and fifth photographs do not come up to our demands. Reality has caught up with us. Top photographs do not pop up on command.

»Integrative composition requires the context of all the creative means. This means that the predominant color impressions in the photographs should be congruent with the color code. Integrative Gestaltung verlangt Kontextualisierung aller gestalterischen Maßnahmen, d.h. die dominierenden Farbeindrücke in den Fotos sollten kongruent mit dem Farbcode sein.«
[URB]

Bilder ausstellen heißt für KODAK: Fotografie präsentieren auf höchstem Niveau. Um diesem Anspruch gerecht zu werden, ist jedes Shooting immer wieder eine Herausforderung an Kreativität und Technik, um den Auftrageber sowie die kritische Zielgruppe der Fotografen mit fotografischen Höchstleistungen überzeugen zu können. Um diese Spitzenqualität zu erzielen, gibt es verschiedene Möglichkeiten. Man beauftragt einen international anerkannten Fotografen, der außerhalb jeglicher Kritik bei seinen Kollegen steht, oder man nimmt einen jungen aufstrebenden Fotodesigner, dem KODAK für seine berufliche Zukunft eine Bühne zur Verfügung stellt. Doch Vorsicht: Weder das Auftragsbild mit exakten Vorgaben noch die freie Arbeit als Auftragsbild garantieren automatisch außergewöhnliche Fotos.

Ein renommierter Fotograf erhält den Auftrag für eine Serie von 5 Bildern zu einem Thema. Es gibt ein Briefing, das Pre-Production-Meeting, die Auswahl der Modelle, das Styling, die Location, alles ist klar. Die Erwartungen sind hoch. Das Ergebnis: Ein Foto übertrifft die Erwartungen, es ist einfach Weltklasse. Ein Foto trifft die Erwartungen voll und ganz, wir sind zufrieden. Ein Foto entspricht den Erwartungen mit leichten Abstrichen, wir können es noch akzeptieren. Zwei Fotos erfüllen nicht unsere Ansprüche. Die Realität hat uns eingeholt. Spitzenfotos entstehen nicht auf Knopfdruck.

KODAK RED

POTENTIAL OF PHOTOGRAPHY

Igor Panitz

»The photograph by Igor Panitz was an instant success. An idea, a shot, a hit. Bei dem Foto von Igor Panitz hat es sofort ›geklickt‹. Eine Idee, ein Schuss, ein Treffer.«
[SJ]

The colors specified for the KODAK@home area:

PANTONE 382
KODAK@HOME
ZONE 6+6A

PANTONE 100

PANTONE PROCESS
YELLOW

PANTONE 343

NO DIVING INTO COLD WATER - A NEW APPROACH TO ASSIGNMENT PHOTOGRAPHY
KEIN SPRUNG INS KALTE WASSER – AUFTRAGSFOTOGRAFIE EINMAL ANDERS

In the spring of the year 2000 KODAK introduces a new generation of color negative films with the product names Max and Farbwelt. The progress: additional uses in photographic applications. The higher speed films have significantly improved color rendition, sharpness, grain, contrast and skin tone rendition. The 400-speed film becomes the all-around film – greater flash range, better for use with long focal length lenses, faster shutter speeds for better sharpness. The objective is to demonstrate the benefits simply and convincingly. In cooperation with Walter Fogel, a former performance sportsman who specializes in sports photography and who operates a studio in the town of Angelbachtal, we strive to prove the product benefits dramatically by means of fast action photographs. We came up with the idea of photographing a diver in action, using four cameras loaded with the four different films and fired simultaneously. The shoot takes place in the public swimming pool of the town of Sinsheim. The charming sports student has to repeat the dive into cold water (17°C / 63°F) again and again. The result is dramatic. Not only is this picture sequence praised at Photokina as an outstanding example of the versatility of these new KODAK films, they are subsequently used successfully around the world in press releases, advertising and sales promotion.

»How can products be showcased effectively when there is no aura of quality? The potential is often contained in the applications, especially in the case of films ... Wie können Produkte nachhaltig in Szene gesetzt werden, wenn keine auratische Qualität vorhanden ist? Das Potential steckt häufig in der Anwendung, wie z.B. bei Filmen.« [FOM]

Four cameras, fired simultaneously, demonstrate the differences

Im Frühjahr 2000 führt KODAK eine neue Generation von Color-negativfilmen mit den Produktbezeichnungen Max und Farbwelt ein. Der Fortschritt: mehr Einsatzmöglichkeiten in der fotografischen Anwendung. Die höher empfindlichen Filme sind in den Bereichen Farbe, Schärfe, Korn, Kontrast und Hauttonwiedergabe wesentlich verbessert. Der 400er wird zum Allround-Film – größere Blitzreichweite, besser für den Einsatz von langen Brennweiten, kurze Verschlusszeiten für bessere Bildschärfe. Diese Vorteile gilt es einfach und überzeugend darzustellen. Zusammen mit dem Fotodesigner Walter Fogel, ein ehemaliger Leistungssportler, der seine Wurzeln in der Sportfotografie hat und heute ein Studio in Angelbachtal betreibt, versuchen wir am Beispiel von »fast action« die Produktvorteile eindrucksvoll in einer Bilderserie umzusetzen. Wir haben die Idee, einen Sprung ins Wasser mit vier Kameras, geladen mit den vier unterschiedlichen Filmen, die wir gleichzeitig auslösten, zu fotografieren. Das Shooting findet im öffentlichen Schwimmbad in Sinsheim statt. Immer und immer wieder

POTENTIAL OF PHOTOGRAPHY

muss die charmante Sportstudentin den Sprung ins kalte Wasser (17 Grad) wiederholen. Das Ergebnis kann sich sehen lassen. Diese Bildserie findet nicht nur die Anerkennung auf der photokina als hervorragendes Beispiel für die Versatility der neuen KODAK Filme, sondern wird danach weltweit in Presse, Werbung und Verkaufsförderung erfolgreich eingesetzt.

Walter Fogel

FROM CORPORATE COLORS TO THE NEW WORLD OF COLOR
VON DER HAUSFARBE ZUR NEUEN FARBWELT

pages and links Verweise
II. 138 – 139
III. 226 – 227

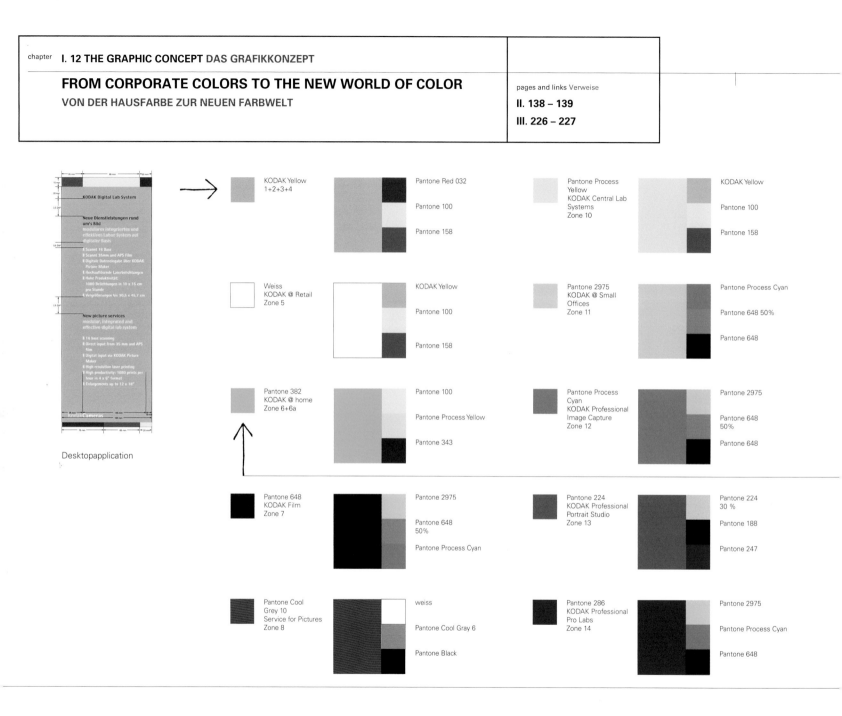

Desktopapplication

KODAK Yellow
1+2+3+4

Pantone Red 032

Pantone 100

Pantone 158

Pantone Process Yellow
KODAK Central Lab Systems
Zone 10

KODAK Yellow

Pantone 100

Pantone 158

Weiss
KODAK @ Retail
Zone 5

KODAK Yellow

Pantone 100

Pantone 158

Pantone 2975
KODAK @ Small Offices
Zone 11

Pantone Process Cyan

Pantone 648 50%

Pantone 648

Pantone 382
KODAK @ home
Zone 6+6a

Pantone 100

Pantone Process Yellow

Pantone 343

Pantone Process Cyan
KODAK Professional Image Capture
Zone 12

Pantone 2975

Pantone 648 50%

Pantone 648

Pantone 648
KODAK Film
Zone 7

Pantone 2975

Pantone 648 50%

Pantone Process Cyan

Pantone 224
KODAK Professional Portrait Studio
Zone 13

Pantone 224 30 %

Pantone 188

Pantone 247

Pantone Cool Grey 10
Service for Pictures
Zone 8

weiss

Pantone Cool Gray 6

Pantone Black

Pantone 286
KODAK Professional Pro Labs
Zone 14

Pantone 2975

Pantone Process Cyan

Pantone 648

»Could you finally use the colors we´ve selected! They look
different every time! Könnt ihr endlich mal die verbindlichen
Farben einsetzen? Jedesmal sehen die anders aus!«
[FOM]

»... my heart bled when I saw the cut-up fan of
Pantone colors. ... da hat mir das Herz geblutet,
beim Anblick des zerschnittenen Pantonefächers.«
[BK]

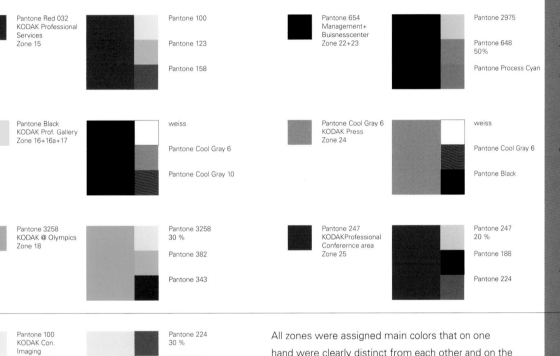

Pantone Red 032 KODAK Professional Services Zone 15	Pantone 100 / Pantone 123 / Pantone 158
Pantone Black KODAK Prof. Gallery Zone 16+16a+17	weiss / Pantone Cool Gray 6 / Pantone Cool Gray 10
Pantone 3258 KODAK @ Olympics Zone 18	Pantone 3258 30 % / Pantone 382 / Pantone 343
Pantone 100 KODAK Con. Imaging International Conference Area	Pantone 224 30 % / KODAK Yellow / Pantone 247
Zone 20 Pantone 158 KODAK Con. Imaging Conference Area Zone 21	Pantone 100 / KODAK Yellow / Pantone Process Yellow

Pantone 654 Management+ Buisnesscenter Zone 22+23	Pantone 2975 / Pantone 648 50% / Pantone Process Cyan
Pantone Cool Gray 6 KODAK Press Zone 24	weiss / Pantone Cool Gray 6 / Pantone Black
Pantone 247 KODAK Professional Conference area Zone 25	Pantone 247 20 % / Pantone 188 / Pantone 224

All zones were assigned main colors that on one hand were clearly distinct from each other and on the other hand were harmoniously tailored to one another in similar areas. The KODAK corporate colors yellow and red served as basic colors for the new world of color and for the orientation system. 30 m^2 (323 ft^2) test printings with laminates had to be made in order to achieve the Pantone colors with digital printers.

Für alle Zonen werden Hauptfarben definiert, die sich einerseits klar unterscheiden und andererseits für ähnliche Bereiche harmonisch aufeinander abgestimmt sind. Die Hausfarben von KODAK, das Gelb und das Rot, dienen als Basisfarben der neuen Farbwelt und des Orientierungssystems. 30 m^2 Testausdrucke mit Laminat sind erforderlich, um mit Digitalprintern die Pantonefarben zu erreichen.

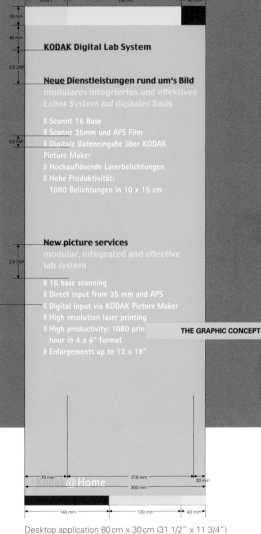

KODAK Digital Lab System

Neue Dienstleistungen rund um's Bild
modulares integriertes und effektives Labor System auf digitaler Basis

▮ Scannt 16 Base
▮ Scannt 35mm und APS Film
▮ Digitale Dateneingabe über KODAK Picture Maker
▮ Hochauflösende Laserbelichtungen
▮ Hohe Produktivität: 1080 Belichtungen in 10 x 15 cm

New picture services
modular, integrated and effective lab system

▮ 16 base scanning
▮ Direct input from 35 mm and APS
▮ Digital input via KODAK Picture Maker
▮ High resolution laser printing
▮ High productivity: 1080 prin hour in 4 x 6" format
▮ Enlargements up to 12 x 18"

THE GRAPHIC CONCEPT

Kodak@Home

Desktop application 80 cm x 30 cm (31 1/2" x 11 3/4")
Type size 38 pt/52 for zones 6 and 6a

GRAPHIC DESIGN ON THE WAY TO THE THIRD DIMENSION
GRAFIK AUF DEM WEG IN DIE DRITTE DIMENSION

First there is a plan, then comes a scale model for simulating the spatial
effect and it all culminates in an impressive result when it becomes reality.
Am Anfang steht der Plan, gefolgt von einem maßstabsgetreuen Modell zur
Simulation der Wirkung im Raum, und es endet als überzeugendes Resultat
beim Übertragen in die Realität.

THE GRAPHIC CONCEPT

»Using two-dimensional graphic design as a spatial visual medium requires thinking in three dimensions while creating graphic designs – something that up to now is still seldom taught in German colleges. Zweidimensionale Grafik als raumbildnerisches Medium einzusetzen verlangt von Grafikern, dreidimensional zu denken, etwas, das an deutschen Hochschulen bisher kaum wahrgenommen wird.«
[URB]

SYNCHRONIZATION OF IMAGE NARRATION AND COLOR CODING
SYNCHRONISATION VON BILDNARRATION UND FARBCODIERUNG

pages and links Verweise

II. 140 – 141

III. 228 – 229

1

2

3

Kodak@Olympics

KodakHighlights

Kodak Cameras Advantix Cameras

Kodak@Retail

Kodak@Home

Kodak Film

Kodak@Small Offices

Kodak Film

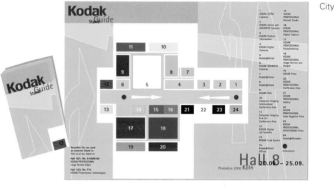

City-Guide

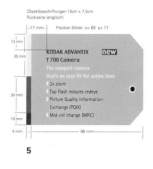

Objektbeschriftungen 10cm x 7,5cm
Rückseite (englisch)

–17 mm–   Position Störer: x= 65 y= 17

13 mm

KODAK ADVANTIX new
T 700 Camera
35 mm

The compact camera
that's an easy fit for active lives

☐ 2x zoom
30 mm   ☐ Top Flash reduces redeye
☐ Picture Quality Information
Exchange (PQIX)
10 mm   ☐ Mid-roll change (MRC)

4 mm |——————— 96 mm ———————|

5

4

1
Paper bag

2
Ad catalog

3
Staff identification badges

4
Stand floorplan

5
Product labels

All the required means of communication were developed and produced for use on the stand in accordance with the specified graphic design guidelines in order to achieve a KODAK presence that is uniformly coordinated down to the smallest application. That presents visitors with a corporate design concept of the KODAK brand that is very homogeneous in spite of the different lines of business. Only a small portion of the extensive array is shown on this page.

Für die Grafikproduktion werden alle erforderlichen Kommunikationsmittel nach den speziell für diesen Messestand entwickelten Gestaltungsrichtlinien definiert und umgesetzt, um den einheitlichen Auftritt des Messestandes bis zur kleinsten Anwendung abzurunden. Dadurch wird dem Besucher ein Corporate-Design-Konzept der Marke KODAK vermittelt, das trotz der unterschiedlichen Geschäftsbereiche sehr homogen wirkt. Auf dieser Seite ist nur eine kleine Auswahl des sehr umfangreichen Sortiments zu sehen.

THE GRAPHIC CONCEPT

Kodak Product Information — Pantone Cool Gray 6

Kodak Capture / Kodak Portrait Studio — Pantone 224

Kodak Services — Pantone Red 032

Kodak Pro Labs — Pantone 272

Kodak Gallery — alternate schwarz

Kodak Press — 247

Conference Area — cyan

THE ARCHITECTURAL CONCEPT
DAS ARCHITEKTONISCHE KONZEPT

pages and links Verweise
II. 142 – 145
III. 232 – 239

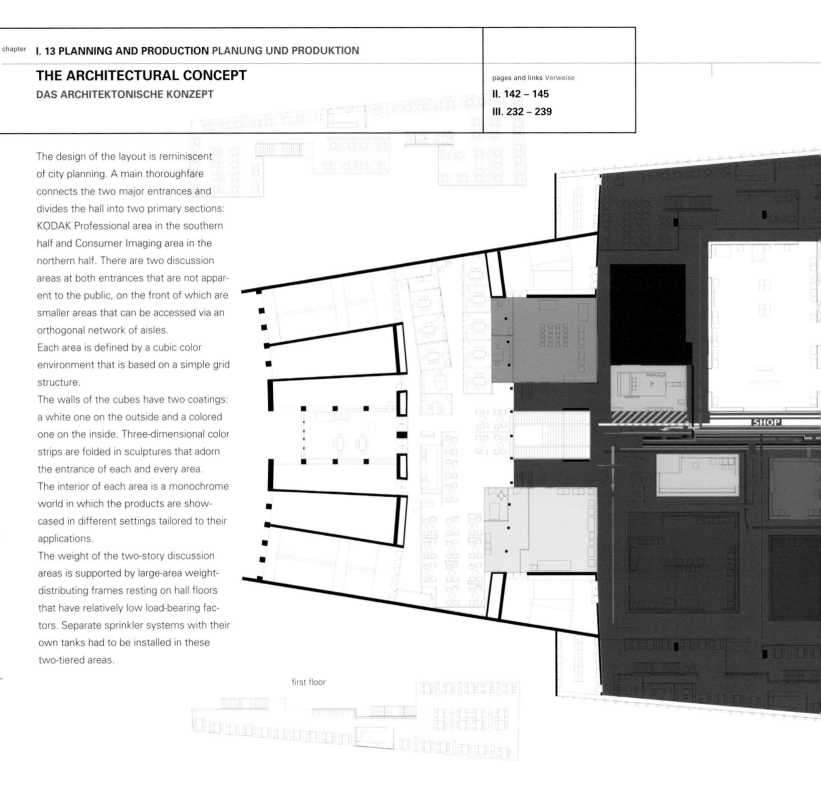

The design of the layout is reminiscent of city planning. A main thoroughfare connects the two major entrances and divides the hall into two primary sections: KODAK Professional area in the southern half and Consumer Imaging area in the northern half. There are two discussion areas at both entrances that are not apparent to the public, on the front of which are smaller areas that can be accessed via an orthogonal network of aisles.

Each area is defined by a cubic color environment that is based on a simple grid structure.

The walls of the cubes have two coatings: a white one on the outside and a colored one on the inside. Three-dimensional color strips are folded in sculptures that adorn the entrance of each and every area.

The interior of each area is a monochrome world in which the products are showcased in different settings tailored to their applications.

The weight of the two-story discussion areas is supported by large-area weight-distributing frames resting on hall floors that have relatively low load-bearing factors. Separate sprinkler systems with their own tanks had to be installed in these two-tiered areas.

first floor

Der Entwurf macht Anleihen an städtebaulichen Strukturen. Eine Hauptachse verbindet die beiden Eingänge und gliedert die Halle schwerpunktmäßig in zwei Bereiche: den KODAK Professional-Bereich im Süden und Consumer-Imaging-Bereich im Norden. An den Hallenfassaden befinden sich die vom Besucher nicht einsehbaren, doppelstöckigen Besprechungszonen, diesen vorgelagert sind kleinere Bereiche (Räume), die durch ein orthogonales Wegenetz erschlossen werden.

Jeder Bereich wird durch einen kubischen Farbraum definiert; eine einfache Gerüstkonstruktion dient hierfür als Grundlage. Die Wände der Kuben sind zweischichtig bespielt: außen mit einer weißen und innen mit einer farbigen Schicht.

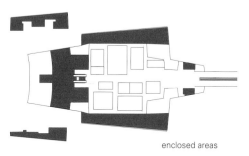

enclosed areas

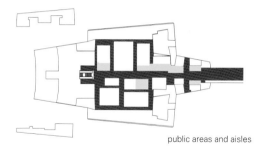

public areas and aisles

3-dimensional aufgefaltete, farbige Bänder werden zu Eingangsskulpturen eines jeden Bereiches.

Im Inneren der Bereiche entsteht eine eigene monochrome Welt, in der die Produkte je nach Anforderung in unterschiedlichen Atmosphären inszeniert werden. Die Last der doppelgeschossigen Besprechungsbereiche wird durch großflächige Lastverteilungsrahmen auf den nur gering belastbaren Hallenboden abgetragen. Für diese Bereiche musste jeweils eine Sprinkleranlage mit eigenem Tank nachgerüstet werden.

PLANNING AND PRODUCTION

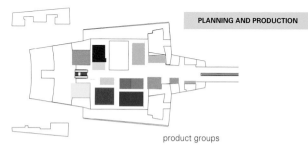

product groups

STEEL FRAMEWORK WITH FABRIC COVERING
STAHLGERÜST MIT STOFFBEZUG

In order to remain as flexible as possible and to create lightweight, optically translucent room partitions that can be set up and taken down quickly and at moderate cost, steel framework units with fabric covering were selected.

Standard zinc-plated pipes with a 48 mm (2 7/8") diameter are arranged in a vertical plane and connected by means of the "Tubeclamp" System by KeeClamp. The result is a series of two-layered, self-standing walls with an overall height of 3.5 to 6.5 m (11'6" to 21'4") and a thickness of 50 cm (19 11/16").

This basic structure serves as a support for the illumination rigs and they also serve as a framework on which will be suspended such items as

- Lengths of cloth: translucent, white Trevira CS fabric on the outside; opaque dyed Trevira CS on the inside.

A total of 450 m² (4.844 ft²) of fabric will be imprinted;
- Lightboxes;
- Display cases
- Graphic designs, information- and product carriers of diverse shapes and sizes.

Um möglichst flexibel zu bleiben, eine leichte, optisch durchlässige Raumbegrenzung zu erhalten, die schnelle Auf- und Abbauzeiten bei moderaten Kostenstrukturen gewährleistet, wird ein mit Stoff bespanntes Stahlgerüstsystem gewählt.

Verzinkte Standardrohre mit einem Durchmesser von 48 mm werden in einer Ebene geführt und mit dem System »Tubeclamp« von KeeClamp verbunden. Daraus entstehen zweischalig aufgebaute, selbst stehende Wände mit einer Gesamthöhe von 3,5 bis 6,5 m bei einer Stärke von 50 cm.

Diese Unterkonstruktion dient als Auflager der Beleuchtungsriggs sowie als Rahmen für eingehängte Elemente. Daran befestigt werden so verschiedenartige Dinge und Materialien wie:

- Stoffbahnen: außen transluzentes, weißes Trevira-CS-Gewebe; innen eingefärbte Trevira CS in blickdichter Ausführung. Insgesamt werden 450 m² Stoff bedruckt
- Leuchtkästen
- Vitrinen und Schaukästen
- Grafik-, Informations- und Objektträger unterschiedlichster Ausformungen

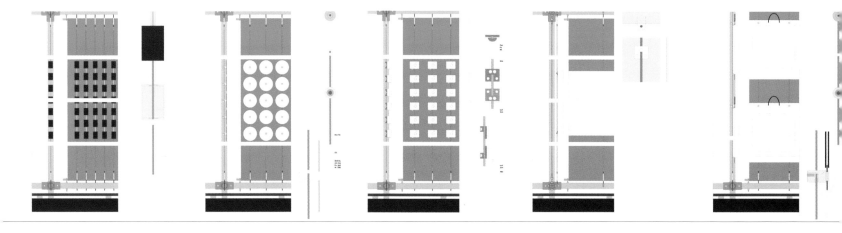

Hundreds of KODAK products, such as cameras, film cartons, CDs and print envelopes must mounted on steel cables as high as the room in the shortest possible time. The number of steel cables and the total weight of the items on display cause the framework in this section to sag, so that it has to be reinforced. This in turn caused a considerable time delay. The easiness of this product collage fascinated the designers, the client, and later on the visitors.

Hunderte von KODAK Produkten, wie Kameras, Filmschachteln, CDs oder Bildertaschen, mussten in kürzester Zeit raumhoch und an Stahlseilen montiert werden. Die Anzahl der Stahlseile sowie das Gesamtgewicht der Exponate bewirkte, dass die Rahmenkonstruktion in diesem Bereich sich durchbog und verstärkt werden musste, was eine erhebliche Zeitverzögerung zur Folge hatte. Die Leichtigkeit dieser Produktcollage hat die Gestalter, den Auftrageber und die Besucher fasziniert.

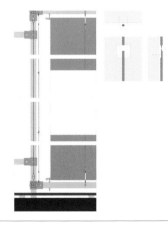

»Even for a trade show that lasts only six days, a meticulously planned execution is worthwhile. Auch für einen nur 6-tägigen Messeauftritt lohnt sich eine detailgenaue Werkplanung.«

[DH]

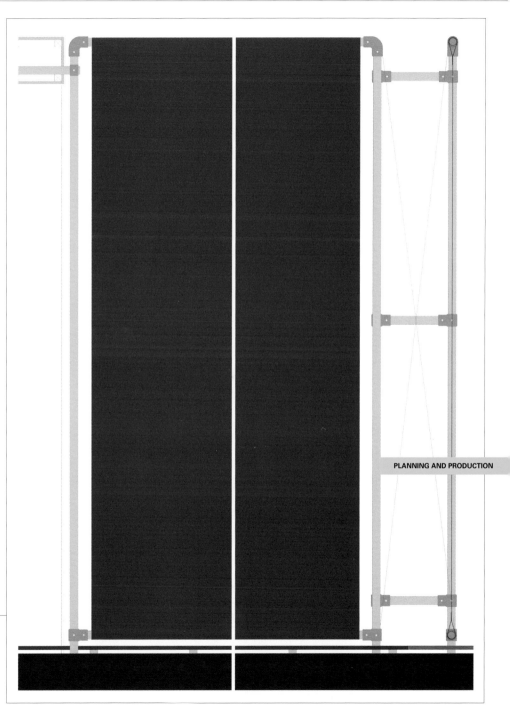

PLANNING AND PRODUCTION

A BRAND NEW WAY OF UTILIZING CARPETING

MIT DEM TEPPICHBODEN NEULAND BETRETEN

»You'll never be able to apply carpeting like that ... So einen Teppich kriegt ihr doch nie hin ...«
[FOM]

29 x 36 cm

29 x 48 cm

29 x 60 cm

29 x 72 cm

29 x 84 cm

15 m x 13,5 cm

15 m x 30 cm

,5 m x 80 cm

SHOP

5,5 m x 80 cm

2,61 m x 35 cm

1,47 m x 30 cm

10,5 m x 30 cm

1,50 m x 98,5 cm

2,93 m x 35 cm

17 cm x 45 cm

1,00m

»If we can manage a veritable tornado, then we should also be able to get this carpet installed. Wenn wir einen veritablen Tornado hinbekommen, dann werden wir doch auch diesen Teppich verlegt bekommen.«
[URB]

THE WALK-UPON ORIENTATION SYSTEM
– what a fabulous idea. Yet it was promptly followed by an objection: »But how do you expect to accomplish that…?« Paint it on the carpet, cut it into the carpet, print it and many other ideas were discussed. Many doubts are raised about this plan – too expensive, too time-consuming, too complicated. The short set-up time of 17 days is an additional problem that has to be kept in mind. Because the aisles are in extremely heavy use by workers and vehicles during the set-up phase, possible damage before the show opens has to be taken into account. Covering the carpet with chipboard would entail additional costs. There are many initial obstacles to the implementation of this floor covering treatment, but no one

wants to give up this creative masterpiece. Gray carpeting is an alternative.This safe variation is the Sword of Damocles for the »creative types«. A supplier is located and the cost estimate is surprisingly favorable. All the participants are enthusiastic. Nevertheless, the concerns remain. A telephone discussion with the supplier increases the skepticism when it is learned that this supplier has never before tried this kind of carpet imprinting, so that it is an absolutely new procedure for him. The decision is made nonetheless to take on the risk of this adventure. The first attempts are encouraging and the result is really attractive. Now a new problem emerges, as the supplier tells that a dimensional tolerance of 30 to 50 cm (11 3/4'' to 19 3/4'') in the direction of travel must be taken into account. That poses a great risk for the design of the orientation lines. The intersections might not match and there could be utter chaos. Still, the daring approach will be taken. The plan: The carpet is to be installed at night, two days before the opening of the trade show, in order to minimize the chances of possible damage. Replacements would have been impossible, both because of time constraints and also because of the special color specifications. The problem was how to clear the aisles. Obviously all of them had to be cleared completely, not just some of them. Everything had to be removed in order to roll out the entire length of the carpet and to match the connections to the lateral aisles accurately. The action is delayed. The carpet installers arrive too late and there are too few of them. They explain that they had already worked through three nights and that they were going to leave right away. Now the nerves are raw. A phone call is placed to the general manager of the supplying company and he is told to come to Cologne immediately with additional carpet layers. The original statement by [FOM] is an ultimatum: »I am now going to leave the stand, and when I return tomorrow morning, I expect to find the carpet fully installed …«. End of the phone message. On the next morning, the stand looks very good indeed. The action succeeded completely. All the participants are happy.

DAS BEGEHBARE ORIENTIERUNGSSYSTEM
Tolle Idee. Doch es folgt sofort der Einwand: »Aber wie wollt ihr das machen … ?« Aufmalen, einschneiden, drucken und viele andere Ideen werden diskutiert. Vieles spricht gegen diesen Plan – zu teuer, zu zeitaufwändig, zu kompliziert. Die kurze Aufbauzeit von 17 Tagen ist ein weiteres Problem, das zu berücksichtigen ist. Da die Gangzonen in der Aufbauphase extrem genutzt und befahren werden, muss eine mögliche Beschädigung im Vorfeld der Messe in Kauf genommen werden. Eine Abdeckung mit Spanplatten hätte weitere Kosten verursacht. Gegen diese Realisierung der Bodengestaltung spricht zunächst einiges, aber keiner will dieses kreative Meisterstück aufgeben. Grauer Teppichboden ist die Alternative.

Die Sicherheitsvariante als Damokles-Schwert für die Ideen der »Kreativen«. Ein Produzent wird gefunden und der Preis ist überraschend günstig. Alle Beteiligten sind begeistert. Dennoch bleiben Zweifel. Ein Telefonat mit dem Hersteller nährt die Skepsis, als klar wird, dass diese Art der Bedruckung von Teppichboden von diesem Unternehmen nie zuvor probiert wurde und absolutes Neuland ist. Es wird entschieden, das Abenteuer dennoch zu wagen. Die ersten Versuche verlaufen positiv, und das Ergebnis sieht wirklich gut aus. Jetzt gibt es ein weiteres Problem, der Produzent teilt mit, dass mit Toleranzen in der Maßhaltigkeit von 30 bis 50 cm in der Laufrichtung gerechnet werden muss. Das ist für die Leitliniengestaltung ein großes Risiko. Die Anschlüsse würden nicht passen, und das Chaos wäre perfekt. Das Wagnis wird dennoch eingegangen. Der Plan: Den Teppich erst in der Nacht, zwei Tage vor Messebeginn verlegen zu lassen, um möglichst keine Beschädigungen zu riskieren. Ersatz wäre sowohl zeitlich als auch farbverbindlich nicht zu beschaffen gewesen. Das Problem ist es, die Gänge frei zu bekommen. Notwendigerweise nicht partiell, sondern komplett. Alles musste raus, um die ganze Rollenlänge auszulegen und die Anschlüsse zu den Seitengängen passgenau treffen

zu können. Die Aktion verzögert sich. Die Bodenleger kommen zu spät und es sind nur sehr wenige Leute. Sie erklärten, sie hätten bereits drei Nächte durchgearbeitet und würden gleich wieder gehen. Jetzt liegen die Nerven blank. Der Geschäftsführer der Lieferfirma wird angerufen und aufgefordert, sofort mit zusätzlichen Leuten nach Köln zu kommen. Originalton [FOM]: »Ich werde jetzt den Stand verlassen und morgen früh erwarte ich, dass alles verlegt ist …«. Ende der Durchsage. Am nächsten Morgen sieht der den Stand sehr gut aus. Die Aktion ist absolut gelungen. Alle Beteiligten sind zufrieden.

COLOR ADVENTURE OR ATTRACTIVE STANDARD GRAY
FARBERLEBNIS ODER ATTRAKTIVES EINHEITSGRAU

For the planning of the carpet production, a nodal point was established in the hall, from which all the measurements will emanate. After much brainstorming, the complex carpet pattern emerges, which also takes into account the tolerances and the maximal number of eight colors per track than can be produced. The go-ahead for the production of the carpet was only given because a neutral gray replacement carpet was ready nearby. Because the installation of the carpet progresses very slowly, many KODAK staff members rebel because they are prevented from transporting their equipment along the main aisles of the hall. The nerves of the stand set-up team are on edge because they had to struggle with the problems of a very flexible carpet. Without the expert help of supplemental carpet installers, the ingenious orientation system that had become so well liked would have to be sacrificed altogether on the following morning.

»Thank heaven we have been spared the gray carpeting! Der graue Teppich blieb uns Gott sei Dank erspart.«
[BK]

»Using a design on the floor covering for an orientation system is an ingenious idea that contributes significantly to the success of the stand. Die Bodengestaltung als Orientierungssystem zu nutzen war eine geniale Idee und trug maßgeblich zum Messeerfolg bei.«
[FOM]

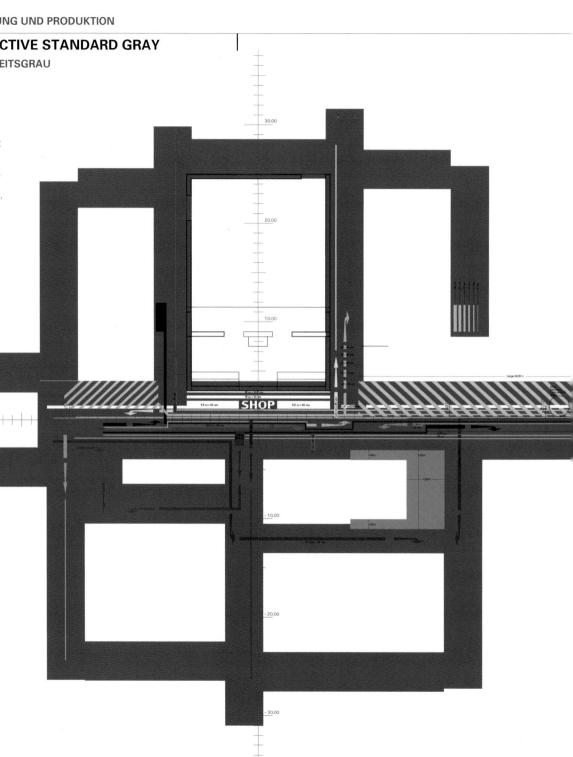

SHOP

Die Halle wird für die Teppichproduktion in der Mitte
mit einem Nullpunkt versehen, von dem aus alles
eingemessen wird. Nach viel Tüftelarbeit entsteht so
das komplexe Verlegemuster, das auch die Toleranzen und die maximal produzierbare Anzahl von
acht Farben pro Bahn berücksichtigt. Das Go für die
Umsetzung hat es nur gegeben, weil ein neutral-
grauer Ersatzteppich in Reichweite bereit liegt. Als
die Verlegearbeiten sehr schleppend vorangehen,
rebellieren viele KODAK Mitarbeiter, weil sie ihre

PLANNING AND PRODUCTION

Geräte nicht mehr problemlos über den Hauptweg
in die Halle transportieren können. Beim Messeteam
gibt es blank liegende Nerven, weil gegen die Tücken
eines sehr flexiblen Teppichs gekämpft werden
muss. Ohne zusätzliche Verlegehelfer hätte man am
nächsten Morgen dem liebgewordenen Orientierungssystem den Todesstoß versetzen müssen.

THE CONTDOWN BEGINS

DER COUNTDOWN LÄUFT

Day 1 Der 1. Tag

At last the hall is empty. Measurements can now be made. We note that once again the hall has shrunk but we are used to that. Die Halle ist endlich leer. Mit dem Einmessen kann begonnen werden. Wir stellen fest, dass die Halle wieder einmal geschrumpft ist, aber das kennen wir schon.

Day 2 Der 2. Tag

More than 20.000m (65.600 ft) of cable are laid for power, networks and telecommunications. Compressors for the compressed air that is needed are installed on the exterior of the hall. Für Strom, Netzwerk und Telekommunikation werden mehr als 20.000 m Kabel verlegt. Für die benötigte Pressluft werden die Kompressoren außerhalb der Halle aufgestellt.

Day 5 Der 5. Tag

The suspensions for the light fixtures are installed, the secondary floor covering of chipwood can now be laid. Die Abhängungen für das Licht werden installiert, der Doppelboden aus Spanplatten kann verlegt werden.

Day 7 Der 7. Tag

The steel structures for the colored areas begin to show their contours. 9.000 m (29.520 running feet) of galvanized steel pipe are used to create the framework for 16.000 m² (172.220ft²) of fabric. (B4) Die Stahlgerüste für die Farbräume zeigen erste Konturen. 9.000 lf. Meter verzinktes Stahlrohr bilden die Haltekonstruktion für 16.000 m² Stoff (B4).

»As a stage designer, I had to learn to let go and not to keep fiddling with the set until the last minute – that is the hour of the
production team. Als Bühnenbildner musste ich lernen, loszulassen und nicht bis zur letzten Sekunde am Set rumzufummeln
– das ist die Stunde der Produktionsteams.«
[URB]

Day 10 Der 10. Tag

The stand begins to take shape. The assembly of the displays has begun. The spotlights are brought into the correct positions. Today the furniture arrives. Room is needed for 200 sideboards, 200 tables, 800 chairs – this is pure logistics. Der Stand nimmt Gestalt an. Die Displaymontage hat begonnen. Die Scheinwerfer werden in die richtige Position gebracht. Heute rollen die Möbel an. Platz wird benötigt für 200 Sideboards, 200 Tische, 800 Stühle – das ist Logistik pur.

Day 12 Der 12. Tag

The first transparencies are in place, the lightboxes no longer blind us. More than 1.000 product labels are placed, 450 camera securing fixtures are assembled, more than 3.500 film cartons are set up. Die ersten Bilder hängen, und die leeren Leuchtkästen blenden uns nicht mehr. Über 1.000 Produktschilder werden verteilt, 450 Kamerasicherungen montiert, über 3.500 Filmschachteln aufgerichtet.

Day 13 Der 13. Tag

The last fabric panels are searched for and located. Now the aisles have to be cleared completely, so that the carpet can be installed overnight. Die letzten Stoffbahnen werden gesucht und gefunden. Die Gangzonen müssen jetzt freigeräumt werden für die Verlegung des Teppichbodens in der Nacht.

PLANNING AND PRODUCTION

THE LONGEST DAY, THE SHORTEST NIGHT

DER LÄNGSTE TAG, DIE KÜRZESTE NACHT

6:00 Am 6:00 Uhr

The set-up personnel are tired, the movements of the workers are becoming slower and slower, there was hardly any sleep during the last three nights. The strain increases. Das Aufbaupersonal ist müde, die Bewegungen der Monteure werden immer langsamer, die letzten drei Nächte gab es kaum Schlaf. Die Anspannung steigt.

7:00 Am 7:00 Uhr

The penetrating sounds of electric saws and wrenches have ceased, only the monotonous humming of vacuum cleaners dominates the scene. Die aufdringlichen Geräusche von Sägen und Schraubern sind verstummt, nur das monotone Brummen der Staubsauger beherrscht die Szene.

8:00 Am 8:00 Uhr

The first colleagues arrive. The first complimentary words "You accomplished it after all – as always". The security people from Rochester are very nervous and just in case they check all the security-related emergency exits, because the CEO will arrive momentarily. Die ersten Kollegen treffen ein. Erste anerkennende Worte »Ihr habt es ja doch geschafft – wie immer.« Die Sicherheitsleute aus Rochester sind mächtig nervös und prüfen vorsichtshalber alle sicherheitsrelevanten Fluchtwege, weil gleich der CEO kommt.

8:30 Am 8:30 Uhr

The vice-presidents suddenly question things that have been cleared with the responsible people long before. That is precautionary obedience, therefore nothing is done for the moment. Die Vize-Präsidenten stellen plötzlich Dinge in Frage, die lange vorher mit den Verantwortlichen geklärt wurden. Das ist vorauseilender Gehorsam, deshalb wird zunächst nichts unternommen.

9.00 Am 9:00 Uhr

One hour to go. The myriad of questions continues: When can we get coffee, we have no power, we need more light. The stand is filling up with KODAK people from all over the world. Eine Stunde noch. Weiter geht die Fragerei: Wann gibt es Kaffee, wir haben keinen Strom, wir brauchen mehr Licht. Der Stand wird immer voller mit KODAK Leuten aus aller Welt.

9:58 Am 9:58 Uhr

The last piece of protective plastic sheeting is removed, the vacuum cleaners fall silent. Das letzte Stück Folie wird entfernt, die Staubsauger verstummen.

10:00 Am 10:00 Uhr

The first journalists arrive on the stand; press day begins. The test run has begun. Die ersten Journalisten betreten den Stand, der Pressetag beginnt. Der Probelauf hat begonnen.

12:00 Am 12:00 Uhr

Questions, questions, more questions from all sides. Where is this and I need that. The expensive presentations, the newsletter and the staff information, nobody seems to have read them – actually it's like it has always been ... Fragen, Fragen, von allen Seiten Fragen. Wo ist dies, und ich brauche das. Die aufwändigen Präsentationen, den Newsletter und die Staff-Infos hat wohl niemand gelesen – eigentlich alles wie immer.

PLANNING AND PRODUCTION

THE RIGHT SERVICE, THE RIGHT PERSONNEL, THE RIGHT CATERING
DER RICHTIGE SERVICE, DAS RICHTIGE PERSONAL, DAS RICHTIGE CATERING

A trade show stand with an area of 6.500 m² (69.965 ft²) requires appropriate staffing. The KODAK exhibit staff is composed of 1.200 individuals – of which 850 are from the distribution and marketing departments. The remaining trade show staff consists of presenters, demonstrators and service. Proper planning of an effective workforce requires ample experience and the right partners. KODAK entrusts this task to the Inter Cris Company of Laatzen, Germany, with which excellent experience was gained in the course of many years. The information and reception counters are largely staffed by our own personnel, because good familiarity with customers leads to faster connections with the appropriate discussion partners.Beginning in the sixties, the standard snacks and refreshments served on the stand consist of coffee, juices and sausages. The sausages in particular, became a tradition with customers as well as staff members. One would meet on the KODAK stand for the famous long sausages on a short slice of rye bread. According to the sales people, the »KODAK sausages« are the key to many a good customer conversation and the key to a successful sale. But the sausages are also the main sustenance for many staff members, who eat them to save their daily expense allotments. During the six-day duration of the show, approximately 28.000 sausages are served. Placed end-to-end, the resulting length would amount to a 7.280 m (23.878 ft) long sausage. Much has changed in the field of trade shows and events. A modern and future-oriented trade show presence therefore requires appropriate and contemporary catering. A trade show stand is successful only when the sales volume is good and when staff members are satisfied. In order to ensure this success, there should be no shortcuts in catering, very especially not with the sustenance of staff members. Customers have the choice of snacks, mini-pizzas, quiche, stuffed croissants, wraps, various pastas, fruit and ice cream. Beverages include coffee (360 kg / 794 lb), espresso, cappuccino, latte macciato, cola, water, Sprite (260 beverage containers) and a different daily fruit salad.

»Following the maxim that one should first eat well, because the work then goes faster, means that every day staffers from around the world should be served varied meals that take into account cultural and religious customs. To be recommended are light meals, such as noodles, vegetarian dishes, salads, sweets and cakes, which are very well received by stand personnel and which lead to a good atmosphere. Unter dem Motto: Erst gut essen, gearbeitet ist dann schnell, heißt es, täglich für 1.200 Mitarbeiter aus aller Welt ein abwechslungsreiches Essen anzubieten, das die kulturellen und religiösen Eigenheiten berücksichtigt. Zu empfehlen sind leichte Speisen wie Nudeln, vegetarische Gerichte, Salate, Süßspeisen und Kuchen, was bei den Mitarbeitern sehr gut ankommt und zu einer guten Stimmung beiträgt.«

[RS]

The trade show stand is good because the food is good. Never neglect the human factor! The positive acceptance leads to success. Messe gut, weil Essen gut. Niemals den Faktor Mensch vergessen! Die positive Rezeption macht den Erfolg.

Ein Messestand mit 6.500 m² Fläche braucht entsprechendes Personal. Die Standbesatzung besteht aus 1.200 Personen – davon sind 850 aus dem Bereich Vertrieb und Marketing. Weitere 350 Messe-Mitarbeiter sind Präsenter, Demonstratoren und Service-Personal. Diese große Anzahl von Arbeitskräften zu planen erfordert große Erfahrung und die richtigen Partner. KODAK vertraute diese Jobs der Firma Inter Cris aus Laatzen an, mit der über viele Jahre die besten Erfahrungen gemacht wurden. Die Informations- und Empfangscounter werden zum großen Teil mit eigenem Personal besetzt, weil durch gute Kundenkenntnis eine schnellere Kommunikation zu den gewünschten Gesprächspartnern möglich ist.

Seit den 1960er Jahren besteht die Standardverpflegung aus Kaffee, Saft und Würstchen. Speziell das Würstchen hat Tradition, bei Kunden wie bei Mitarbeitern. Man trifft sich zum Würstchenessen bei KODAK. Nach Meinung der Vertriebsleute ist das »KODAKwürstchen« der Schlüssel für ein gutes Kundengespräch und schafft die Grundlage für einen erfolgreichen Vertragsabschluss. Die Würstchen sind aber auch Hauptnahrungsmittel für viele Mitarbeiter, die so ihr Spesenkonto schonen. In sechs Tagen werden durchschnittlich 28.000 Würstchen ausgegeben, in Meter umgerechnet ergibt das eine 7.280 m lange Wurst.

Im Messe- und Eventbereich hat sich vieles verändert. Deshalb gehört zu einem modernen und zukunftsorientierten Messeauftritt auch ein passendes und zeitgemäßes Catering.

Eine Messe ist dann ein Erfolg, wenn die Verkaufszahlen gut und die Mitarbeiter zufrieden sind. Um diesen Erfolg sicherzustellen, darf nicht beim Catering gespart

THE OPENING

werden, schon gar nicht bei der Versorgung der Mitarbeiter. Für die Kunden gibt es Snacks, Mini Pizzas, Quiche, gefüllte Hörnchen, Wraps, verschiedene Pastas, Obst und Eis. Als Getränke werden Kaffee (360 kg), Espresso, Cappuccino, Latte macciato, Cola, Wasser, Sprite, (260 Getränkecontainer) und ein täglich wechselnder Fruchtcocktail angeboten.

THE LASTING IMPRESSION

DER BLEIBENDE EINDRUCK

Print@

@Home

Kodak PhotoNet Online

Kodak

THE OPENING

»The powerlessness of the designer now gives
way to the fascination of the result. Jetzt weicht
die Ohnmacht des Gestalters der Faszination des
Ergebnisses.«
[URB]

PRODUCT-RELATED STAGING IN THE COLOR SPACE
PRODUKTADÄQUATE INSZENIERUNG IM FARBRAUM

THE OPENING

»160.000 visitors discover the new world of KODAK. Orientation and encounters in an unmistakable environment. Product-related gestures in the color space convey an associative and positive image of the brand. 160.000 Besucher entdecken die neue Welt von KODAK. Orientierung und Begegnung im unverwechselbaren Umfeld. Produktbezogene Gesten im Farbraum hinterlassen ein assoziatives und schlüssiges Bild der Marke.«
[FOM]

THE ACCESSIBLE COLOR SPACE

DER BEGEHBARE FARBRAUM

Central Data

KODAK Wedding Portrait CD

KODAK PROFESSIONAL
Film Scanners

KODAK PROFESSIONAL
Digital Color Printers

KODAK PROFESSIONAL
Color Management

KodakPhotofinishing

KodakPhotofinishing

KodakPhotofinishing

THE OPENING

»It is around midnight that trade show stands are at
their most beautiful. Um Mitternacht sind Messestände am schönsten.«
[DG]

chapter **I. 15 PRESS AND EVALUATION** PRESSE UND ECHO

THE SUCCESS AND ITS RESULTS
DER ERFOLG UND SEINE AUSWIRKUNGEN

pages and links Verweise
II. 156 – 157
III. 254 – 255

Once again, media coverage of photokina 2000 was overwhelming. Every significant radio and television station highlighted the KODAK stand. 103 TV reports and 87 radio commentaries were broadcast about the World's Fair of Imaging. Both the public media and the photographic press devoted prominent attention to KODAK in their reports. End result: Millions of contacts through a brilliant trade show presence.

Die Medienresonanz ist bei der photokina 2000 wieder überwältigend. Alle bedeutenden TV- und Rundfunkanstalten haben den KODAK Stand im Blickpunkt. 103 Fernsehberichte und 87 Hörfunkberichte werden über die Weltmesse des Bildes ausgestrahlt. Die Publikums- und Fachpresse räumt KODAK in der Berichterstattung einen herausragenden Platz ein. Bilanz: Viele Millionen Kontakte durch einen brillanten Messeauftritt.

Die Welt, Berlin
25. SEP. 2000

KODAK
Mit Photokina zufrieden

Eine „neue Ära in der Bilderwelt" sieht Kodak auf der Jubiläums-Photokina in Köln angebrochen. „Standen sich bis vor kurzer Zeit die analoge Fotowelt und die digitale Informations- und Computerwelt konkurrierend gegenüber, demonstriert die Photokina 2000 harmonisches Miteinander", sagte das Vorstandsmitglied Dieter Werkhausen der Nachrichtenagentur dpa. Kodak erwarte von der Messe „einen ganz wesentlichen Impuls für das Weihnachtsgeschäft", sagte Werkhausen einen Tag vor Messeschluss. „Wir sind in einer positiven Aufbruchsstimmung, und wir sind mit der Photokina hoch zufrieden." Die Stuttgarter Tochter des US-Fotokonzerns Eastman Kodak hat 1999 rund 1,7 Mrd. DM umgesetzt. Auf der 50. Photokina stellen 1700 Aussteller aus 45 Ländern ihre Neuheiten vor. ; dpa

KODAKS FARBEN DES GLÜCKS

Ein riesiger Sprung vorwärts

Die Weltmesse des Bildes feierte die Verbrüderung der Technologie-Welten – perfekt inszeniert zum Beispiel auch in der Kodak-Halle

Keine Orgie in Gelb, sondern eine fröhliche Farbwelt empfing die Besucher des Kodak-Standes in Köln diesmal. Obwohl die traditionell größte Standfläche durchaus per Farbgestaltung in einzelne Bereiche eingeteilt war, wurde das Verschmelzen der technischen Möglichkeiten beim gelben Riesen im Obergeschoss der Halle 8 ganz besonders deutlich.

Rundum Zufriedenheit strahlte auch Kodak-Vorstand Dieter Werkhausen im Gespräch mit FOTOwirtschaft aus. „Eine neue Ära in der Bilderwelt bricht h...

Kodak Vors...
Dieter Werkha...
„Das war für K...
die erfolgreic...
photokina aller Zei...

...will Farbwelt-Erfolg ...übertragen

Resonanz und Akzept... die wir mit den Farb... Filmen beim Verbrau... erzielten, sind wir n... lich besonders erfreu... wir ja stets betonten, ... wir das Farbwelt-Kon... auf die Verbrau... wünsche und die spezielle Zielgr... in Deutschland und Österreich ... geschneidert haben.

„Erwartungen übertroffen"
Interview mit Kodak Vorstand Dieter Werkhausen

...totypen, mit dem man Bilder aus einer Mobilbox abrufen und verschicken kann. Schöne Aussichten, wenn der Branchenführer im traditionellen Filmgeschäft so ...

...cher die Vorzüge des APS-Systems nahebringen." Diejenigen, die bereits eine APS-Kamera besitzen, scheinen die Vorteile des Systems ja schon eifrig zu nutzen,

Subject: thank you
Date: Tue, 10 Oct 2000 14:34:43 +0200
From: 917194N@knotes.kodak.com
To: Kontakt@atelier-brueckner.de

Alle, Alle Alle

From: Detlev Gehrke

Hallo Frau Kölz, hallo Herr Hegemann, *Frau Nagel.*

dieses Lob geht auch und vor allem an Sie!

Mit Dank & Gruß
D.Gehrke
------------------- Forwarded by Detlev Gehrke/917194/Germany/Europe/EKC
on 10/10/2000 02:30 PM --------------------------

Gerard Meijs
09/28/2000 01:46 PM

Subject: thank you

From: Gerard Meijs

Hello Photokina team!!!!

If this was the Eurovision song contest I would say: Stuttgart 12 points,
douze points!

This was the best show ever. All the other companies were using the same
old booth they have been using for years. Ours was different and really
reflected a new spirit and a new vision. I just talked to Tiina in Sweden
and she said that the Finnish reps told her that they were proud to work
for a company like Kodak who can put a show like this together. I fully
agree with them. You have done a great job in putting Picture Maker and all
the related products on center stage.

Hope to see you soon!

Gerard

IS SUCH A MAJOR EFFORT REALLY WORTHWHILE?

Considering the fact that 1 1/2 years of painstaking work precede a KODAK stand at photokina, this question is absolutely justified. photokina is no longer a purely order-taking trade show – today it is the world's most important meeting point and showcase for the photographic industry, a prime opportunity for »testing the waters«, for gathering information, as well as for taking orders. The KODAK presence at photokina has traditionally been large and impressive, designed to foment long-term massive external and internal image enhancement. KODAK has been profiting from this positive effect for many years. Trade shows are highlights in marketing that produce long-lasting impressions.

LOHNT SICH DER GANZE AUFWAND?

Wenn man davon ausgeht, dass fast 1 1/2 Jahre an einer photokina gearbeitet wird, ist diese Frage absolut berechtigt. Vom Marktführer im Fotobereich wird einiges erwartet. Die photokina ist keine reine Ordermesse mehr, viel mehr ist sie heute weltweit der wichtigste Treffpunkt und Schaufenster der Fotobranche, wo es darum geht, zu sondieren, sich zu informieren und auch Verkaufsabschlüsse zu tätigen. Der Messeauftritt von KODAK ist traditionell groß und anspruchsvoll gestaltet, weil damit langfristig eine massive Imagebildung nach außen und innen betrieben wird. Von dieser positiven Wirkung profitiert KODAK seit Jahren. Messen sind Bergetappen im Marketing, und deshalb bleiben sie für lange Zeit unvergesslich.

PRESS AND EVALUATION

The photokina Obelisk was awarded to the KODAK trade show team. Friedrich Mueller and his team are very pleased with this recognition.

Appeal of the Kodak Booth 2000

I like the Kodak booth...

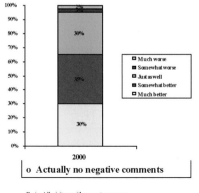

| Much worse |
| Somewhat worse |
| Just as well |
| Somewhat better |
| Much better |

2000

o **Actually no negative comments**

Basis: All visitors with concrete answers

photokina 2000
Exhibition Evaluation

Detlef Baur / BR CI Kodak Germany
October 2000

Visitor survey of photokina 2000.
1039 visitors are interviewed.
Evaluation of the KODAK stand:

- The KODAK stand was rated as »very good« and substantially better than the 1998 stand.
- 2/3 of the individals who were interviewed indicated that the KODAK stand was better than the stands of the competitors.
- Compared to earlier slogans, the claim »KODAK pictures.The Universal Language« was understood very well.

TIME OUT – WITHOUT KODAK
DIE ZEIT OHNE KODAK

WITHOUT KODAK THERE IS NO VACATION
OHNE KODAK GIBTS KEINEN URLAUB

WHEREVER YOU GO, KODAK HAS ALREADY BEEN THERE
ÜBERALL WO DU HINKOMMST, IST KODAK SCHON DA

KODAK FOR KLICKS
ZUM KLICK GIBTS KODAK

CHAPTER OVERVIEW KAPITELÜBERSICHT

KODAK. Share moments. Share life.

A SLOGAN FOR SIX DAYS?
EIN SLOGAN FÜR SECHS TAGE?

pages and links Verweise
I. 22 – 23
III. 162 – 169

KODAK has invested a great deal of time and money in the development of an appropriate slogan for every photokina. A few advertising agencies made a lot of money with the development of slogans. With the structure of products and services that are offered remaining roughly similar over the years, one cannot help wondering whether a special trade show slogan for only a few days makes any sense at all. Experience shows that the selection of a claim (or slogan) is always a very lengthy process and usually politically motivated.

Depending on the decision-making persons, the claims that are chosen are usually company image slanted or more, sales-oriented. For example: »KODAK World Leader in Imaging« or »KODAK Solid Business Solutions for Today and Tomorrow«. These statements are intended to underscore the leadership claim of KODAK. But their real effect on dealers and consumers is a matter of critical conjecture. It is more of an internal patting-on-the-back to confirm that: We are the best and the greatest. The final decision as to which claim is to be used is the prerogative of top management, and therefore, as far as the trade show stand designers are concerned, are always announced much too late. This often has the consequence that the selected slogan does not match the overall concept of the trade show stand. Of course the advertising literature is also imprinted with the design of the trade show slogan. This in turn has the consequence that it becomes waste paper once the show has ended.

A company's trade show slogan that is touted for only six days will never take hold and much less make a lasting impression. It is an interesting observation that during the briefing the stand designers always ask for the theme or the stand slogan in order to perform their task on the basis of the principle that »design follows content«. The slogan is a constraint that restricts the latitude of the design. The recommendation of the team is to employ the current corporate claim of the company in the stand design. If it is right for the company, then it should also be right for the presence at a trade show. The colleagues at company headquarters understood that and gave an early ›go-ahead‹. A slogan is chosen that pleases everyone and that really makes sense: »KODAK. Share Moments. Share Life.«

KODAK hat zu jeder photokina sehr viel Zeit und Geld investiert, um passende Messe-Slogans zu entwickeln. Einige Agenturen haben mit den Sloganentwicklungen gutes Geld verdient. Bei der über Jahre annähernd gleichbleibenden Struktur des Angebotes von Produkten und Dienstleistungen muss dennoch die Frage gestellt werden, ob ein spezieller Messe-Slogan für nur wenige Tage überhaupt Sinn macht. Die Claim-Entscheidung ist, wie die Praxis zeigt, immer sehr langwierig und meistens »politisch« motiviert.

Abhängig von den entscheidenden Personen werden eher imageträchtige Claims oder mehr vertriebsorientierte Claims ausgewählt. Zum Beispiel: »KODAK World Leader in Imaging« oder »KODAK Solid Business Solutions for Today and Tomorrow«. Die Aussagen sollen den Führungsanspruch von KODAK unterstreichen. Die Intensität der Wirkung auf Händler und Verbraucher darf dennoch kritisch beurteilt werden. Es ist vielmehr ein internes Schulterklopfen zur Bestätigung: Wir sind die Besten und die Größten. Die letztendliche Entscheidung, welcher Claim verwendet wird, behält sich das Topmanagement vor und kommt deshalb aus der Sicht der Messe-Macher immer viel zu spät.

Das hat zur Folge, dass häufig das Design des Messeslogans nicht zum Gesamtkonzept des Messestandes passt. Selbstverständlich werden auch die Werbemittel mit dem Design des Messe-Slogans bedruckt. Dies hat zur Folge, das sie nach Abschluss der Messe Makulatur sind.
Ein Messe-Slogan, der nur sechs Tage präsent ist, wird sich niemals etablieren und schon gar nicht nachhaltig durchsetzen. Eine interessante Beobachtung ist, dass die Gestalter beim Briefing immer nach dem Thema, beziehungsweise dem Messe-Slogan fragen, um im Sinne von »design follows content« an die Aufgabe herangehen zu können. Diese Vorgabe ist ein Korsett und schränkt den Gestaltungsspielraum ein. Die Empfehlung des Teams ist, den gültigen Corporate Claim auch auf der Messe einzusetzen. Wenn er für die Company richtig ist, dann ist er auch richtig für den Messeauftritt. Das haben dann auch die Kollegen in den Staaten verstanden und geben frühzeitig das Go. Es gibt einen Slogan, mit dem alle gut leben können und der wirklich Sinn macht:
»KODAK. Share Moments. Share Life.«

»We press the button, you do the rest«
[FOM]

»Now everything starts all over again. Every two years KODAK has to re-invent itself. What madness ... Jetzt geht das alles wieder von vorne los. Alle zwei Jahre muss sich KODAK neu erfinden, was für ein Wahnsinn ...«
[URB]

94 **95**

THE NEW LOCATION WITH THE CHARM OF A PARKING GARAGE

DIE NEUE HALLE MIT DEM CHARME EINES PARKHAUSES

Sometimes changes require new strategies or just more time. As mentioned earlier, Hall 8, the so-called KODAK hall, is strategically located at the junction of the old and the new fairgrounds, therefore it is a key nodal point for all trade show visitors. This location has served as the ideal site for the stand of market leader KODAK since 1960. Hall 8 was originally conceived, not as a building for trade shows, but as a facility for events, and that has considerable technical disadvantages. Even so in 2001, it was very difficult to persuade the managers in the USA to relocate the KODAK stand in another hall. The first suggestion for moving the stand had already been made in 1998. The reasons that prompted that suggestion were the substantial difficulties involved in setting up the stand. The following arguments were cited: The load capacity of the floor was too low, requiring costly load distribution schemes and additional expenses. Not enough room for dealer discussion areas, because a two-story construction was possible only along the peripheral area of the hall. An inadequate electrical power supply, which required the installation of supplemental generators. Fixtures could only be suspended from the ceiling at a few points, which made the installation of the illumination fixtures difficult and which hindered the proper light distribution throughout the hall. Ventilation is inadequate, because the air conditioning system cannot cope with the heat generated when a show is in progress. The delivery and removal of supplies for the set-up and the dismantling of the stand has to be handled by two antiquated elevators that are too small, which causes delays and additional expenses. Nevertheless, these arguments did not convince the powers that be, on the grounds that the KODAK stand was always located on this site and that our customers only visit us in Hall 8. But a well thought-out strategy eventually leads to success. A new approach. Based on the premise »When a prophet does not prevail in his own country, he looks for allies«. The idea: The management of the Cologne Trade Fair Organization is the right partner for this persuasion project. A new attempt is made in 2001. During an official visit by the Cologne Trade Show Organization executives to KODAK headquarters in Rochester, NY, the suggestion made in 1998 that the KODAK stand should be relocated to Hall 4 is presented as an official recommendation. Shortly after that visit, an inquiry from Rochester is received in Stuttgart, asking what KODAK AG thought of the suggestion of moving the KODAK stand to Hall 4. The reasons stated earlier were formulated in the reply, and a few days later the approval was granted for 8.500 m² (91.492 ft²), i.e. the entire Hall 4. The change makes everything better, faster and easier, with a proven team and the extensive KODAK experience. They are the very best prerequisites for continuing the successful cooperation with the Brückner studio. As that wise saying goes: Never change a winning team.

Manchmal brauchen Veränderungen neue Strategien oder einfach nur Zeit. Die Halle 8, die sogenannte KODAK Halle auf der photokina, liegt – wie bereits beschrieben – an der Schnittstelle zwischen altem und neuem Messegelände und ist deshalb Dreh- und Angelpunkt für alle Messebesucher. Seit 1960 gilt dieser Standort als der ideale Platz für den Marktführer KODAK. Zur Erinnerung: die Halle 8 wird beim Bau ursprünglich nicht als Messe-, sondern als Veranstaltungshalle konzipiert, was technisch erhebliche Nachteile hat. Es ist dennoch 2001 äußerst schwierig, die Manager in den USA davon zu überzeugen, den Stand in eine andere Halle zu verlegen. Der erste Vorschlag eines Umzugs datiert bereits aus dem Jahr 1998. Damaliges Ziel: Umzug in die Halle 4. Als Begründung dienen die erheblichen technischen Probleme beim Aufbau des Messestandes. Die Argumente sind: Zu geringe Bodenbelastung, was aufwendige Lastverteilungen und Mehrkosten bedeutet. Zu wenig Platz für Besprechungsbereiche, weil eine zweigeschossige Bauweise nur im Randbereich der Halle möglich ist. Eine schlechte Elektroversorgung, was zusätzliche Aufstellung von Generatoren zur Folge hat. Abhängungen von der Decke sind nur an wenigen Punkten möglich, was die Lichtinstallation erschwert und die Hallenausleuchtung beeinträchtigt. Die Belüftung ist mangelhaft, weil die Klimaanlage mit der Wärmeentwicklung nicht zurechtkommt. Die Anlieferung für den Auf- und Abbau kann nur über zwei alte und zu kleine Aufzüge erfolgen, was zu Zeitverzögerungen und Mehrkosten führt. Alle Argumente zählen jedoch nichts und werden mit der Begründung abgelehnt: KODAK war immer an diesem Platz, das ist die KODAK Halle, unsere Kunden kommen nur in die Halle 8. Mit wohlüberlegter Strategie zum Erfolg. Ein erneuter Anlauf. Nach dem Motto: »Wenn der Prophet im eigenen Land nichts gilt, dann sucht er sich Verbündete.« Die Idee: Das Management der Kölnmesse ist der richtige Partner für diese Überzeugungsarbeit. Im Jahr 2001 wird ein neuer Versuch gestartet. Im Rahmen eines offiziellen Besuches der photokina-Verantwortlichen der Kölnmesse in der KODAK Zentrale in Rochester, USA, wird der Vorschlag aus dem Jahr 1998, dass KODAK in die Halle 4 umziehen möge, als offizielle Empfehlung präsentiert. Kurz darauf kommt die Anfrage aus Rochester in Stuttgart auf den Tisch: Was ist von diesem Vorschlag, in die Halle 4 umzuziehen, zu halten? Als Antwort werden die Anforderungen formuliert, und wenige Tage später kommt die Genehmigung für die 8.500 m², also die komplette Halle 4. Alles wird durch den Wechsel besser, schneller und einfacher mit bewährter Mannschaft und dem großen Erfahrungsschatz von KODAK. Das sind die besten Voraussetzungen, um die erfolgreiche Zusammenarbeit mit dem Atelier Brückner fortzusetzen. Wie heißt es so schön: Never change a winning team.

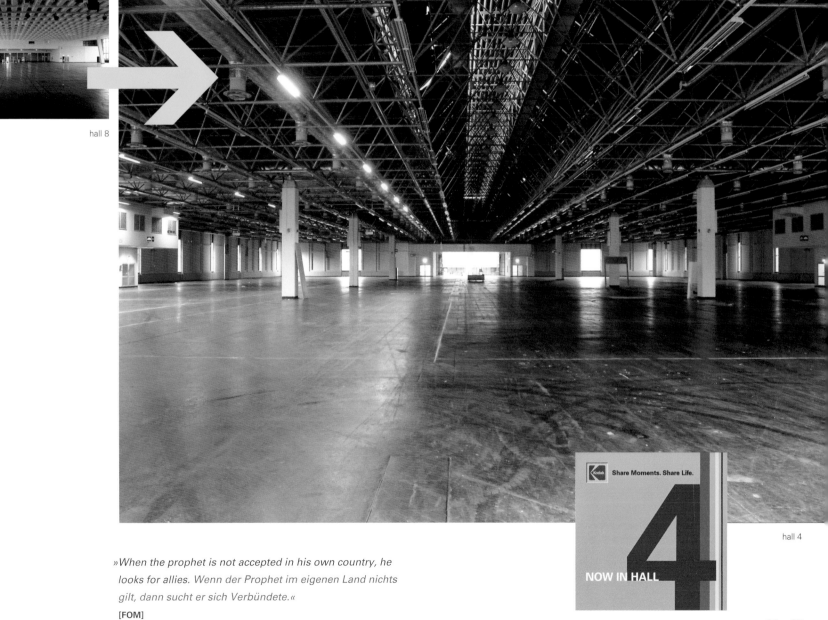

hall 8

hall 4

»When the prophet is not accepted in his own country, he looks for allies. Wenn der Prophet im eigenen Land nichts gilt, dann sucht er sich Verbündete.«

[FOM]

OBJECTIVES, CONTENTS, MESSAGE
ZIELE INHALTE BOTSCHAFT

GENERAL INFORMATION

Film maintains strength position. Digital image increase overall and professional photography. Digital capture has reached mass market appeal. Use digitization services to anhance enjoyment. Convergence of imaging and information.

EMPHASIZE:

Working together from capture to output
Share moments. Share life.
Output and digitization categories.
Industry leadership in digital and digitization products.
Clear vision of the future of photography
Superior products to take, enjoy and share for greater use.
Technological and innovative leadership.

ROLES:

Clear focus on output, digitization and digital products.
Leadership in developing products for all consumers photographic needs.
Demonstrate »Share moments. Share life«.
Present high speed film story.
Present the vision for the future of photography.

GOALS:

Strong focus on output.
Highlight what the visitors must see.
Graphic plans, to define key areas of interest.
Strong brand presence.
Strengthen visual communication through use of clear brand messaging.
Communicate the new location hall 4 by strong advertising on fairgrounds.

MANDATORIES:

Trendsetting design, regardless of the technology.
Bigger than life images, architecture, backwalls.
Share moments. Share life. –a world to enter, represented by pictures and displays.
Color guiding system for better orientation/ communication.
Large format images dominating outer walls, identifying the applications, featuring key benefits, create a emotional and high tech atmosphere.
Staff will be clearly identified as KODAK people.
Project will come in on budget – overruns not acceptable.

OTHER CONSIDERATIONS:

Space requirements

Stand area	8.500 m^2 / 91.492 ft^2

Product areas:

Space requirement:	2/3 of the stand area
Consumer Imaging	50% of the stand area
KODAK Professional	35% of the stand area
Digital & Applied Imaging	10% of the stand area
Olympic Games / Photo Exhibits	5% of the stand area

Discussion areas with controlled access

Space requirement:	1/3 of the stand area

Management offices for VIPs	400 m^2 / 4.306 ft^2
Conference rooms, enclosed	200 m^2 / 2.153 ft^2
Demonstration rooms, enclosed	220 m^2 / 2.368 ft^2
Open discussion areas	1.300 m^2 / 13.993 ft^2
Buisness center	300 m^2 / 3.229 ft^2
Cafeteria	180 m^2 / 1.937 ft^2
Press Center and discussion area	300 m^2 / 3.229 ft^2
Operating Minilab	100 m^2 / 1.076 ft^2
Stand management	50 m^2 / 538 ft^2
Telephone switchboard	20 m^2 / 215 ft^2
Storage, kitchen and facility rooms	800 m^2 / 8.611 ft^2

The following statement only covers a small extract from the briefing document that is more than 30 pages long. Comments about the market situation, the role of competitors, and detailed information about products and services were deliberately omitted.

MESSAGE: FOCUS ON OUTPUT

output

»*Never change a winning team – everything gets better the second time around.* Never change a winning team – beim zweiten Mal wird alles besser.«

[URB]

PROPOSAL 1: NETWORK
KONZEPT 1: NETWORK

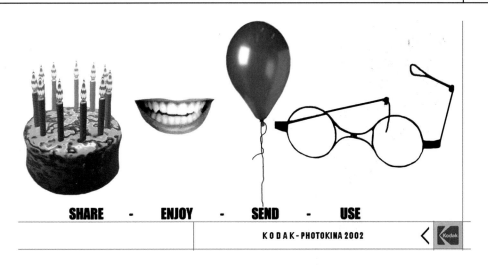

SHARE - ENJOY - SEND - USE

KODAK-PHOTOKINA 2002

THEME

Datastream, wireframe, matrix
Digital network, synergy and continuity across the
entire area, global vision.

MESSAGE

Info imaging – devices, media and service,
infrastructure.

CONTENT

The first concept is an evolution from KODAK I.
Colored lines become stripes that form paths,
locations and spaces. In spite of the complexity, the
stand remains a transparent and cohesive unit.
Each one of the three infoimaging elements is identified with a specific color and represented by one of
the colored stripes.

These three conditions dominate the trade show
stand and they combine to form a coordinated unit.
The background formed by the spatial limitations of
the floor, the ceiling, and the walls is yellow. These
elements constitute the space for the interior structure. The colored stripes are located along Hall 4 both
horizontally as well as vertically.

The creative elements are employed as follows:
Floor – Orientation
Walls – Delineation
Desks and counters – Product bearers
Frames – Picture supports
Panels – Digital information supports

THEMA

Datenstrom, Wireframe, Matrix
Digitales Netzwerk, Synergie und Verbindung über
den ganzen Raum, globale Vision

BOTSCHAFT

Info-Imaging – Geräte, Medien & Dienstleistung,
Infrastruktur

INHALT

Das erste Konzept ist eine Weiterentwicklung von
KODAK I. Farbige Linien werden zu Bändern, die sich
zu Wegen, Orten und Räumen formen. Trotz der Kom-
plexität bleibt dem Messestand ein transparenter und
umfassender Bereich.
Jedes der drei Elemente des »Info-Imaging« trägt
eine Farbe und wird von einem Band repräsentiert.

Diese drei Bedingungen dominieren den Messestand
und bilden eine Einheit. Der Hintergrund, der sich aus
den räumlichen Grenzen des Bodens, der Decke und
der Wand bildet, ist gelb. Sie bilden den Raum für die
Innenstruktur. Die Bänder sind horizontal sowie verti-
kal in der Halle angeordnet.

Die Gestaltungselemente stehen für:
Boden – Orientierung
Wand – Begrenzung
Arbeitstisch / Pult – Produktträger
Rahmen – Bildträger
Tafel – Digitaler Informationsträger.

»The color code stripes dominate the stand. A concentration of such stripes identifies an area. Large format pictures are interspersed between product areas and they are intended to represent the dataflow in a network.
Die Farbcodelinien dominieren den Raum. Die Konzentration von Farbbändern kennzeichnet die Areas. Großformatige Bilder bewegen sich zwischen den Produktareas und sollen den Datenfluss eines Netzwerkes darstellen.«
[URB]

»Think it over again. Keep the color code and come up with something else. Überlegt doch mal. Übernehmt den Farbcode und findet etwas anderes.«
[FOM]

PROPOSAL 2: STREAMING
KONZEPT 2: STREAMING

stream	der Strom
stream	der Fluss
to stream	strömen
job stream	die Aufgabenablauffolge
stream gold	das Flussgold
stream network	das Gewässernetz
business stream	der Geschäftsfluss
business stream	die Geschäftsrichtung
to put on stream	in Betrieb nehmen
data stream	der Datenfluss
electron stream	der Elektronenfluss

Streaming has a large variety of meanings. Common to all of them is the dynamic movement – the processing. It contains the image of change and development.

Therefore streaming is an appropriate word to visualize the manifold actions expressed by the term »Info Imaging«. The exchange between the Devices, Service and Media as well as Infrastructure is a data stream. Those three elements which form parts of the »Info Imaging« strategy are interrelated by streaming.

The spacial connection between the different areas of the KODAK stand is a the yellow back bone, which links the Consumer Imaging and the Professional areas.

The color code lines contain color-coded islands with product stages in a surrealistic pictorial environment.

Streaming hat eine große Anzahl an Bedeutungen. Alle haben dynamische Bewegung gemeinsam, das Verarbeiten. Es beinhaltet das Abbild der Veränderung und Entwicklung. Deshalb ist Streaming ein angemessener Begriff für das Visualisieren der Vielfalt an Aktivitäten, die mit dem Begriff Info-Imaging ausgedrückt werden. Der Austausch zwischen Geräten, Dienstleistung und Medien sowie Infrastruktur ist ein Datenstrom. Diese drei Elemente, die einen Teil der Info-Imaging-Strategie bilden, stehen durch Streaming in wechselseitiger Beziehung.

Die räumliche Verbindung der verschiedenen KODAK Bereiche bildet das gelbe Rückgrat. Der Bereich Consumer Imaging sowie der professionelle Bereich sind dadurch verbunden. Aus den Farbcodelinien entwickeln sich Farbcodeinseln mit Produktbühnen in einem surrealistischen Bilderraum.

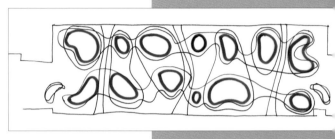

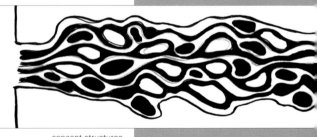

concept structures

»Positive experiences with an attractive central passage make this area especially significant. Why not divide the flow of visitors into several streams? Die positiven Erfahrungen mit einer attraktiven Mittelachse in einer Durchgangshalle machen diese Zone besonders bedeutungsvoll. Warum nicht die Besucher in mehrere Ströme aufteilen?«
[URB]

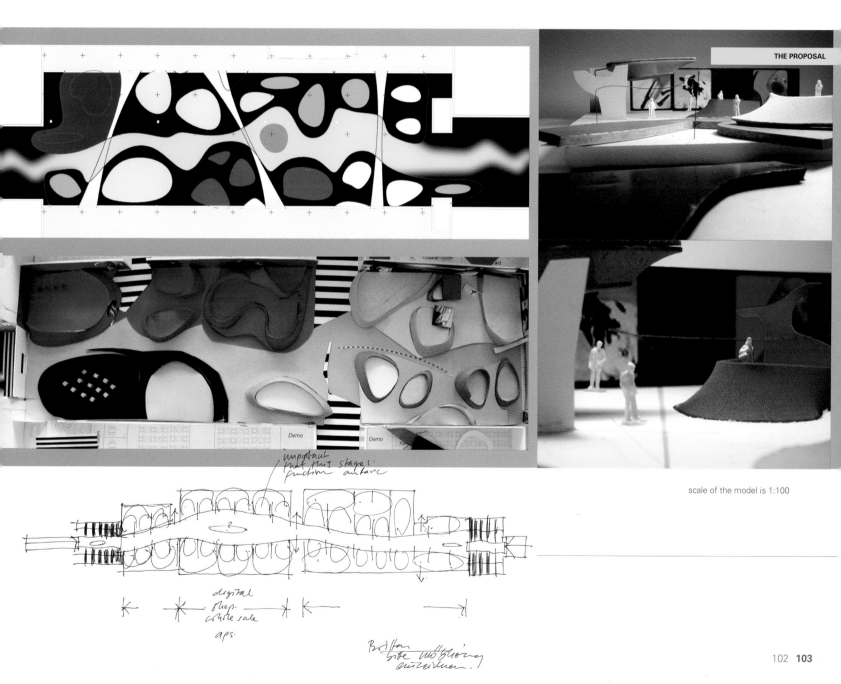

THE PROPOSAL

scale of the model is 1:100

PROPOSAL 3: ALICE IN WONDERLAND
KONZEPT 3: ALICE IM WUNDERLAND

Color is a carrier of emotions. Texture is the secret ingredient for bringing color to life. The objective is to generate an emotional picture and color concept. As with the orientation system used on the KODAK stand at photokina 2000, visitors are guided by means of colors. Visual highlights and key figures create a second level of orientation. Visual highlights – moving pictorial elements, photographs on which things are shown larger than they are in reality – break up the space with their oversized dimensions and their movements. Huge feet dangle from above, an oversized soccer ball appears, a small house is in the way – together they create the atmosphere for the KODAK landscape. The impression of being unreal also simulates a feeling of being virtual. Each key figure represents a KODAK product area. The objective is to incorporate a message that is conveyed by the key figures.

»Why don't we create or own world of images?
Warum gestalten wir nicht unsere eigene Bilder-
welt?«
[BN]

»Great, Britta! This is perfect storytelling! And if these cutouts can be made to
move, new picture worlds will be created continually. Simply fantastic! Großartig,
Britta! Dies ist ein perfektes Story Telling. Und wenn wir diese Bilder auch noch in
Bewegung setzen, entstehen ständig neue Bilderwelten. Einfach phantastisch.«
[URB]

THE PROPOSAL

Farbe als Träger von Emotionen. Textur ist die magische Zutat, um Farbe lebendig zu machen. Ziel ist es, ein emotionales Bild-Farbkonzept zu erstellen. Der Besucher wird, ähnlich wie beim Orientierungssystem auf dem photokina-Stand 2000, von den Farben geführt. Die visuellen Höhepunkte – die Schlüsselfiguren – kreieren eine zweite Ebene zur Orientierung. Der visuelle Höhepunkt sind bewegende Bildelemente. Fotografien, die größer sind als die Wirklichkeit, lösen dank ihrer übergroßen Dimensionen und Bewegungen den realen Raum auf. Riesige Füße baumeln vom Himmel, ein übergroßer Fußball erscheint, ein kleines Haus steht im Weg. Diese Elemente bilden die Atmosphäre für die KODAK Landschaft. Der Eindruck des »Unrealen« simuliert auch den des »Virtuellen«. Jede Schlüsselfigur repräsentiert einen KODAK Bereich. Das Ziel ist die Vermittlung einer Botschaft durch die Schlüsselfiguren.

»Fantastic, but too expensive! Super, aber zu teuer!«
[FOM]

PROPOSAL 4: STAGES

KONZEPT 4: STAGES

Title:

color meets pattern, KODAK dot com

Message:

change the World with KODAK

Content:

KODAK is mastering the most challenging tasks of image creation.
KODAK achieves what is said to be impossible.

The stand resembles a theatre stage. Viewing the set from the front, one sees a coherent graphic image. The extreme contrasts in the graphic structure cause visual surprises – it is as if the stand is moving dynamically. Walking through the scenery one discovers a neutrally colored area for product and image presentations. The monochrome background creates a relaxing atmosphere.

»This is a perfect idea for a trade show stand. It is a coura-
geous, unconventional, direct attack on our perception. A
profound and lasting memory. Das ist eine perfekte Idee für
einen Messestand. Es ist ein mutiger, außergewöhnlicher,
direkter Angriff auf unsere Wahrnehmung. Eine tiefgreifende
und nachhaltige Erinnerung.«
[URB]

»If we adopt this concept, I'll get fired! Wenn wir das realisieren, schmeißen die mich raus.«
[FOM]

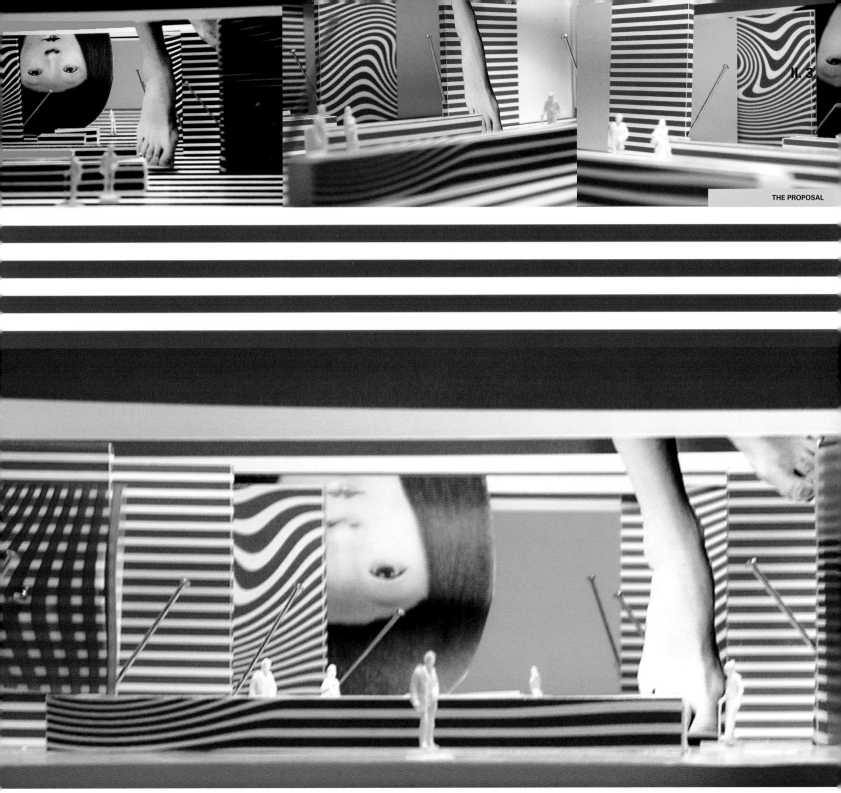

THE PROPOSAL

II, 3

LETS TALK ABOUT SLOGANEERING…
DIE SLOGANDISKUSSION

pages and links Verweise
I. 34 – 35
III. 176 – 177

THE MESSAGE:

SHARE MOMENTS. SHARE LIFE.

What can it achieve? Through the eyes, always in the mind. Share feelings, emotions, memories with others. Focus on output, pictures, pictures without end. Ingenious idea: »Shower of information«. The idea is discussed. Printed-out photographs and their processing technology are to be presented to different target groups in individual story lines. The desired effect is that of a perfect »shower of information«. That would be a truly new approach to brand presentation. Can that concept be implemented at a trade show or will it remain utopian?

DIE BOTSCHAFT:

SHARE MOMENTS. SHARE LIFE.

Was kann das? Aus den Augen, immer im Sinn. Gefühle, Emotionen, Erinnerungen mit anderen teilen. Focus auf Output, Bilder, Bilder ohne Ende. Genialer Einfall: »Informationsdusche«. Die Idee wird diskutiert. Ausgedruckte Fotos und deren Verarbeitungstechnologie sollen in einer individuellen Wegführung für unterschiedliche Zielgruppen präsentiert werden. Die angestrebte Wirkung ist die einer perfekten Informationsdusche. Das wäre ein wirklich neuer Ansatz für den Markenauftritt. Ist das Konzept auf einer Messe durchführbar, oder bleibt es Utopie?

Collage

»KODAK sloganeering – same content, new packaging? With an unmistakable recognition effect. A creative treadmill. KODAK sloganary – gleicher Inhalt, neue Verpackung? Mit unverwechselbarem Wiedererkennungseffekt. Ein gestalterisches Hamsterrad.«

[URB]

»Actually, it is always about pictures, again about pictures and probably about pictures again and again. Eigentlich geht's immer ums Bild, immer noch ums Bild und wahrscheinlich immer wieder ums Bild.«

[FOM]

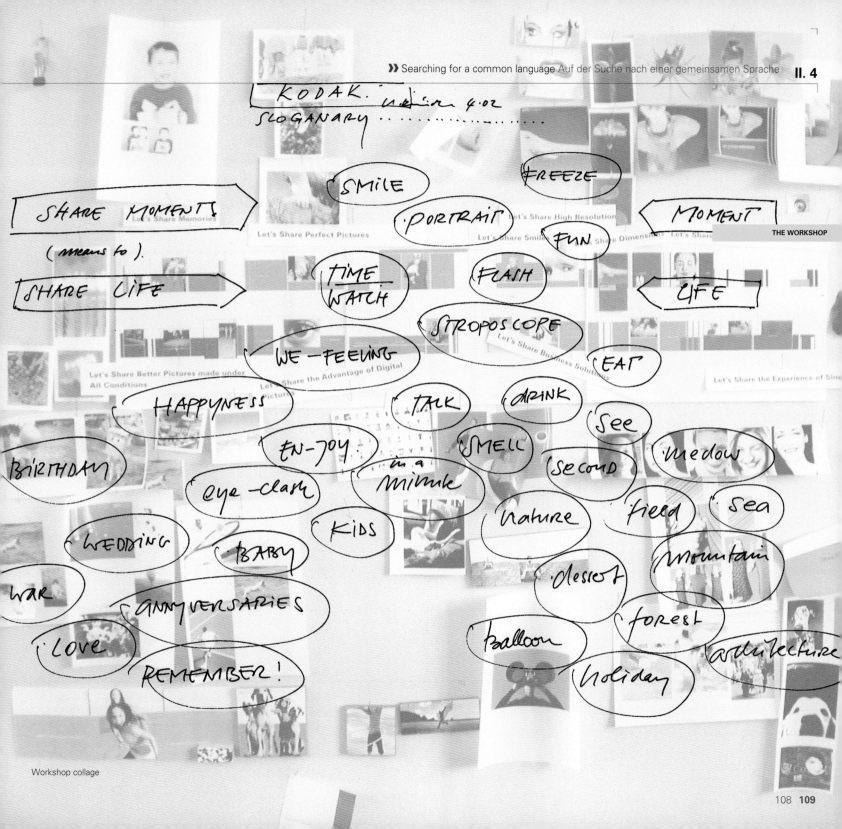

KODAK. *version 4.02*
SLOGANARY · · · · · · · · · · · · · · · · ·

THE WORKSHOP

SMILE

FREEZE

PORTRAIT

MOMENT

FUN

SHARE MOMENTS
(means to).

SHARE LIFE

TIME
WATCH

FLASH

LIFE

STROPOSCORE

WE-FEELING

EAT

HAPPYNESS

TALK

DRINK

SEE

BIRTHDAY

EN-JOY

in a
Minute

SMELL

Second

Medow

eye-clash

Nature

field

Sea

KIDS

mountain

WEDDING

BABY

dessert

forest

WAR

ANNYVERSARIES

architecture

LOVE

Balloon

holiday

REMEMBER!

Workshop collage

LOST IN CONCEPTIONS: FOUR CONCEPTS AND NO SOLUTION

LOST IN CONCEPTIONS: VIER KONZEPTE UND KEINE LÖSUNG

pages and links/Verweise
I. 38 – 39
III. 178 –179

A black hole occurs in every project, a bottomless standstill of aimless helplessness. Bei jedem Projekt gab es ein Loch, einen abgrundtiefen Stillstand der orientierungslosen Hilflosigkeit.

»... have you lost your mind – how many more alternatives??? ... *ja seid ihr denn wahnsinnig, wieviele Alternativen denn noch???«*

[URB TO THE TEAM]

»... you yourself requested the alternatives to be presented with equal emphasis. ... *du selbst verlangst doch, die Alternativen gleichwertig darzustellen.«*

[BN TO URB]

»... that's right, otherwise one wouldn't need alternatives. ... *stimmt, sonst braucht man keine Alternativen.«*

[URB TO EVERYONE]

»We have spoiled the client [FOM] once again with half a dozen alternatives. *Wir haben den Kunden (FOM) mal wieder zu stark verwöhnt mit einem halben Dutzend Alternativen.«*

[URB TO SB]

»Perhaps we were too quick in the beginning, so that we still had time left over. *Vielleicht weil wir am Anfang zu schnell waren und noch Zeit übrig hatten.«*

[SB TO URB]

»There are enough ideas for more than three trade show stands. *Die Ideen reichen für mehr als drei Messestände.«*

[URB]

»Lost in alternatives, the only solution is to make the best of it ... *Lost in Alternatives, da hilft nur, aus der Not eine Tugend zu machen ...«*

[URB TO THE TEAM]

»... I have already heard that saying many times! ... *den Spruch habe ich schon oft gehört!«*

[BN]

»You must be crazy, how do you expect to make any money at all with so many sketches. *Ihr müsst ja wahnsinnig sein, wie wollt ihr bei so vielen Entwürfen überhaupt noch Geld verdienen.«*

[FOM TO THE TEAM]

»Beg your pardon? ... and for whom are we actually creating all this madness. *Wie bitte? ... Und für wen machen wir den ganzen Wahnsinn eigentlich.«*

[URB]

THE SENSE AND NONSENSE
OF REBRIEFINGS.
Briefings often are personal explanations of purposes, not coordinated with participating departments,
so that re-briefings sometimes
cause power struggles among
different depart- | RESET |
ments. Rebrief-
ings frequently result from igno-
rance and negligence. Rebriefings
are permissible only when something significant has changed since
the original task was presented.
Rebriefings become necessary
when the contractor has interpret-
ed the original briefing incorrectly.

SINN UND UNSINN
VON REBRIEFINGS
Häufig sind Briefings persönliche
Absichtserklärungen und nicht
mit den beteiligten Bereichen
abgestimmt, deshalb sind Rebriefings manchmal die Ursache
von Machtkämpfen von verschiedenen Abteilungen untereinander.
Rebriefings sind oft das Resultat
von Ignoranz und Nachlässigkeit.
Rebriefings sind nur erlaubt, wenn
sich etwas Wesentliches seit der
Aufgabenstellung verändert hat.
Rebriefings sind notwendig, wenn
der Auftragnehmer das Briefing
falsch interpretiert hat.

»HORROR VISON – CONDENSE FOUR INTO ONE «

»Die Horrorvision – Aus vier mach eins.«

[URB]

»Three lazy compromises – that's not going anywhere ...
Drei faule Kompromisse, das kann doch nix werden ...«

[BK]

»Always the same schizophrenia – create a sensation, but as
harmless as possible **... immer die gleiche Schizophrenie,
Aufsehen erregen, aber möglichst harmlos.«**

[BN]

BACK TO THE ROOTS. ACTUALLY, WHAT'S THIS ALL ABOUT?
UM WAS GEHT ES EIGENTLICH?

THE COMMUNICATION CONCEPT OF A TRADE
SHOW STAND AS A »WALK-UPON CATALOGUE«
The larger the trade show stand, the greater the
importance of orientation. All the visitor surveys that
were conducted over many years again and again
faulted the lack of overview and problems with orientation on the stand. Every effort is made to provide
visitors with better orientation – obviously with little
success. This includes, for example, information
panels, directional signs, folded pamphlets that are
handed out at the entrances, plus additional personnel for the information counters. All the measures
implemented by us are handled in the same manner
in other trade shows and stands. A clear conclusion is
that trade show visitors are not interested in study-
ing information panels and floor plans. They merely
want to find the desired product and an attendant
easily and quickly. With the large number of diverse
products and different target groups that are characteristic of KODAK, extra care must be taken during
the planning stage for the placement in the floor plan
to have a clear and logical structure. The latter has
to be clearly discernible to the visitor. As is the case
with advertisements, flyers and catalogues, the basic
objective is to generate attention and to create interest. The next step is to facilitate a personal contact
with the appropriate sales representative. This can be
achieved by means of an interesting or provocative
headline, a highly emotional key visual or an attractive
live presentation. Simple and short product descriptions are important. In addition, color codes can be
helpful for better differentiation of product groups.
During the many meetings between the marketing
people and the designers, it became quite apparent
that both sides still had a lot to learn from each other.

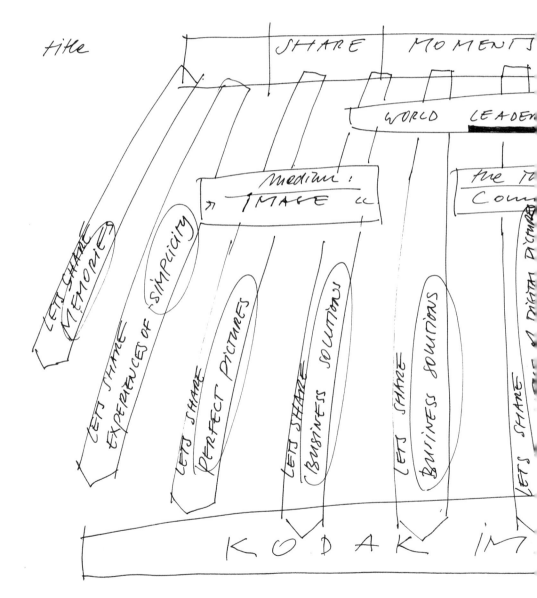

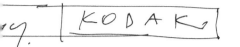

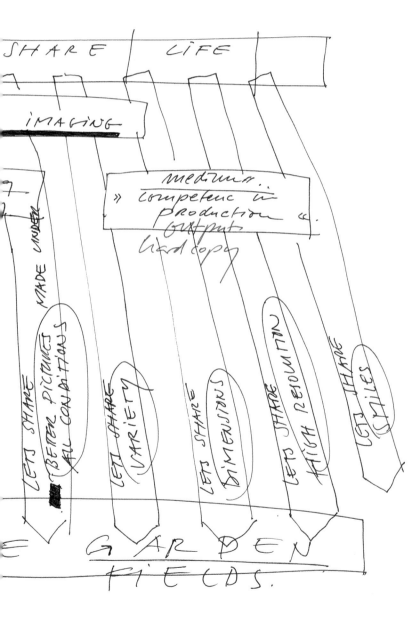

DAS KOMMUNIKATIONSKONZEPT,
DER MESSESTAND ALS BEGEHBARER KATALOG.
Je größer der Messestand, desto wichtiger ist die Orientierung.
Bei allen Besucherbefragungen, die in den vielen Jahren durchgeführt werden, wird immer wieder die Unübersichtlichkeit kritisiert,
und es werden Probleme bei der Orientierung auf dem Stand be-
mängelt. Dabei wird alles getan, um den Besuchern eine bessere
Orientierung zu bieten – offensichtlich mit wenig Erfolg. Da sind
beispielsweise Informationstafeln, Wegweiser, Faltpläne, die am
Eingang ausgegeben werden und zusätzliches Personal für Info-
Counter. Alle diese durchgeführten Maßnahmen werden auf
anderen Messen und Ständen genauso gehandhabt. Ein-
deutiges Fazit: Messebesucher sind nicht daran interes-
siert, Informationstafeln und Grundrisse zu studieren. Sie wollen
nur einfach und schnell das gesuchte Produkt oder einen Ansprechpartner finden.
Bei einer Vielzahl unterschiedlicher Produkte für die sehr unterschiedlichen Zielgruppen, wie sie für KODAK charakteristisch
sind, ist bei der Planung darauf zu achten, dass die Platzierung im
Grundriss eine klare und logische Struktur hat. Diese muss für den
Besucher leicht erkennbar sein. Wie bei Anzeigen, Prospekten
oder Katalogen geht es zunächst darum, Aufmerksamkeit zu
generieren und Interesse zu wecken. In einem weiteren Schritt gilt
es, den persönlichen Kontakt mit dem Kundenberater herzustellen. Dies wird erreicht mit einer interessanten oder provokativen
Headline, einem hochemotionalen Key-Visual oder einer attraktiven
Lifepräsentation. Wichtig sind einfache und kurze Produktbeschrei-
bungen. Zur besseren Unterscheidung der Produktgruppen können
dazu noch Farbcodes hilfreich sein. In den vielen Meetings zwischen den Marketingleuten und den Gestaltern hat sich gezeigt,
dass beide Seiten noch viel voneinander lernen können.

THE DISCOVERY

»The message of sharing pictures with others and presenting
this message from different points of view – that is the task.
Die Botschaft, Bilder mit anderen zu teilen, und dies aus verschiedenen Blickwinkeln darzustellen, das ist die Aufgabe.«
[URB]

BACK TO THE STORYTELLING
ZURÜCK ZUR EIGENTLICHEN GESCHICHTE

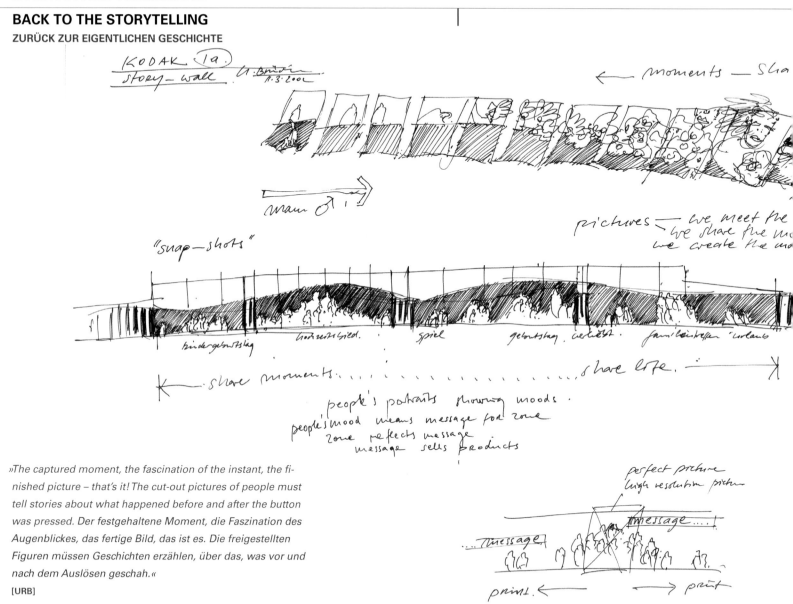

»The captured moment, the fascination of the instant, the finished picture – that's it! The cut-out pictures of people must
tell stories about what happened before and after the button
was pressed. Der festgehaltene Moment, die Faszination des
Augenblickes, das fertige Bild, das ist es. Die freigestellten
Figuren müssen Geschichten erzählen, über das, was vor und
nach dem Auslösen geschah.«
[URB]

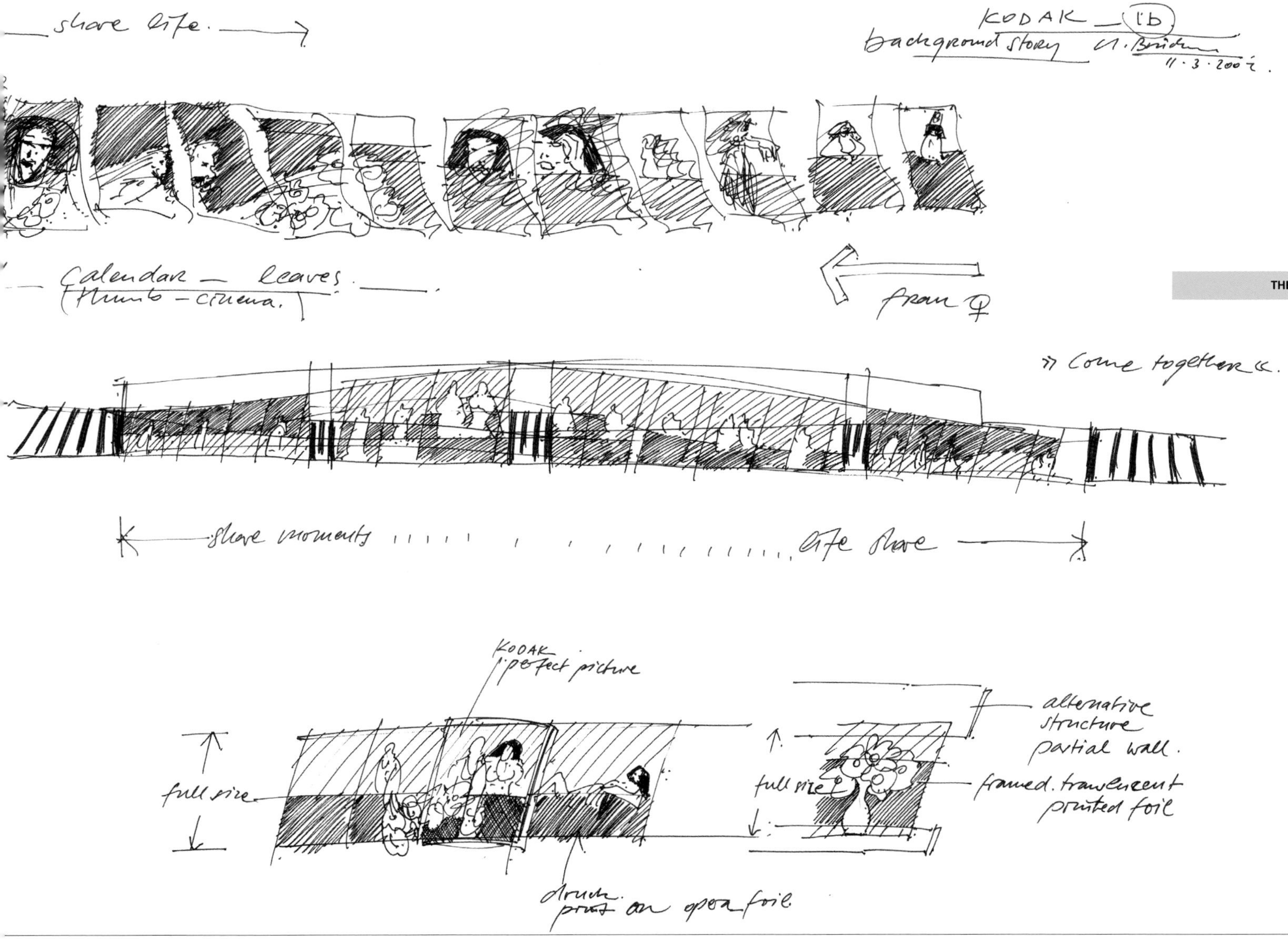

share life. →

KODAK 1b
background story U. Brüderin
11·3·2002

Calendar — leaves.
(thumbs – cinema.)

from φ

THE DISCOVERY

» Come together «

share moments , , , , , , , , , , , , , , life share →

KODAK
perfect picture

full size

alternative
structure
partial wall.

framed. translucent
printed foil

full size

druck
print on open foil

»Storytelling is the core message of KODAK.
Storytelling ist die Kernbotschaft von KODAK.«
[FOM]

THE YELLOW PORTALS
DIE GELBEN RAHMEN

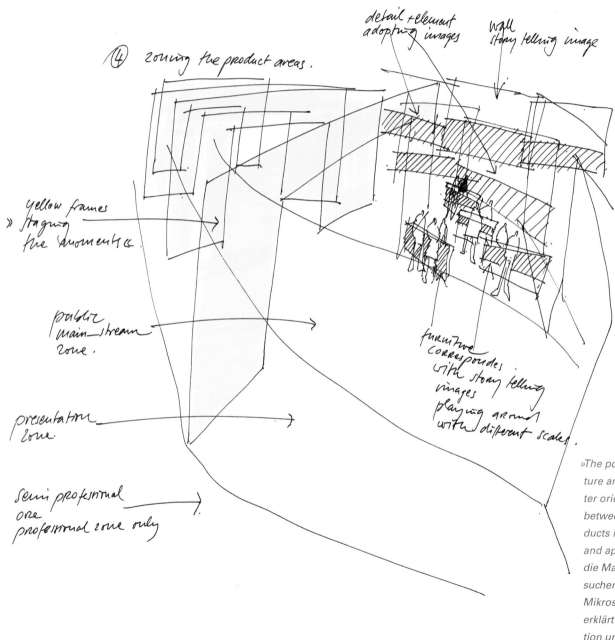

④ zoning the product areas.

detail + element
adopting images

wall
story telling image

yellow frames
» staging
the "moment" «

public
main-stream
zone.

presentation
zone.

semi professional
one
professional zone only

furniture
correspondes
with story telling
images
playing around
with different scales.

»The portals constitute the macrostructure and serve the visitors with better orientation. The microstructures between the portals describe the products in detail, including their functions and applications. Die Rahmen bilden die Makrostruktur und dienen dem Besucher zur besseren Orientierung. Die Mikrostruktur zwischen den Rahmen erklärt im Detail die Produkte, ihre Funktion und Anwendung.«

[URB TO BN]

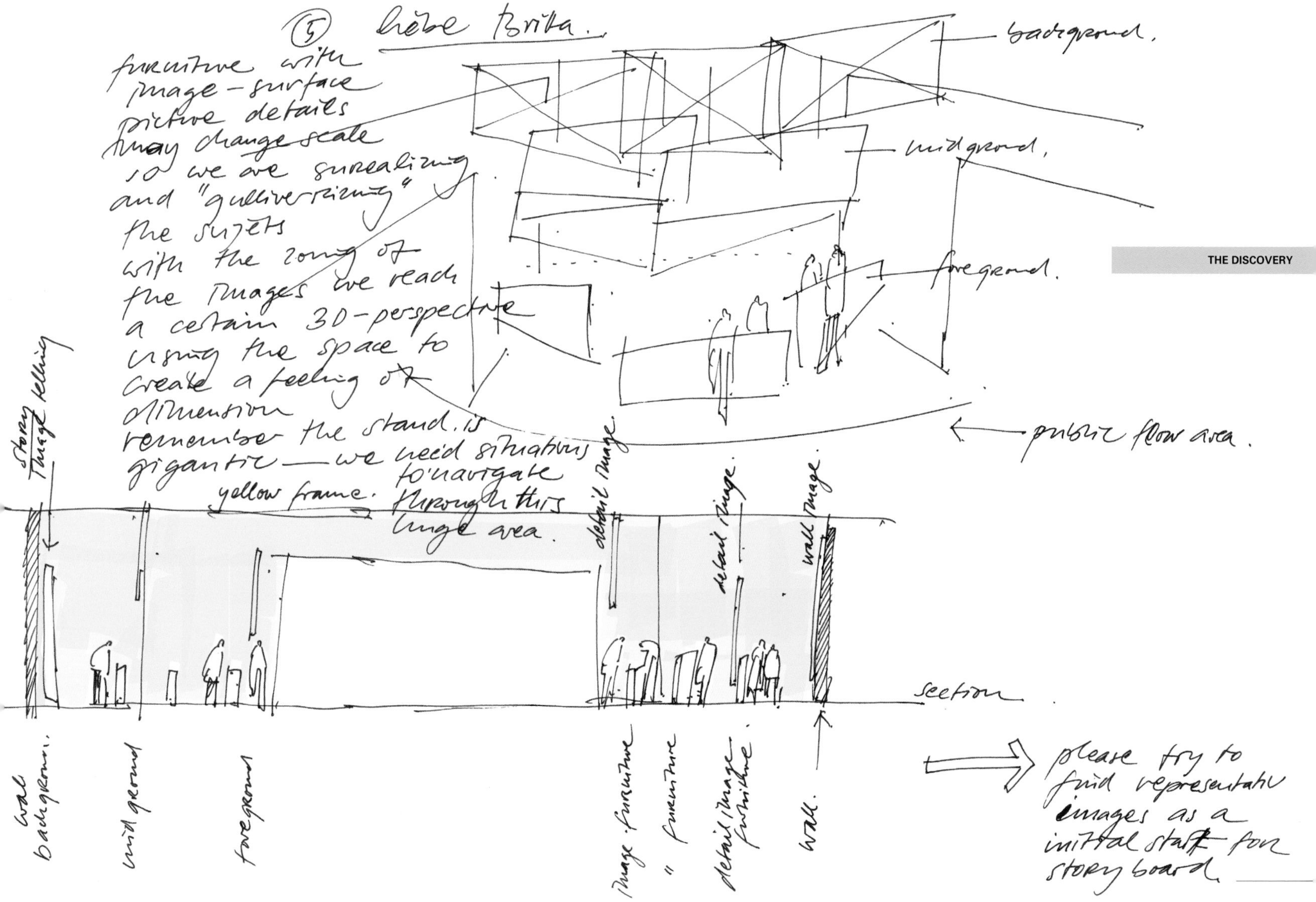

⑤ liebe Brita.

furniture with
image-surface
picture details
may change scale
so we are surealizing
and "gulliverizing"
the subjects
with the zoom of
the images we reach
a certain 3D-perspective
using the space to
create a feeling of
dimension
remember the stand is
gigantic — we need situations
to navigate
yellow frame. through this
huge area.

THE DISCOVERY

background.

midground.

foreground.

public flow area.

story telling

detail image

detail image

wall image

section

wall background.

midground

foreground

image furniture

" furniture

detail image furniture

wall.

→ please try to
find representativ
images as a
initial start for
story board.

PROPOSAL 5: STAGING THE MOMENTS
KONZEPT 5: STAGING THE MOMENTS

pages and links Verweise
I. 41 – 45
III. 180 – 183

KODAK SHARE MOMENTS. SHARE LIFE. Ideally this slogan should not hover all by itself as an arbitrarily chosen header above Hall 4. The designers will give it content and meaning. Everything that is conjured up in the KODAK world by the somewhat abstract notions »Share Moments. Share Life« is described realistically to the visitors in the various areas. Always under the umbrella concept of »Sharing«. KODAK does not boast »We are the greatest, just follow us blindly«. Instead it presents itself as a fair partner who offers visitors and customers a mutual and logical sharing in all the various areas. In other words, not a blaring advertising blast, not an intricate technical dissertation, but an inviting sequence of ambitious, encompassing concepts lead into a world of mutual experiences. Every area of the stand is identified with »Let's share …« and the respective benefit. With this treatment, the corporate claim is carried through as a stand philosophy that can be experienced by everyone.

KODAK SHARE MOMENTS. SHARE LIFE. Idealerweise sollte dieses Motto nicht isoliert – als willkürlich gewählter Messe-Slogan – über der Halle 4 schweben. Die Gestalter geben ihm Inhalt und Sinn. Alles, was sich zwischen den beiden eher abstrakten Begriffen »share Moments, share Life« in der KODAK Welt bewegt, wird in den einzelnen Areas für die Besucher konkret vorgestellt. Immer unter dem Gesichtspunkt des »Sharing«. KODAK brüstet sich nicht nach dem Motto »We are the greatest, just follow us blindly«, sondern ist der faire Partner, der dem Besucher und Kunden ein gemeinsames »Sharing« konsequent in allen Bereichen bietet. Also kein dröhnendes Reklamegewitter, kein klein-kleines Technologie-Latinum, sondern eine einladende Abfolge anspruchsvoller, übergreifender Begriffe führt in die Welt gemeinsamen Erlebens.
Jeder Bereich auf dem Messestand ist gekennzeichnet mit »Let's share« und dem jeweiligen Benefit dazu. So wird der Corporate Claim zu einem erlebbaren und durchgängigen Messekonzept.

»By means of a judicious ratio of curiosity and overview, it is possible to create a dialog between the trade show stand and product placement – a kind of tension field between the expectations of the visitors and the surprising offerings of the brand. Durch ein geschicktes Verhältnis von Neugierde und Übersicht lässt sich ein Dialog zwischen dem Subjekt und dem Productplacement herstellen – eine Art Spannungsfeld zwischen der Erwartung der Besucher und dem überraschenden Angebot der Marke.«
[URB]

THE CONCEPT

»*Clearly legible messages, attractive product areas, banning of small items into the background, generous central area – that's o.k. Klar lesbare Messages, übersichtliche Produkt-zonen, Verbannung des Kleinkrams in die Tiefe, großzügige Mittelzone, das ist o.k.*«

[FOM]

»*... a little too much yellow for my taste.
... für meinen Geschmack etwas zu gelb.*«

[BK]

TELLING THE STORY IN THE PRODUCT AREAS
ERSCHEINUNGSBILD DER PRODUKTBEREICHE

? are we shure
that we want
a red lady in the
yellow yellow area?

lady with red costume
and white dog,
dog invades
the fur looks perfect
area 6 KODAK

12.3.2007

>> Don't bore visitors with the obvious. Challenge them and stimulate their associative potential. Surprise them with unexpected surroundings cleverly connected to the product. Provide an inviting opportunity to explore and visitors will automatically participate in the scene. Langweile nicht mit Alltäglichem. Fordere den Betrachter und aktiviere seine Vorstellungskraft. Überrasche mit unerwarteten Ideen, die eine Verbindung zum Produkt haben. Biete dem Besucher die Möglichkeit, zu entdecken, dass er und sie automatisch Teil der Inszenierung sind.

THE CONCEPT

Working model

» easy share «
aps — panorama.
area 3   K O D A K   12.3.2002

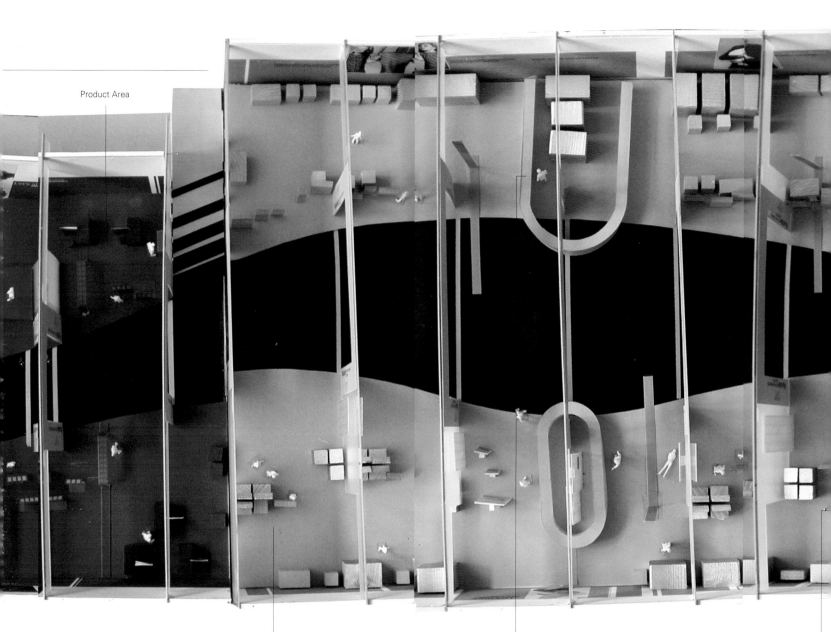

Product Area

Digital Area

Digital Area

Professional Area

THE PRESENTATION MODEL: PUBLIC AREA

DAS PRÄSENTATIONSMODELL: DER ÖFFENTLICHE RAUM

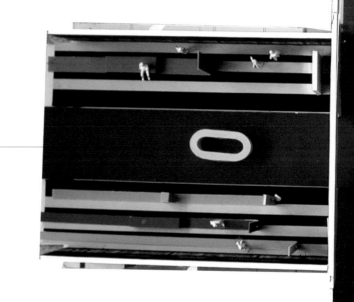

Entrance Area

chapter **II. 8 THE PRESENTATION** DIE PRÄSENTATION

8.500 SQ. METERS (91.492 SQ. FEET) OF CREATIVE SPACE
8.500 QUADRATMETER KREATIVER SPIELRAUM

pages and links Verweise
I. 46 – 47
III. 184 – 187

»The pictures of a detailed model provide a realistic impression of the proposed stand and are the best medium for convincing the client. Der Eindruck eines detailgetreuen Modells vermittelt eine realistische Vorstellung und ist dadurch am besten geeignet, den Kunden zu überzeugen.«
[BN]

DESIGNERS' DREAM

GESTALTERS TRAUM

»The vision: Pictures are composed of color impressions – in the head and on the completed trade show stand. That's how I'd like it! *Die Vision: Bilder setzen sich aus Farbeindrücken zusammen – im Kopf und auf dem fertigen Messestand. So hätt´ ichs gern!*«
[URB]

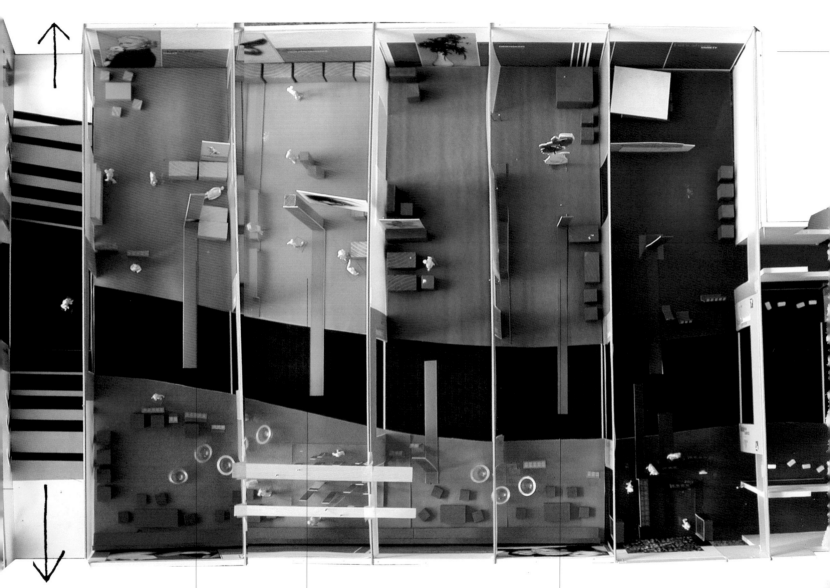

Dealers Area

Dealers Area

Area

Professional Area

Professional Area

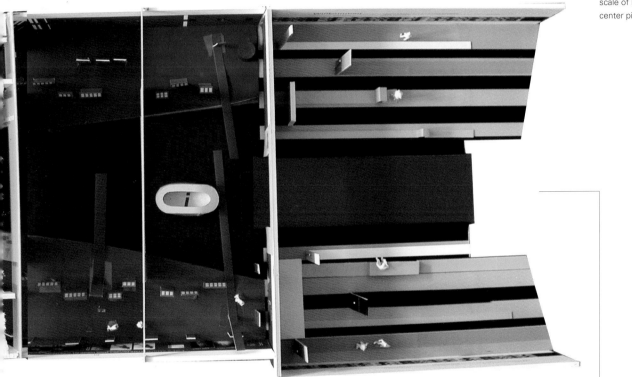

scale of Modell 1:100
center piece, display zone

»... the way is the destination – or is it?
 ... der Weg ist das Ziel, oder?«
[FOM]

Entrance Area

Share Moments. Share Life.

Scale = 1 : 100

»The model still has the best effect. Viewed and judged to
be good. Das Modell hat immer noch die beste Wirkung.
Gesehen und für gut befunden.«
[FOM]

THE PRESENTATION

»Actually, it is an ideal case for the designers. Neither products, displays nor texts interfere with the installation – free space – indeed pure aesthetics ... *Eigentlich der Idealfall für die Gestalter. Weder Produkte noch Displays oder Texte verstellen die Inszenierung – freier Raum – pure Ästhetik halt ...*«
[FOM]

BEYOND SOLUTIONS / THE HORRIBLE »YES, BUT ...« MEETING
DAS GEFÜRCHTETE »JA, ABER ...«-MEETING

pages and links Verweise

I. 34 – 35

III. 198 – 199

»*All is well, at last we have succeeded.*
My God, that took a lot of energy again
... Alles bestens, endlich sind wir
soweit! Mein Gott, hat das wieder mal
Energie gekostet ...«
[URB]

»*I can hardly believe it: not*
another chess move. Ich
kann's nicht glauben: nicht
schon wieder eine Rochade.«
[URB]

»*Visitors should be able to*
take something away. Like
paper airplanes, for instance.
Die Leute müssen etwas mit-
nehmen können. Wie z.B. Papier-
flieger.«
[FOM]

»*Paper airplanes. Only over my dead*
body! ... Papierflieger – nur über
meine Leiche.«
[URB]

»*How about cut-outs?*
... wie wäre es mit den Cutouts?«
[BN]

»*Only in combination with the stripes.*
... nur in Kombination mit den Streifen.«
[URB]

»*It's much too late for the stripes.*
... für die Streifen ist es längst zu spät.«
[BK]

»*... something's missing*
here... ... da fehlt noch
etwas.«
[FOM]

The team is convinced: we have a good stand design. All requirements appear to have been met. Visitor guidance, orientation system, branding, product highlights, an entire range of core points conjured the impression of an optimal solution. Before a dangerous state of satisfaction can set in, and contemplating the project from a critical distance, a very basic question begins to worry me: What will be retained in the minds of the visitors? What is our »key take-away«? With that question in mind, we once again review the creative elements. The portals are not key take-aways. Neither are the large pictures. Nor the color codes. What then, are they? The search continues – a painful process. In a situation like this one, everyone is challenged. Criticism by itself is not sufficient. New ideas must be found and solutions developed. Almost flippantly I set off on a daring thought process: Paper is the basis of a print. Why don't we do something with paper? Like paper airplanes, for example, since the paper print is our core message.

Uwe R. Brückner is already fantasizing about thousands of KODAK paper airplanes flying all over the entire Cologne fairgrounds, including, of course, the stands of our competitors. A great idea – or is it? A goofy idea is literally in the air. The whole studio spends days creating paper airplanes. Flying them is a lot of fun. But the team soon lands back on earth. After that temporary euphoria, the gag is relegated to the proverbial bin after all. Please note: Constructive suggestions are not always objective, as this action has shown. After this wonderful crash landing came the recollection that an outstanding idea was contained in the »Alice in Wonderland« concept proposed in the initial stages of our project – an idea that needed only a few creative modifications. Oversized heads in profile were placed in the path of the visitors and at a given perspective, they formed the "Larger-than-life kiss" that became the most photographed subject of the entire photokina.

Das ist die Überzeugung im Team: Wir haben einen guten Standentwurf. Alle Anforderungen scheinen erfüllt. Besucherführung, Orientierungssystem, Branding, Produkthighlights, eine ganze Skala von Kernpunkten vermitteln den Eindruck einer optimalen Lösung.

Bevor sich gefährliche Zufriedenheit einstellen kann, drängt sich bei kritischer Distanz dann doch eine sehr zentrale Frage auf: Was wird in den Köpfen unserer Standbesucher nachhaltig hängen bleiben? Was ist unser – schönes Wort – »Key Take-Away«?

Wir gehen die Gestaltungselemente unter diesem Aspekt nochmals durch. Die Tore sind es nicht. Die großen Bilder sind es nicht. Die Farbcodes sind es nicht. Was ist es dann?

Die Suche wurde fortgesetzt. – ein quälender Prozess. In so einer Situation ist jeder jeder gefordert. Kritik allein reicht nicht. Es müssen neue Ideen und Lösungsansätze her.

Leichtfertig setzte ich zu einem kühnen gedanklichen Höhenflug an: »Papier ist doch die Grundlage eines Bildes. Warum machen wir nicht etwas mit Papier? Beispielsweise Papierflieger, wo doch das gedruckte Papierbild unsere Kernbotschaft ist.«

Uwe R. Brückner sieht bereits in seiner Fantasie Tausende von KODAK Papierfliegern auf dem gesamten Kölner Messegelände herumliegen, natürlich auch auf den Ständen der Mitbewerber.

Großartige Idee, oder doch nicht? Da liegt buchstäblich eine verrückte Idee in der Luft. Das ganze Atelier bastelt tagelang Papierflieger. Überfliegerei macht Spaß. Aber dann bekommt das Team doch wieder Bodenkontakt.

Der wundervolle Gag wird dann doch lieber wieder in die berühmte Tonne getreten. Merke: Nicht immer sind Vorschläge konstruktiv und zielführend, wie diese Aktion beweist.

Nach dieser herrlichen Bruchlandung kommt die Erinnerung, dass bereits mit dem Konzept »Alice im Wunderland«, aus der Anfangsphase unseres Projektes, eine hervorragende Idee vorhanden ist, die nur ein wenig modifiziert werden müsste. Übergroße Köpfe im Profil stellten sich dem Besucher in den Weg, und bei entsprechender Perspektive wurde der »Kiss bigger then life« erlebbar und wird zum meistfotografierten Motiv auf der photokina.

THE KEY TAKE-AWAY

THE COMEBACK OF ALICE ...
DAS COMEBACK VON ALICE ...

»Motor-driven – no way! Guard rails, blinking lights and emergency cut-out switches and nobody notices the expenses! Motorbetrieben – no way – Absperrgitter, Blinklichter und Notausschalter, und niemand merkt den Aufwand.«

[FOM]

THE KEY TAKE-AWAY

»It looks very easy on the Polaroids. Auf den Polas
sieh das ganz simpel aus.«
[MV]

»I hope that we can use such moving cut-outs
again somewhere else. Hoffentlich können wir das
mit den bewegten Cutouts nochmal woanders
realisieren.«
[URB]

THE BIGGEST KISS OF THE YEAR
DER GRÖSSTE KUSS DES JAHRES

Searching for ideas for the »grand gesture«. First comes the scan with a huge amount of data. The Mac needs more than five minutes to open the file – one of the difficulties with high resolution large formats. Retouching the necktie is no problem, but it becomes a challenge to reproduce the colors of the transparency with a large format inkjet printer. Test printing takes a long time, fine-tuning the most delicate nuances. Another challenge: The largest width of a KODAK Inkjet Paper Roll is 1,5 m (almost 5 ft). But Satchmo's head (as it was nicknamed in the meantime) is 4,10 m high and 4,20 m wide (13'5" x 13'9"). And what kind of support material is available in this format? Now things really become complicated, because in this size it is simply impossible to mount a print on a previously contoured support board with precision. That means that the print will first have to be mounted on the board before the profile is cut out. For technical reasons, Plexiglas and aluminum cannot be used for the support board, so that only wood remains as a viable material. But chipboard is only available worldwide in a maximal size of circa 2,10 x 5,30 m (5' x 17'5"), so that a vertical joint has to be taken into account.

A solution for each giant cut-out gradually evolves. First, the two halves of each side of the printed profile are aligned exactly and mounted on two separate panels and the mirror image prints are mounted on two additional panels for a total of four panels for each of the two faces. The edges are very carefully retouched, so that the joint will not be noticeable. A master carpenter uses a special jig saw to cut the contours of the two heads with absolute accuracy. The panels are then assembled in a 10 cm (4") wide supporting framework. This support is very light, yet sturdy enough to accept the more than 2 m (6'7") high square steel tube that will hold the cut-out. That tube is welded to an appropriately sized steel plate that is installed under the double base on site. The contour edges of the heads are sealed with a special compound.

For the assembly on site, the two halves of the head can be inserted into the steel framework. The two halves are joined by means of long threaded rods and »Satchmo« and »Red Riding Hood« are ready They stand upright and secure, the joint is hardly visible and the impression is gigantic. The effort was eminently worthwhile.

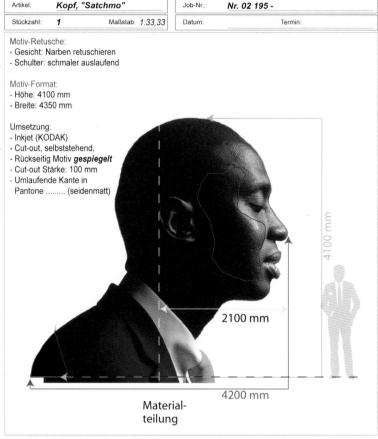

Fax

Name/Name:	
Firma/Comp.:	
Abt./Dep.:	
Messe:	**Photokina 2002, Köln**
Area:	**5**
Pos.-Nr.:	**5.4.2., neben Tor 6 A**
Artikel:	**Kopf, "Satchmo"**
Stückzahl: **1**	Maßstab: **1:33,33**

HEINZE & MALZACHER GMBH
FACHSERVICE EXPO-DISPLAY
Dornhaldenstraße 10/1
70199 Stuttgart
Telefon 0711/ 60 17 18-60
Fax   0711/ 60 17 18-70
ISDN   0711/ 60 17 18-80
e-mail   heinze.malzacher@t-online.de

Job-Nr.:	**Nr. 02 195 -**
Datum:	Termin:

Motiv-Retusche:
- Gesicht: Narben retuschieren
- Schulter: schmaler auslaufend

Motiv-Format:
- Höhe: 4100 mm
- Breite: 4350 mm

Umsetzung:
- Inkjet (KODAK)
- Cut-out, selbststehend,
- Rückseitig Motiv *gespiegelt*
- Cut-out Stärke: 100 mm
- Umlaufende Kante in
  Pantone .... (seidenmatt)

4100 mm

2100 mm

4200 mm

Material-
teilung

Fax

Name/Name:	
Firma/Comp.:	
Abt./Dep.:	
Messe:	**Photokina 2002, Köln**
Area:	**6**
Pos.-Nr.:	**6.4.2., neben Tor 10 B**
Artikel:	**Kopf, "Rotkäppchen"**
Stückzahl:	**1** Maßstab: **1:33,33**

HEINZE & MALZACHER GMBH
FACHSERVICE EXPO-DISPLAY
Dornhaldenstraße 10/1
70199 Stuttgart

Telefon 0711/ 60 17 18-60
Fax 0711/ 60 17 18-70
ISDN 0711/ 60 17 18-80
e-mail heinze.malzacher@t-online.de

Job-Nr.:	**Nr. 02 195 -**
Datum:	Termin:

Motiv-Retusche:
- Gesicht: Haut retuschieren

Motiv-Format:
- Höhe: 4550 mm
- Breite: 3758 mm

4550 mm

2100 mm

3767 mm

Material-
teilung

Umsetzung:
- Inkjet (KODAK)
- Cut-out, selbststehend,
- Rückseitig Motiv *gespiegelt*
- Cut-out Stärke: 100 mm
- Umlaufende Kante in
- Pantone .... (seidenmatt)

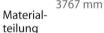

Kopfzerbrechen für die »große Geste«. Zuerst kommt der Scan mit unvorstellbaren Datenmengen. Der Mac braucht über fünf Minuten, um die Datei zu öffnen, das ist eine der Schwierigkeiten bei großen Formaten mit hoher Auflösung. Die Retusche der Krawatte ist kein Problem, eine Herausforderung wird es, die Farben des Diafilms mit einem Large Format Inkjetdrucker hinzukriegen. Die Andruckbemusterung zieht sich hin, es geht um feinste Nuancen. Eine weitere Herausforderung: KODAK Inkjet Papierrollen sind maximal anderthalb Meter breit. Der Kopf von »Satchmo«, wie er inzwischen liebevoll genannt wird, ist 4,10 m hoch und 4,20 m breit. Und was für ein geeignetes Trägermaterial gibt es in diesem Format? Jetzt wird es wirklich kompliziert, denn bei dieser Größe ist es schlicht unmöglich, einen Ausdruck millimetergenau auf eine zuvor dekupierte Trägerplatte zu kaschieren. Das bedeutet, es wird zuerst aufgezogen und danach freigestellt. Nachdem Plexiglas und Aluminium aus technischen Gründen als Trägermaterial ausscheiden, bleibt nur noch Holz übrig. Spanplatten werden weltweit aber nur bis zu einer Größe von ca. 2,10 x 5,30 m gefertigt, es muss folglich eine vertikale Teilung vorgenommen werden. Nach und nach entsteht die Lösung für das riesige »Cutout«. Zuerst werden je zwei Bahnen des gedruckten Motivs exakt aneinander auf insgesamt vier Spanplatten kaschiert. Der unschöne Papierstoß wird retuschiert und ist danach nicht mehr zu sehen. Der Schreinermeister dekupiert mit einer Spezial-Stichsäge das Motiv absolut akkurat, um danach die Vorder- und Rückseite deckungsgleich auf eine zehn Zentimeter starke Rahmenkonstruktion zu montieren. Diese Konstruktion ist sehr leicht und stabil und hat den Vorteil, dass sie das über zwei Meter hohe Vierkant-Stahlrohr zur Halterung des »Cutouts« aufnehmen kann. Das Rohr wird mit einer ausreichend großen Stahlplatte verschweißt, die vor Ort unter den vorhandenen Doppelboden platziert wird. Die Konturkante des Kopfes wird mit einem speziellen Umleimer geschlossen. Zur Montage vor Ort können die beiden Hälften des Kopfes seitlich an das stabilisierende Stahlrohr geschoben werden. Die beiden Teile

THE GRAPHIC CONCEPT

werden durch lange Gewindestangen mit dem Rohr verbunden, und fertig ist »Satchmo«. Er steht gerade und fest, die Teilung ist fast nicht sichtbar, und der Eindruck ist gigantisch. Die Mühe hat sich gelohnt.

»It has to look exactly like it does on the transparency. No, the necktie is to be red instead of green. The heads protrude freely into the room and I don't want to see any supporting elements at all. A two-sided cutout. Printing will be on KODAK material. Top quality and super sharp. Perfect as always. And watch the costs – they will only be used for six days. Er muss genauso aussehen wie auf dem Dia hier. Nein, die Krawatte wird rot statt grün. Der steht frei im Raum, und ich will auf keinen Fall irgendwelche Halterungen sehen. Ein »Cutout«, beidseitig. Gedruckt wird auf KODAK Material. Top-Qualität und superscharf. Perfekt wie immer. Und denkt an die Kosten, es steht ja nur sechs Tage.«
[FOM]

GRAPHIC DESIGN MEETS PHOTOGRAPHY
GRAFIK UND FOTOGRAFIE ERGÄNZEN SICH

It is not an egocentric demand on the part of designers when they request an integrative selection of photographic subjects. Nor is it an unacceptable intrusion into the artistic freedom of the photographer, but a necessity for an overall work of art. That is when all the artistic contributions benefit from one another.

Es ist keine egozentrische Forderung der Gestalter, wenn sie für eine integrative Motivauswahl der Fotos plädieren. Es ist auch kein unzulässiger Eingriff in die künstlerische Autarkie der Fotografen, sondern eine Notwendigkeit für ein Gesamtkunstwerk. Dann profitieren alle künstlerischen Beiträge voneinander.

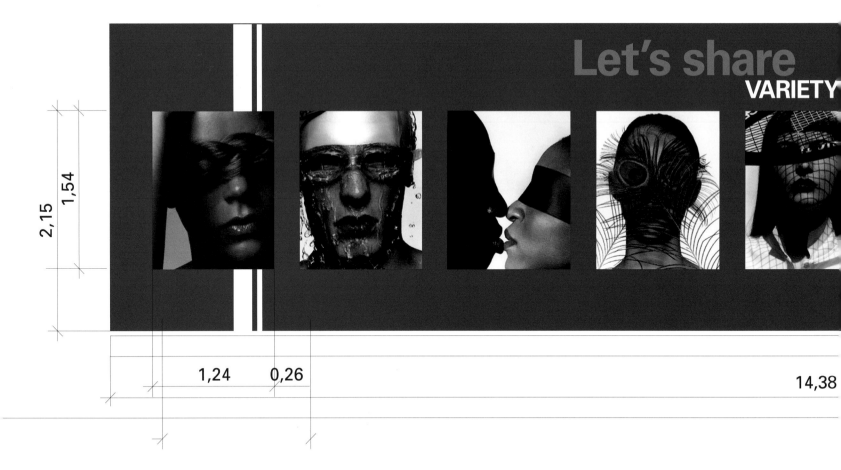

»Seen – unseen«, the intellectual among German photo-designers, Christian von Alvensleben, is one of the creative photographic artists who accomplishes a consistent photographic theme at nearly every one of the photokina trade shows. He proved that seeing is more than the physical effect on the retina by creating a series of delicate and double-meaning photographs. Share moments – these are very special moments that captivate the viewer.

»Sehen – ungesehen«, der Intellektuelle unter den deutschen Fotodesignern, Christian von Alvensleben, ist bei fast jeder photokina einer der Kreativen mit der Kamera, die ein tragendes Bildthema realisieren. Dass Sehen mehr ist als der physikalische Netzhauteindruck, hat er in einer Serie von fein- und doppelsinnigen Fotografien inszeniert. Share moments – hier sind es ganz spezielle Augenblicke, die den Betrachter in den Bann ziehen.

4,00

3,00

2,15

THE GRAPHIC CONCEPT

Layout

1,24

Implementation

FURTHER REFINEMENT OF THE COLOR CONCEPT
DAS FARBKONZEPT WEITERENTWICKELT

The well-functioning KODAK I color concept is adopted, the colors and their juxtapositions are judiciously tailored to the concept. Each product area is assigned a color and a theme, which will constitute the background.

A colored surface and the interplay with the horizon embed the picture into the space. The horizon and the use of colored surfaces are creative elements that are used throughout the stand. They appear again and again, in different scales, from the design of the exterior wall to the design of the displays, giving them distinctive identities.

Das gut funktionierende Farbkonzept von KODAK I wird übernommen, die Farben und die Farbstellung zueinander dem Konzept entsprechend angepasst. Jedem Produktbereich ist eine Farbe und ein Motiv zugeordnet, welches den Hintergrund bildet.

Eine farbige Fläche, das Spiel mit dem Horizont, bindet das Bild in den Raum ein. Der Horizont und der Einsatz von Farbflächen sind durchgängige Gestaltungselemente, tauchen in verschiedenen Maßstäben von der Gestaltung der Außenwand bis zu Gestaltung der Displays immer wieder auf und wirken identitätsstiftend.

 KODAK Consumer Imaging International Conference Area Zone 24 + 25

 KODAK WholeSale + Retail+ Photofinishing Zone 4+5+6 Pantone 1375

 Image Communication Zone 7 Pantone 185

 OTUC Zone 3 Pantone 187

 CI Film Story Zone 8 Pantone 224

 Digital Capture and Output Zone 2 Pantone 382

Portrait Photography Zone 14 Pantone 3258

KP Capture Zone 13 Pantone Process Blue

Large Inkjet Service House Zone 12 Pantone 286

KODAK Professional Film Story Zone 11 Pantone 286

pages and links Verweise
I. 58 – 59
III. 226 – 227

SHARE MOMENTS SHARE LIFE

1

2

3

4

5

6

7

8

THE GRAPHIC CONCEPT

Beyond the obligatory two-dimensional transmittal of information graphic design is rich in atmospheric and experiential potential. Jenseits der obligatorischen 2-dimensionalen Vermittlung von Information birgt Grafikdesign im Raum atmosphärische und erlebnishafte Potentiale.

GRAPHICDESIGN MEETS CORPORATE DESIGN
GRAFIKDESIGN WIRD CORPORATE DESIGN

pages and links Verweise
I. 63 – 64
III. 228 – 229

1

HE WHO WANTS TO MOVE SOMETHING MUST FIRST MOVE HIMSELF.
After nearly 50 years in the old KODAK Hall 8 at photokina, the move to Hall
4 has to be communicated effectively. From billboards in trams and busses
to literature bags and a folded floorplan of the stand for better orientation,
everything is designed logically and uniformly. Therefore communication in
the area is no longer confined to the sections within the stand, it extends
well beyond the stand.
WER WAS BEWEGEN WILL, MUSS SICH BEWEGEN.
Nach fast 50 Jahren in der alten KODAK Halle 8 auf der photokina muss der
Umzug in die Halle 4 entsprechend kommuniziert werden.
Von Plakaten in Bahn und Bussen bis zur Tragetasche und einem Stand-
faltplan zur besseren Orientierung, alles ist konsequent durchgestaltet. Die
Kommunikation im Raum ist dadurch nicht mehr örtlich begrenzt, sondern
geht vielmehr weit über die Grenzen des Messestandes hinaus.

2

»The texts, graphic designs, themes and the orientation
system require common elements to facilitate their use for
navigating through a complex trade show stand.
Orientierungssysteme, Text, Grafik und Bilder brauchen
merkfähige Elemente, um die Struktur eines großen Messestandes besser zu verstehen.«
[BK]

3

4

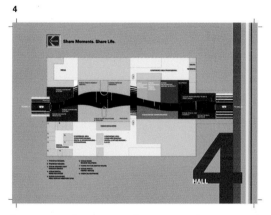

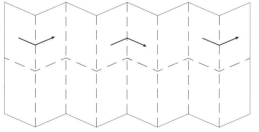

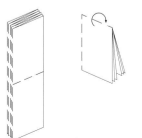

Color swatches as an orientation idea

1
Billboard

2
Paper bag

3
Advertisement

4
Stand guide

5
Tulip cut out

4,30

THE GRAPHIC CONCEPT

5

EXPERIENCING NEW CHALLENGES, PORTAL BY PORTAL
RAHMEN FÜR RAHMEN NEUES ENTDECKEN

pages and links Verweise
I. 64 – 65
III. 232 – 233

The large yellow portals frame the main stages. Individual product areas are located along the central aisle. The floor between the portals is black. The aisle is enlivened by offset cutouts of pictures that trigger moments of curiosity. The yellow portals are followed by semi-transparent white fabric panels in the product areas. This creates individual side stages, some of which are connected by means of openings. Specific colors are assigned to the individual product areas. The floor as well as parts of the back wall in these areas are identified with the respective colors.

The conference areas are positioned along the outer walls of the hall, isolated from the exhibition area by a high partition. When a visitor looks into one of the lateral stages from the central aisle, he sees a very large picture on that partition. The floor configuration: the central aisle and the presentation areas have a slightly raised floor that accommodates the supply lines. The floor in those areas consists of 16 mm (1 5/8") soft fiberboards covered with glued 22 mm (1 7/8") tongue-and-groove tiles. The central aisle is covered with dark gray double-rib carpeting and the display areas feature velour carpeting that has been specially dyed by the Vorwerk Company. Embedded in the floor covering are bands of MDF painted in corresponding colors that protrude into the central aisle.

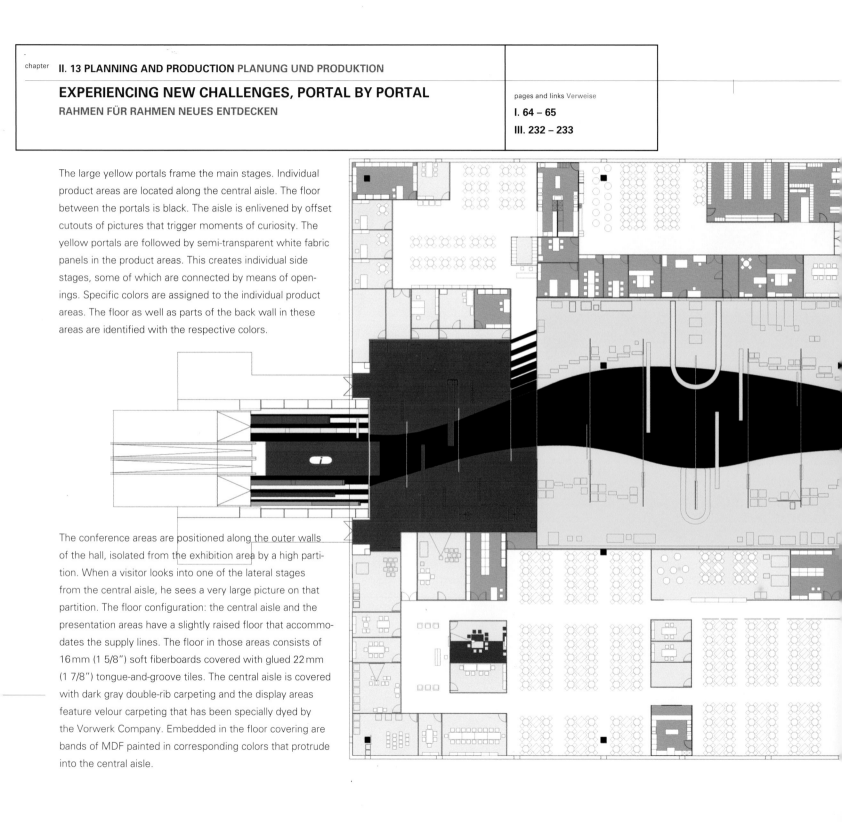

Die gelben Rahmen bilden die Hauptbühne. Entlang des zentralen Gangs befinden sich rechts und links die einzelnen Produktbereiche. Der Boden zwischen den Rahmen ist schwarz. Der Gang wird durch Versatzstücke belebt – große Cutouts von Bildern schaffen einen attraktiven Irritationsmoment.

Die gelben Rahmen werden in den Produktbereichen durch semitransparente, weiße Wände aus Stoff fortgesetzt. Es entstehen dadurch einzelne Seitenbühnen, welche zum Teil durch Öffnungen verbunden sind. Den jeweiligen Produktbereichen sind Farben zugeordnet. Der Boden sowie Teile der Rückwand sind mit dieser Farbe bespielt.

Die Besprechungsbereiche sind an die Längswände der Halle angegliedert und durch eine raumhohe Wand vom Ausstellungsbereich abgetrennt. Blickt der Besucher vom zentralen Gang in eine

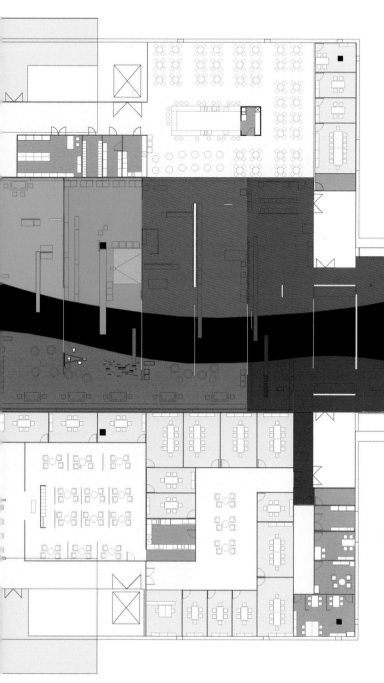

der Seitenbühnen, sieht er vor dieser Wand ein großformatiges Bild. Der Bodenaufbau: Mittelgang und Präsentationsbereiche haben einen leicht aufgeständerten Boden, um Versorgungsleitungen zu verlegen; dort liegen Verlegeplatten (22 mm nut- und federverleimt) auf Weichfaserplatten (16 mm) als Bodenbelag wird im Mittelgang schwarzgraue Doppelrippe, in den Ausstellungsbereichen wird ein von Vorwerk speziell eingefärbter Velours eingesetzt; im Boden eingelassen ragen Bänder aus farbig lackiertem MDF in den Mittelgang.

Grundriss

Project:
Photokina 2002

Client:
Kodak GmbH

Hedelfinger Straße 60
70327 Stuttgart

Design:

Quellenstraße 7   Tel.0711/500077-0
70376 Stuttgart   Fax.0711/500077-22

Number: Index
GR_026
Scale:
1:100

Editor:
bn/dh/sb/gd

THE PORTALS IN CONTEXT

DIE RAHMEN-HANDLUNG

The illumination rigging also serves as an overhead support structure for room dividers and for suspended elements. It traverses the hall and delineates it with soffits and framework. In this stand too, room dividers made of framed fabrics are a key to fast set-up and take-down times. The yellow portals also have a lightweight construction that consists of sandwiched painted panels supported by T-profiles. They stand on the floor and are anchored to the overhead rig to stop them tilting. Every frame consists of four components held together by screws. All room dividers of semi-transparent Trevira CS fabric are fastened to rails at the top and the bottom, which are also anchored to the overhead rigging and to the floor.

Self-standing walls made of painted MDF material serve as carriers for graphics and lightboxes. They are also a part of the orientation system and serve as the background for the display areas.
Oversized cutout pictures (also laminated to sandwiched panels for support) serve to intrigue by distorting the scale in the line of sight.
The spatial separation of public and semi-public areas is accomplished by means of stripes with presentation furniture of yellow painted MDF material decorated with sample photographs.

Das Beleuchtungsrigg dient gleichzeitig den räumlichen Elementen sowohl als Unterkonstruktion wie auch als Abhängpunkte. Es zeichnet die Halle in Querrichtung durch Soffitten und Rahmen nach. Wände aus Stoff sind auch bei diesem Stand Garanten für schnelle Auf- und Abbauzeiten. Auch die gelben Rahmen sind dem Leichtbau verpflichtet, sie sind aus lackierten Sandwichplatten gefertigt, die in T-Profilen gehalten werden. Sie sind auf dem Boden aufgestellt und am Rigg gegen Kippen gesichert. Jeder Rahmen besteht aus vier Segmenten, die miteinander verschraubt werden. Sämtliche Wände aus semitransparentem Trevira-CS-Gewebe sind oben und unten in Kederschienen gefasst, zwischen Rigg und Boden verspannt.
Selbststehende Wände aus lackiertem MDF dienen sowohl als Träger von Grafik und Leuchtkästen wie auch als Leitsystem und geben den Ausstellungsbereichen ihren Background.
Übergroße ausgeschnittene Bilder (ebenfalls auf Sandwichplatten als Träger) sorgen in Blickrichtung für Maßstabsverzerrung.
Die räumliche Trennung zwischen öffentlichem und halböffentlichem Bereich übernimmt ein Band mit Präsentationsmöbeln aus gelb lackiertem MDF, das mit Musterbildern bestückt wird.

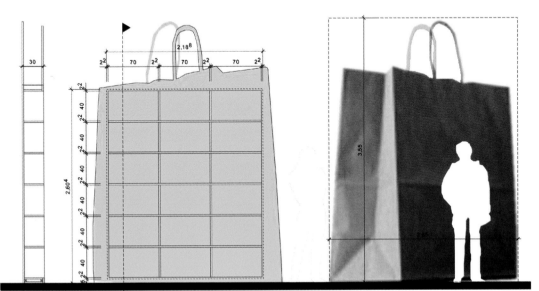

Schnitt a-a

a-a ▶

Literature bag shelf of 22 mm (7/8") painted MDF material. Back wall with a mounted picture of a shopping bag on a support base of Alucobond or Forex.

Tütenregal
aus 22 mm Mdf lackiert
Rückwand mit aufkaschiertem Bild einer Einkaufstüte
auf einer Trägerplatte aus Alucobond oder Forex
Outline der Einkaufstüte um die Tiefe des Regals extrudiert
Regalkonstruktion aus Regalböden konstruktiv überkreuz ineinandergesteckt

KODAK Photokina 2002

Plan No.	DM_5.IV.3.3
Planstoff	Tüten-Regel
Maßstab	M1:20
Datum / gez.	22.03.2002/an
Konzeption/ Gestaltung	atelier brückner architekturen und szenografie Quellenstraße 7 70376 Stuttgart Fon. +49-(0) 711-5060 77-0 Fax. +49-(0) 711-5050 77-22

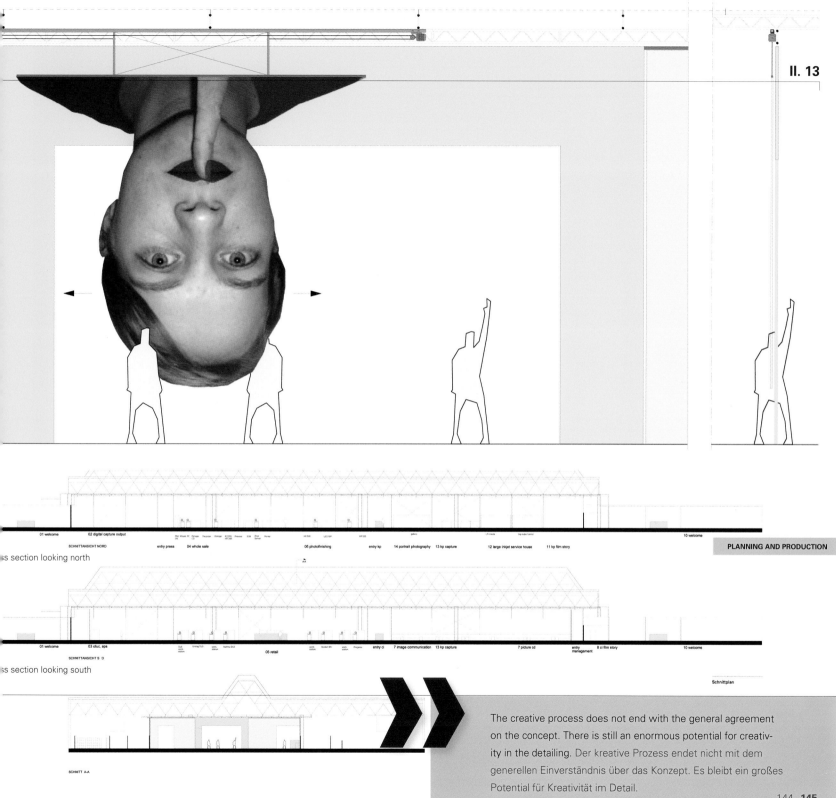

01 welcome 02 digital capture output P&2 Mosaic PC Panage Tecolour Storage ECOPS iView IDM Riot Server Panap HX 500 LEO RIP HX 500 gallery LFI media big output (prini) 10 welcome
OS
HX 300

SCHNITTANSICHT NORD entry press 04 whole sale 06 photofinishing entry kp 14 portrait photography 13 kp capture 12 large inkjet service house 11 kp film story

ss section looking north

A-A

PLANNING AND PRODUCTION

01 welcome 03 ofuc, aps DLS work station Graig DLS work station Nofilm DLS 05 retail work station System 89 work station Progeno entry ci 7 image communication 13 kp capture 7 picture cd entry management 8 ci film story 10 welcome

SCHNITTANSICHT S D

ss section looking south

Schnittplan

SCHNITT A-A

The creative process does not end with the general agreement on the concept. There is still an enormous potential for creativity in the detailing. Der kreative Prozess endet nicht mit dem generellen Einverständnis über das Konzept. Es bleibt ein großes Potential für Kreativität im Detail.

PRESS DAY AS A TEST RUN
DER PRESSETAG ALS PROBELAUF

More than a year of preparation has just come to an end. Now it will be seen whether the creative ideas that have been implemented will work successfully in a hard practical test. The big clean-up has been completed, the last protective plastic covering has been removed. The stand shines in beautiful light and color. Except for the sales reps, all staff members are at their assigned stations. Everything is functioning, the show can now begin. Exactly at 10 o'clock, the first journalists, coming from all over the world, arrive on the stand. The suspense ebbs, top managers give interviews in front of live cameras, reporters want to take attractive product shots with models. This too, has been foreseen and good-looking models have been hired especially for this purpose. The first positive comments about the stand please the managers. One of the vice-presidents pats Friedrich O. Müller on the shoulder and says »Looks great, that's KODAK for me …«. More than 2.000 journalists visited the stand on press day to report their impressions to readers around the world. All the reviews about KODAK were favorable. The reaction of the press was overwhelming.

Über ein Jahr an Vorbereitungen ist nun abgeschlossen. Jetzt zeigt es sich, ob das, was an kreativen Ideen umgesetzt wurde, im harten Praxistest funktioniert. Das große Reinemachen ist vorbei und die letzte Folie ist entfernt. Der Stand erstrahlt in schönstem Licht und Farbe. Außer der Vertriebsmannschaft sind alle Mitarbeiter an Bord. Alles funktioniert, jetzt kann es losgehen. Punkt 10 Uhr betreten die ersten Journalisten, die aus aller Welt kommen, den Stand. Die Anspannung legt sich, die Topmanager geben Interviews vor laufender Kamera, andere wollen attraktive Produktfotos machen, auch für diese Situation ist vorgesorgt, und speziell für diesen Zweck sind gutaussehende Models engagiert. Die ersten positiven Äußerungen über den neuen Stand erfreuen das Management. Einer der Vize-Präsidenten klopft Friedrich O. Müller auf die Schulter und sagt: »Looks great, that´s KODAK for me …« Mehr als 2.000 Journalisten haben den Stand an diesem Tag besucht, um über ihre Eindrücke in alle Welt zu berichten. Das Urteil über KODAK fällt in allen Berichten positiv aus. Die Presseresonanz ist überwältigend.

THE OPENING

»*The test run was successful, everything worked perfectly. Now we are ready for the first official day of the trade show. Der Probelauf war gelungen, alles funktionierte bestens. Der erste offizielle Messetag konnte kommen.*«
[FOM]

THE KISS
DER KUSS

»Be careful during the set-up. You must handle these cutouts carefully. Like a
4,5 m (14'9"), 150 kg (331 lb) raw egg. *Aufpassen beim Aufstellen! Ihr müsst diese*

THE FIRST REACTIONS
ERSTE KOMMENTARE

»Messages could not have been communicated more effec-
tively and harmlessly. Effektiver und harmloser kann man
Botschaften nicht unterbringen.«
[BK]

»It worked better than I expected. Es hat besser funktioniert,
als ich dachte.«
[URB]

»I have never seen more satisfied customers. So zufrieden
habe ich den Kunden noch nie gesehen.«
[BN]

»The first trade show stand (KODAK I) was not as clear and
so well organized. So klar und übersichtlich war der erste
Messestand (KODAK I) nicht.«
[SB]

Let's share
HIGH PERFORMAN

**KODAK
PROFESSIONAL
DCS PRO 14N**

Let's share
DIMENSIONS

THE OPENING

PERFECT VISUAL MARKETING
VISUAL MARKETING IN PERFEKTION

Professional output area

E BIENVENUE BIENVENIDO VELKON
A HOS GELDINIZ BENVENUTO BEM-VINDO VÄLKON
ISTEN HOZOTT

EXCITING
SELLING IDEAS
FOR SUCCESSFUL
PRODUCTS

THE OPENING

Entrance area

EXPIRATION DATE: 6 DAYS
VERFALLSDATUM 6 TAGE

The last hours before the show closes. A general mood of unrest begins to set in. It is 5:58 PM and a gong signals an official trade show announcement: »Ladies and gentlemen, we wish to inform you that photokina 2002 will close its doors at 6:00 PM. Please proceed to the exits. We thank you for your visit«. Staffers feel a bit of nostalgia. The take-down crew is about to arrive. After six strenuous days and nearly 160.000 visitors, the stand still looks superb and the carpeting hardly shows any wear. In a matter of hours the »temporary building« is history.

Die letzten Stunden vor Messeschluss. Eine allgemeine Unruhe macht sich breit. Es ist 17:58 Uhr, der Gong kündigt die offizielle Messedurchsage an. »Meine Damen und Herren, wir dürfen Sie darauf aufmerksam machen, dass die photokina 2002 um 18:00 Uhr ihre Tore schließt. Bitte begeben Sie sich zu den Ausgängen. Wir danken für Ihren Besuch.« Alles ist vorbei. Etwas Wehmut ist nicht zu verleugnen. Gleich kommt das Abrisskommando. Nach strapaziösen sechs Tagen mit fast 160.000 Besuchern sieht der Stand noch immer super aus, und der Teppich zeigt kaum Gebrauchsspuren. Stunden später ist das »Temporary Building« Geschichte.

THE BEST PRESS REVIEWS IN MANY YEARS
DIE BESTE PRESSERESONANZ SEIT JAHREN.

pages and links Verweise

I. 88 – 89

III. 254 - 255

The official press photo of the opening of photokina 2002 distributed by the German dpa press agency shows »The Kiss« as the visual highlight of the KODAK stand. This picture was published in nearly every daily newspaper. Every one of the important television and radio stations broadcast from the KODAK stand, which generated millions of additional contacts. In the official closing report about photokina, a dpa picture of the KODAK stand is once again the first choice. The giant KODAK digital camera symbolizes the favorable reports about the outstanding business results enjoyed by the photographic industry. Mission accomplished. Expectations exceeded.

Das offizielle »dpa Pressebild« zur Eröffnung der photokina zeigt das visuelle Highlight »The Kiss« vom KODAK Stand. In fast allen Tageszeitungen ist dieses Bild abgedruckt. Alle wichtigen TV- und Hörfunkstationen berichten vom KODAK Stand, was weitere Millionen von Kontakten zur Folge hat. Zum offiziellen Abschlussbericht der photokina ist wieder ein dpa-Bild vom KODAK Stand die erste Wahl. Der Aufmacher für die positiven Meldungen über die hervorragenden Geschäftsabschlüsse der Fotobranche ist die übergroße Digitalkamera von KODAK. Ziel erreicht. Erwartungen übertroffen.

artin Wolgschaft

e- und Produktneuheiten prä-
amerikanische Unternehmen
ftsorientierter Konzepte und
ndelspartner, Profifotografen
enten. Messegästen sei emp-
Besuch des Kodak-Standes
zuplanen, denn am neuen
4 steht Kodak eine um rund
sere Ausstellungsfläche zur
photokina 2000.

Intime Einblicke aus großer Entfernung

Photokina-Aussteller ziehen gute Bilanz

Die Aussteller auf der photokina in Köln haben am letzten Messe-tag eine positive Bilanz gezogen. Bei der sechstägigen Leitmesse für die Fotoindustrie hätten sich mehr als 160000 Besucher über die Neuheiten der Branche infor-miert. Insgesamt seien mehr als

1540 Aussteller aus fast 140 Län-dern in die Messehallen gekom-men. Wichtige Themen waren die neuesten Trends bei Foto-Kame-ras, Camcordern und Druckern so-wie die Weiterentwicklungen bei der analogen und digitalen Foto-grafie. Foto: dpa

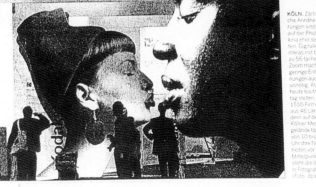

KÖLN. Zärtli-
che Annähe-
rungen sind
auf der Photo-
kina eher sel-
ten. Digitalka-
meras mit bis
zu 56-fachen
Zoom machen
geringe Entfer-
nungen auch
unnötig. Ab
heute bis Mon-
tag stellen
1550 Firmen
aus 46 Län-
dern auf dem
Kölner Messe-
gelände täglich
von 10 bis 18
Uhr ihre Neu-
heiten vor. Im
Mittelpunkt
steht die digita-
le Fotografie.
(Foto: dpa)

Ins rechte Bild gerückt

Zwischen übergroßen Bildern am Stand von Kodak laufen am gestrigen Dienstag die ersten Fachbesucher der heute in Köln beginnenden Photokina. Zur diesjährigen Fachmesse Photokina, die bis zum 30. September andauert, sind insgesamt 1546 Unternehmen aus 46 Ländern mit ihren neuesten Produkten vertreten. Mit vielfältigem Design und technischen Neuerungen will die Foto-Industrie den boomenden Foto-Markt weiter anheizen. Im Trend liegen digitale und analoge Designerkameramodelle. Begeistern sollen die Käufer auch Kameras mit drahtlosen Netzwerkfunktionen.

Photokina 2002 - die große Welt der kleinen Digi-Cams

VON HANS STENGLEIN,
MICHAEL BISCHOFF
Die Welt der
er wird immer
inierender. Das
eist die neueste
otokina" in Köln.
Messe titelt
rld of Imaging" -
zieht Profis wie
teure ab heute
ren Bann
»Welt der Zukunft
natürlich der
Techni. Die
igilen die Fro-
dotke. Fur die
Wie viel Profi
auf ince der Spie-
ones wie
ist die neue
...
nate Nachricht
le Branche vor

weg. Die Preise für so-
genannte DigiCams
sinken langsam, aber
stetig. Und die Qua-
litätsmaßstäbe auf dem
"Hobby Markt" können
sich mit dem Profi
messen.
Die "Photokina" be-
ginnt heute, dauert
bis Montag in
den Messehal-
len 1 bis 11
und 14 präsen-
tieren 1.546
Unternehmen
aus 46 Ländern
die neuesten
Neuigkeiten
aus der Welt
der Photo und
Videokameras,
Dia- und Film-
projektion.

Home-Cinema und al-
les rund um Digital...
von 10 bis 16 Ut
Dauerkarte 51 Eur
3-Tages-Karte 41 E
ro. Tageskarte 17 E
ro. Tageskarte
Wochenende 12 E
ro. Katalog 18 Eur

Am imposantesten ist der
Kodak-Stand. Die gesamte
Halle 4 ist in intensivem Blau
und Gelb gehalten und an den
Seiten buhlen Animateure
lautstark um Aufmerksam-
keit. Beiden Produkt-Neuhei-
ten bietet Kodak vor allem für
den professionellen Fotografen ein Schmuckstück an:
Ganze 13,89 Megapixel und
ein volles Kleinbildformat von
24 mal 38 Millimeter hat die
Kodak Professional DCS Pro
14n. Die Bilder haben eine gi-
gantische Auflösung von 4536
mal 3024 Pixel. Diese Kamera
für den Profi hat allerdings
auch ihren Preis. Knapp unter
6000 Euro soll das Modell kosten.
Ganz auf das Ausprobieren
der Kameras hat das Traditi-

Die einfache Kamera soll die
junge Generation mit bunten
Farben und ungewöhnlichem
Design locken. Zielgruppe
sind Personen, die einfach nur
Fotos machen wollen.
Aber nicht nur die Kameras
werden immer aufwendiger -
auch das Design, der Drucken
...
ben mit einem beigen, kant-
gen Kasten nichts mehr gemeinsam. In schwarz und mit
silbernem Tastein sieht der HP
Photosmart 7350... einfach
schicke aus. Unter der Abdeckung sind drei Druckpatro-
nen, dafür verantwortlich,
dass bis zu sieben verschiedene Farben gleichzeitig gedruckt werden. Zudem kann
man sich Fotos vor dem Drucken auf dem Display des Foto-
marts anschauen, Digitalfo-
os zu bearbeiten und aus

160 000 Besucher auf Kölner Photokina

Die Aussteller auf der Photokina in Köln haben am letzten Messetag eine positive Bilanz gezogen. Bei der sechstägigen Leitmesse für die Fotoindustrie hätten sich mehr als 160.000 Besucher über die Neuheiten der Branche informiert, teilte die KölnMesse gestern in Köln mit. Auch diese Rie-senkamera fand besonders bei Kindern großes Interesse. dpa / Foto: Scheidemann

tofans: Die Photokina in Köln

In Köln eröffneten Messe Photokina. Die Profi-Digital-
... leistung. Mehr als 1500 Aussteller zeigen
... Siehe auch den Bericht auf Seite 22

otokina als Blickfang

Zwei - Hits von Kodak: Links für
Amateure die kleine Easy Share
LS 444 (4 Megapixel) für rund 650
Euro. Rechts für Profis die Professional DCS Pro 14n, die erste Spie-
gelreflex mit 13,89 Megapixel für
knapp 6000 Euro

PRESS AND EVALUATION

Photokina-Aussteller ziehen gute Bilanz

Die Aussteller auf der photokina in Köln haben am letzten Messe-tag eine positive Bilanz gezogen. Bei der sechstägigen Leitmesse für die Fotoindustrie hätten sich mehr als 160000 Besucher über die Neuheiten der Branche infor-miert. Insgesamt seien mehr als

1540 Aussteller aus fast 140 Län-dern in die Messehallen gekom-men. Wichtige Themen waren die neuesten Trends bei Foto-Kame-ras, Camcordern und Druckern so-wie die Weiterentwicklungen bei der analogen und digitalen Foto-grafie. Foto: dpa

großem Besucherandrang hat gestern in Köln die Leitmesse
Fototechnik photokina begonnen. Mehr als 1500 Unterneh-
... aus 46 Ländern zeigen bis zum 30. September Innovationen
... den Bereichen Bildtechnik und Bildanwendung. Bild: dpa

TIME OUT – WITHOUT KODAK
DIE ZEIT OHNE KODAK

AUF DEN BILDERN IN MEINEM KOPF STEHT HINTEN KODAK
THE PICTURES IN MY MIND SAY KODAK ON THE BACK.

CLICK, CLICK, AND KODAK IS HERE AGAIN
KLICK, KLACK UND KODAK IST SCHON WIEDER DA

CHAPTER OVERVIEW KAPITELÜBERSICHT

KODAK. Anytime. Anywhere. >

»Welcome to the digital world of KODAK. Willkommen in der digitalen Welt von KODAK.«

[FOM]

KODAK GOES DIGITAL

pages and links Verweise
I. 22 – 25
II. 94 – 99

(N)EVER CHANGE A WINNING TEAM

Times are changing ... the world of pictures has gone digital. A new KODAK must reinvent itself. This demands new thinking and a new way of seeing. We are faced with the choice of continuing with the same team, with which we were very satisfied, or with raising a new team to face the new tasks with an open mind. Old knowledge and experience should not be allowed to influence the new tasks. But this means much more work for the client. The challenge of risking a change is accepted with the motto »ever change a winning team«. KODAK is happy with the decision.

Die Zeiten ändern sich … Die Bilderwelt ist digital geworden. Eine neue KODAK muss neu erfunden werden. Dies erfordert neues Denken und neue Sehweisen. Die Entscheidung steht im Raum, mit demselben Team weiterzumachen. Es hat stets einen sehr guten Job gemacht. Oder, das ist die Frage: mit einem neuen Team, das völlig unbelastet an die neue Aufgabe herangeht, antreten? Das Gelernte und die Erfahrung sollen nicht die neue Aufgabe belasten. Das aber bedeutet für den Auftraggeber erheblich mehr Arbeit. Die Herausforderung, einen Wechsel zu riskieren, wird angenommen unter dem Motto: »Ever change a winning team«. KODAK ist damit gut gefahren.

KODAK GOES DIGITAL – WHAT STAYS, WHAT CHANGES?

The successful products, like film, paper, and chemicals have lost their significance much faster than many expected. The world of analog photography must rethink its values. Where in the past qualities like color, sharpness, contrast, brilliance, and film sensitivity were at the focus of all communications and values like safety, trust, tradition, and warmth were emphasized, in the new digital world they have been replaced by technology, pixels, lifestyle, and coolness.

The fascination of digital photography lies in the ability to see the picture immediately and to delete it if desired. Design and technology, together with the demand for more and more pixels drive buying habits. The resulting picture is no longer the primary interest, but the process of photographing itself. Pictures have lost their value. Pictures are stored on CDs and hard discs. Classical albums are out.

What happens to all the recorded moments and the wonderful memories?

Digital photography – the new world of KODAK – consists of cameras, image processing systems, printers, and storage media. The printed picture remains KODAK's core competence, and will be promoted in the future.

THE BRIEF

KODAK GOES DIGITAL – WAS BLEIBT, WAS ÄNDERT SICH?

Die großen Renditebringer wie Film, Papier, Chemie sind schneller als von vielen erwartet nicht mehr das beherrschende Thema. Die heile Welt der Analogfotografie muss umdenken. Wo in der Vergangenheit Qualitätsmerkmale wie Farbe, Schärfe, Kontrast, Brillanz und Filmempfindlichkeit im Fokus der Kommunikation stehen und Werte, die Sicherheit, Vertrauen, Tradition und Wärme vermitteln, treten an ihre Stelle in der Kommunikation in der neuen digitalen Welt: Technologie, Pixel, Lifestyle und Coolness. Die Faszination der Digitalfotografie liegt in der Möglichkeit, sofort das gemachte Bild betrachten zu können und gegebenenfalls gleich wieder zu löschen. Design und Technik, verbunden mit dem Wunsch nach immer mehr Pixeln prägen das Kaufverhalten. Nicht das Bildergebnis steht im Vordergrund, sondern der Vorgang des Fotografierens an sich. Bilder werden gelöscht, Bilder haben an Wert verloren, Bilder bewahrt man auf CDs und Festplatten. Das klassische Album ist out.

Wo bleiben alle die festgehaltenen Momente und schönen Erinnerungen?

Digitalfotografie – die neue Welt von KODAK – sind Kameras, Bildbearbeitungssysteme, Drucker und Speichermedien. Das gedruckte Bild ist die Kernkompetenz von KODAK, und die gilt es in Zukunft zu fördern.

»The new KODAK must be different ...
Die neue KODAK muss anders aussehen.«
[FOM]

MOOD BOARDS FOR BETTER UNDERSTANDING
MOOD BOARDS, ZUM BESSEREN VERSTÄNDNIS

*»The house colors of yellow and red should
not dominate. The stand should be cooler and
more authentic. Die Hausfarben Gelb und Rot
sollen nicht dominieren. Der Stand sollte cooler,
authentischer werden.«*
[FOM]

*»What is the new KODAK, and what does it want
to be? Was ist die neue KODAK, und was will die
neue KODAK sein?«*
[URB]

*»We must change people's perception of us,
modern, younger, more technical, and cooler.
Wir müssen anders wahrgenommen werden,
moderner, jünger, technischer und cooler …«*
[FOM]

*»… exactly like our mood boards.
… genauso, wie unsere Mood boards.«*
[SJ]

*»Mood boards get on my nerves. I prefer a text by
Shakespeare. Mood boards sind nervig, mir ist
ein Text von Shakespeare lieber.«*
[URB]

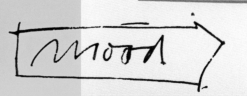

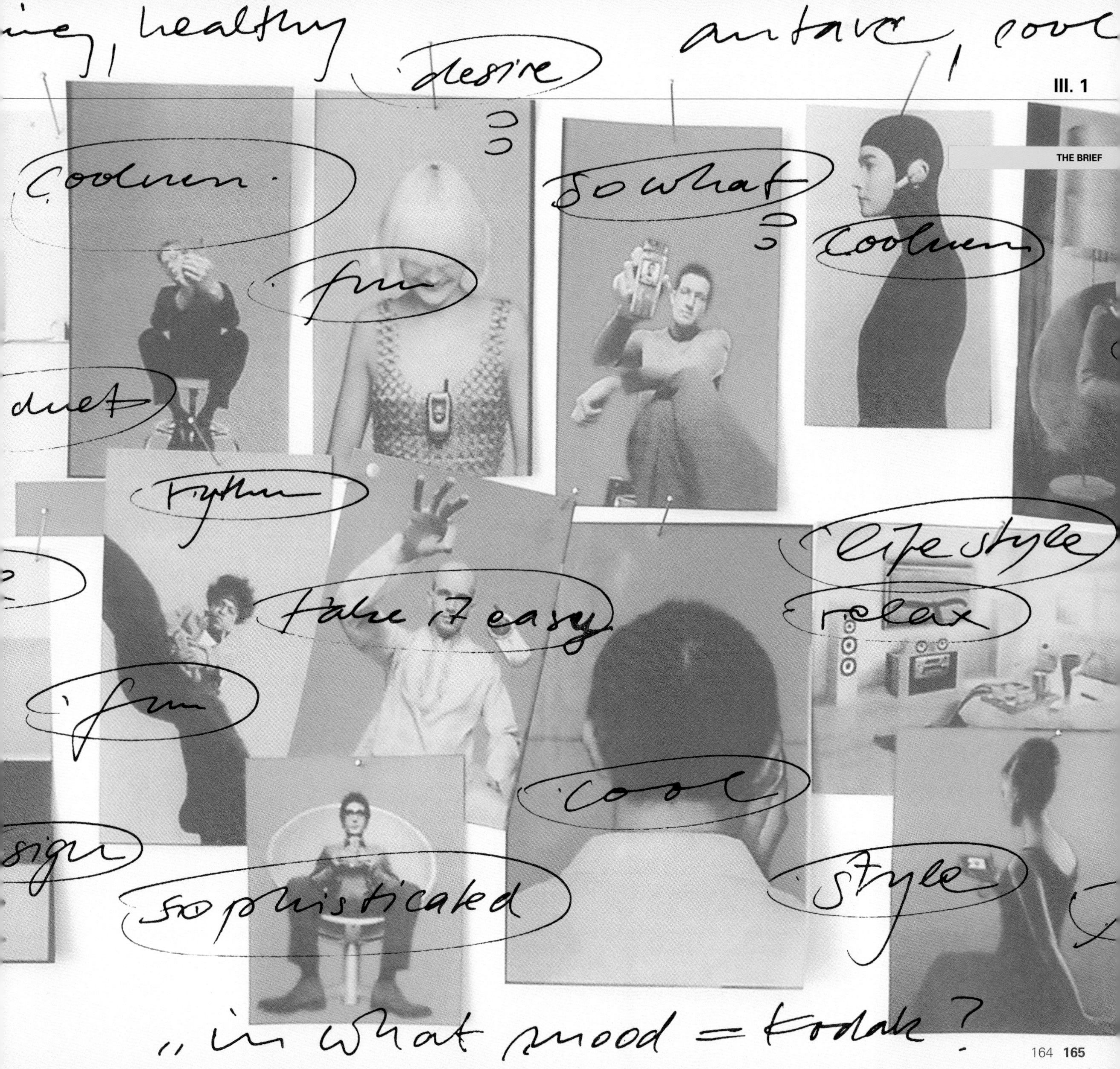
healthy
desire
coolness
so what
coolness
fun
duet
rythm
lifestyle
take it easy
relax
fun
cool
sophisticated
style
„in what mood = kodak?

OBJECTIVES, STRATEGY, MESSAGES
ZIELE, INHALTE, BOTSCHAFTEN

BACKGROUND

KODAK is a brand that is evolving from a traditional film and output business to a digital products and services-focused business by offering the best choices of both worlds.

photokina 2004 will be the first photokina where KODAK can clearly demonstrate the new digital world to consumers, professionals, and retailers and also to the press and strategic and cooperative partners. The new digital world is connected.

The customer in the new digital world demands choice and today he has a wide array of products and services both from KODAK as well as from its competitors.
Customers want to work with a company that has the brand and the power to deliver the best connected systems that provide them with choices

KEY MESSAGE

KODAK is the only company that can deliver a complete, connected range of products and services to its customers around the globe, helping consumers to capture, organize and manage, preserve and share their images anywhere, as they wish.

VISION:

KODAK understands and believes in the value of pictures.
KODAK enthusiastically leads and participates in the shaping of the industry.
In the pursuit of the best choices for capturing, organizing, sharing, printing and preserving memories, KODAK is:

- Relentless
- Passionate
- Innovative
- Contemporary
- Trusted

»Your challenge is to improve on the successful exhibition stands of 2000 and 2002. One advantage is the rich documentation. Take an x-ray view, get inside the client. The danger is in believing that all good things come in threes. My advice to you is to take the client seriously and be confident. Success makes us confident. And one clear and simple rule: three alternatives at the most!
Die Herausforderung an euch ist, dass ihr die überaus erfolgreichen Auftritte von 2000 und 2002 noch übertreffen sollt. Der Vorteil ist die üppige Dokumentation. Verschafft euch ein Röntgenbild, eine Innenansicht des Klienten. Die Gefahr ist, zu glauben, aller guten Dinge sind drei. Nehmt den Kunden ernst, aber seid selbstbewusst. Der Erfolg macht uns sicher. Und die klare und deutliche Ansage: maximal drei Alternativen!«

[URB TO THE NEW TEAM]

COMMUNICATIONS OBJECTIVES

What do we want consumers and customers to think when they leave the KODAK stand?

KODAK offers the best imaging choices for both worlds – digital and analog.

KODAK is a leader and is already delivering on the promise of connected services.

KODAK innovations are world-class (cite awards and/or leadership in DSC, image sensors, printer docks, thermal media, inkjet papers, kiosks, DLS systems, online photo services, image science, color management).

KODAK is relentless in developing the best, easiest-to-understand-and-use products and services to meet the demanding needs of its consumers and customers. Demonstrate this by means of user interface, plug-and-play systems.

KODAK is committed to participate in the long haul and is driving the industry forward by means of a variety of new products and services with continued investment, support and innovation in both film and digital products and services.

OBJECTIVES, STRATEGY, MESSAGES
ZIELE, INHALTE, BOTSCHAFTEN

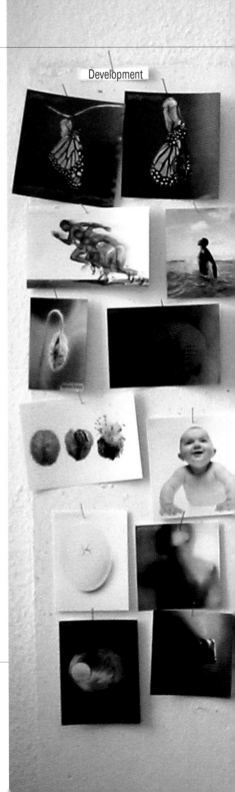

Development

COMMUNICATIONS STRATEGIES:

(How will we communicate and deliver against the objectives?)

– KODAK must demonstrate the choices in the connected digital world through all product areas (i.e. we are One KODAK); including products/services offered by KODAK affiliated companies (i.e.Nexpress, Encad, Pakon, Ofoto).

– Messaging needs to be application/consumer solution focused (i.e. @retail, online, @home, @lab, @ studio).

– KODAK should demonstrate its leadership by reinforcing its relationships with partners (i.e. mobile imaging, retail partners).

– KODAK will demonstrate its innovation through new value propositions supported by product introductions/product enhancements at the show and through proud display of award winning products and services.

– KODAK will not lose site of existing products and services in the market and will display appropriately at the show.

MANDATORIES:

– KODAK must be presented as one company with an integrated vision.

– KODAK presents the best choices for its customers/partners.

– If a connection is possible, it will be connected.

OTHER CONSIDERATIONS:

– Project will come in on budget – overruns not acceptable.

DESIGN MANDATORIES

– Clear, transparent and simple orientation for the visitor/customer within the KODAK booth.

– Logical, understandable and easy structure of the different areas to find products/applications/services.

– Project a strong brand and corporate colors presence.

– Clear focus on (new) highlights, following the company's strategic concept.

– Stand design represents life style, cutting edge design, fancy compelling excitement in the new KODAK Digital World.

– Demonstrate the global connectivity of all KODAK products/services. KODAK Anytime. Anywhere.

– Even for non-experts understandable messages and short copies: Clear take-away for the visitor.

– Integrate the different divisions C&PI, D&AI, ENCAD, NexPress etc. in one corporate appearance (no companies within the company …).

»… I really wonder what KODAK thinks about going digital. … auf das digitale Verständnis von KODAK bin ich wirklich gespannt.«

[URB]

Company Objektives

Kodak Produkte

III. 1

THE BRIEF

Identity

Personality

Moments

Photography

CAPTURE OUTPUT

EIN MOMENT

„sich vor dem Bild verstecken"

EIN

19

chapter **III. 3 THE PROPOSAL** DER VORSCHLAG

THE EXAMPLE OF EXPO 2003
DIE EXPO 2003 ALS VORBILD

pages and links Verweise
I. 32 – 33
II. 100 – 107

Of course the KODAK team visits other exhibitions to get ideas and inspiration. The Expo around Lake Neuchâtel represents the best current exhibition architecture that can be found. The Wedding Pavilion at the Expo in Yverdon was immediately inspiring. The designers have built a massive pier out into the lake and placed on it cubic spaces which can be viewed and entered. Everything is white, giving a strong contrast to the blue sky and the turquoise water.

However, the most impressive element consists of the colored columns lining the walkway. This is not an obstacle course but is a journey of visual discovery studded with new viewpoints and color experiences.

The impression is lasting. The idea is formed of using a similar concept as the basis of the next photokina stand. The columns could be used to carry informa-tion or products. In the cubic spaces along the way we imagine the product demonstrations. In the center of the stand the columns should give way and lead to a projection space in which a highly emotional multimedia show communicates the significance of pictures in the digital world. In our mind the photokina exhibit is already complete.

[FOM] »… But how do I tell that to my architects …«

Natürlich besuchen die KODAK Messemacher auch andere Ausstellungen, um Ideen und Anregungen zu bekommen. Die Expo rund um den See von Neuchâtel ist im Vergleich das Beste, was es an aktueller Aus-stellungsarchitektur zu entdecken gibt.

Der Hochzeitspavillon im Expogelände in Yverdon hat sofort begeistert. Die Gestalter haben einen massiven Steg in den See gebaut, und darauf sind kubische Räume angeordnet – einsehbar und begehbar. Alles ist in Weiß gehalten, was einen hervorragenden Kon-

»*Wow, this time it's going to be a cool project. Wow, diesmal wird das wohl ein lässiges Projekt.*«
[URB]

»*Super, at this rate we'll earn a packet. Super, bei diesem Fortschritt verdienen wir mal ordentlich.*«
[SFB]

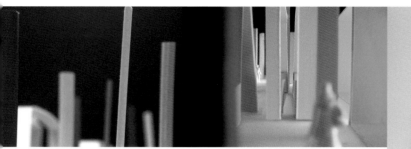

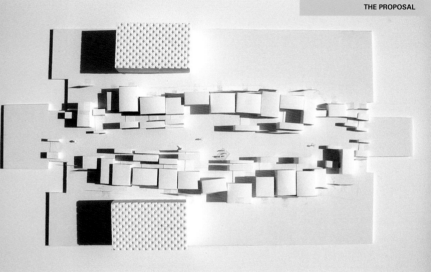

THE PROPOSAL

trast zum blauen Himmel und dem türkisen Wasser darstellt. Das imponierende Element aber sind die farbigen Säulen im Laufbereich, die es zu durchwandern gilt. Dies ist kein Hindernislauf, sondern eine visuelle Entdeckungsreise mit ständig neuen Durchblicken und Farberlebnissen.

Der Eindruck ist nachhaltig. Die Idee entsteht, dieses Konzept als Basis für den nächsten photokina-Stand zu nutzen. Die Säulen sollten als Information- oder Produktträger dienen. In den kubischen Räumen entlang des Gangbereiches werden in Gedanken die Produktdemonstrationen platziert. Im Zentrum des Standes sollen sich die Säulen auflösen und in einen Projektionsraum führen, in dem eine hoch emotionale Multimediashow die Bedeutung des Bildes in der digitalen Welt kommuniziert. In Gedanken ist der photokina-Auftritt bereits fertig.

[FOM] »... Aber wie sage ich das meinem Architekten ...«

Joint excursions for the client and designers are extremely useful. Experiences together make the development of the necessary common language, the description of intentions so much more effective. Gemeinsame Exkursionen von Auftraggebern und Gestaltern sind extrem vorteilhaft. Die notwendige gemeinsame Sprache, Intentionen zu beschreiben, funktioniert anhand gemeinsam erlebbarer Beispiele wesentlich effektiver.

PROPOSAL 1: PIXEL
DER VORSCHLAG 1: PIXEL

The concept must fit in the new world of digital images. The basic idea: a sequence of »pixelated« sectioned spaces, pulled back in the center to leave a free path. On their way through visitors can look at all product areas. The concept envisages the individual spaces for product displays, for meetings, or even as points of access. The protruding single frames contain »capturing« products for recording images. They are directly related to theme frames, which are thus emphasized and constitute individual units. Individual units are configured as back-projection spaces, and fitted out with sufficient space for the necessary technology.

Das Konzept muss in die neue digitale Bilderwelt passen. Die Grundidee: eine Abfolge »gepixelter«, angeschnittener Einzelräume, die in der Mitte auseinandergezogen sind und dadurch einen Durchgangsweg freigeben. Der Besucher hat auf seinem Weg die Möglichkeit, alle Produktbereiche zu erfassen. Die Einzelräume dienen sowohl der Produktpräsentation, sind aber auch als Besprechungsraum und Durchgangsfläche konzipiert. Die vorgesetzten Einzelrahmen beinhalten Produkte der Aufnahmetechnik, des sogenannten »Capturing«. Sie haben direkten Bezug zu Themenräumen, die daraus hervorgehen und sich scheinbar wieder zu Einzelräumen zusammensetzen. Einzelne Räume sind als Rückprojektionsflächen ausgebildet und so angeordnet, dass sie Platz für die dazu erforderliche Technik ergeben.

»I like it a lot, it's a good development of KODAK I and KODAK II. Gefällt mir sehr gut, eine echte Weiterentwicklung von KODAK I und KODAK II.«
[URB]

»The idea's good, but where's the clear view? You must be able to feel a sense of the open hall. Idee gut, aber wo bleibt der Durchblick? Die Halle muss offen und anders wahrgenommen werden.«
[FOM]

»How do you mean different? Wie anders?«
[JH *hesitantly*]

THE PROPOSAL

PROPOSAL 2: FLOW
DER VORSCHLAG 2: FLOW

An alternative concept: flowing meanders display products in the convex parts and form meeting rooms in the concave sections opposite. They form a continuum on both sides of the transit space. The flowing walls are made of individual layers in a changing sequence of different transparent materials. The walls not only define the space but also form a storytelling element. The spatial design is the wall, image, and projection surface at the same time. Here too visitors can perceive the whole space from the main pathway. The wall transitions between path and space contain the capture products. Individual spaces can be used as »product cinemas«. The surfaces facing the path can be used for »all-round projections«.

Ein alternativer konzeptioneller Ansatz: Fließende Mäander, die in ihrer Positivform jeweils Produkte beinhalten, und auf der Gegenseite – in ihrer Negativform – als Besprechungsbereich dienen. Sie bilden einen Gesamtablauf an beiden Seiten der Durchgangszone. Die fließenden Wände bestehen aus einzelnen Schichten in einer Wechselabfolge unterschiedlicher transparenter Materialien. Die Wand beschreibt nicht nur den Raum und führt den Besucher, sondern wird zum erzählerischen Element. Die Raumgestaltung ist gleichzeitig Wand, Bild- und Projektionsträger. Auch hier erfasst der Besucher vom Hauptweg aus alle Bereiche. Die Wandübergänge zwischen Weg und Raum beinhalten die jeweiligen Capture-Produkte. Einzelne Räume können als »Produktkino« bespielt werden. Die Außenflächen zum Gang bieten die Möglichkeit einer »Rundumprojektion«.

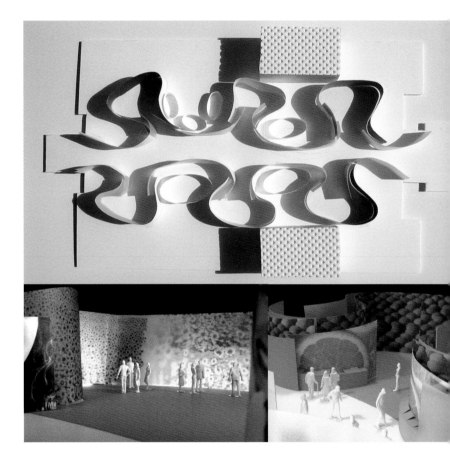

»I'm afraid Müller won't be able to sell the Americans amorphous forms. *Ich fürchte, amorphe Figuren kann Müller den Amerikanern nicht verkaufen.«*

[URB]

»*That was the second alternative. Das war jetzt schon die Alternative zwei!«*

[HV]

»*All dead ends. We need more orientation and an overview. Lauter Sackgassen. Wir brauchen mehr Orientierung und Übersicht.«*

[FOM]

LET'S TALK ABOUT NEW CONTENT
AUF DER SUCHE NACH NEUEN INHALTEN

Formale Idee

pages and links/Verweise
I. 34 – 37
II. 108 – 109

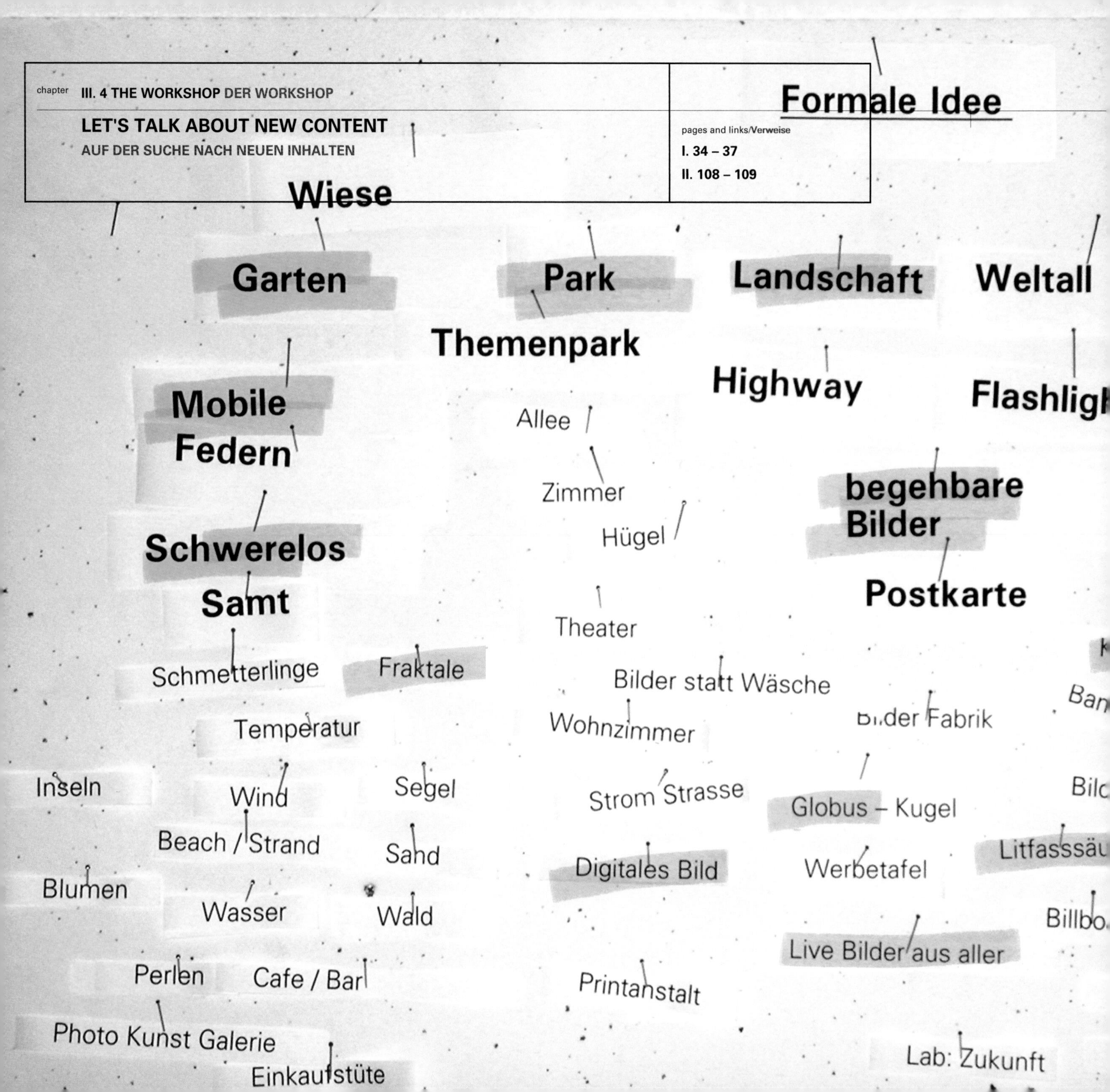

Wiese

Garten   **Park**   **Landschaft**   **Weltall**

Themenpark

Highway   **Flashligh**

Mobile
Federn

Allee

Zimmer   **begehbare**
Bilder

Hügel

Schwerelos

Samt   **Postkarte**

Theater

Schmetterlinge   Fraktale   Bilder statt Wäsche

Temperatur   Wohnzimmer   bii der Fabrik   Ban

Inseln   Segel   Strom Strasse   Bild

Wind   Globus – Kugel

Beach / Strand   Sand   Litfasssäu

Blumen   Digitales Bild   Werbetafel

Wasser   Wald   Billbo

Perlen   Cafe / Bar   Live Bilder aus aller

Printanstalt

Photo Kunst Galerie

Einkaufstüte   Lab: Zukunft

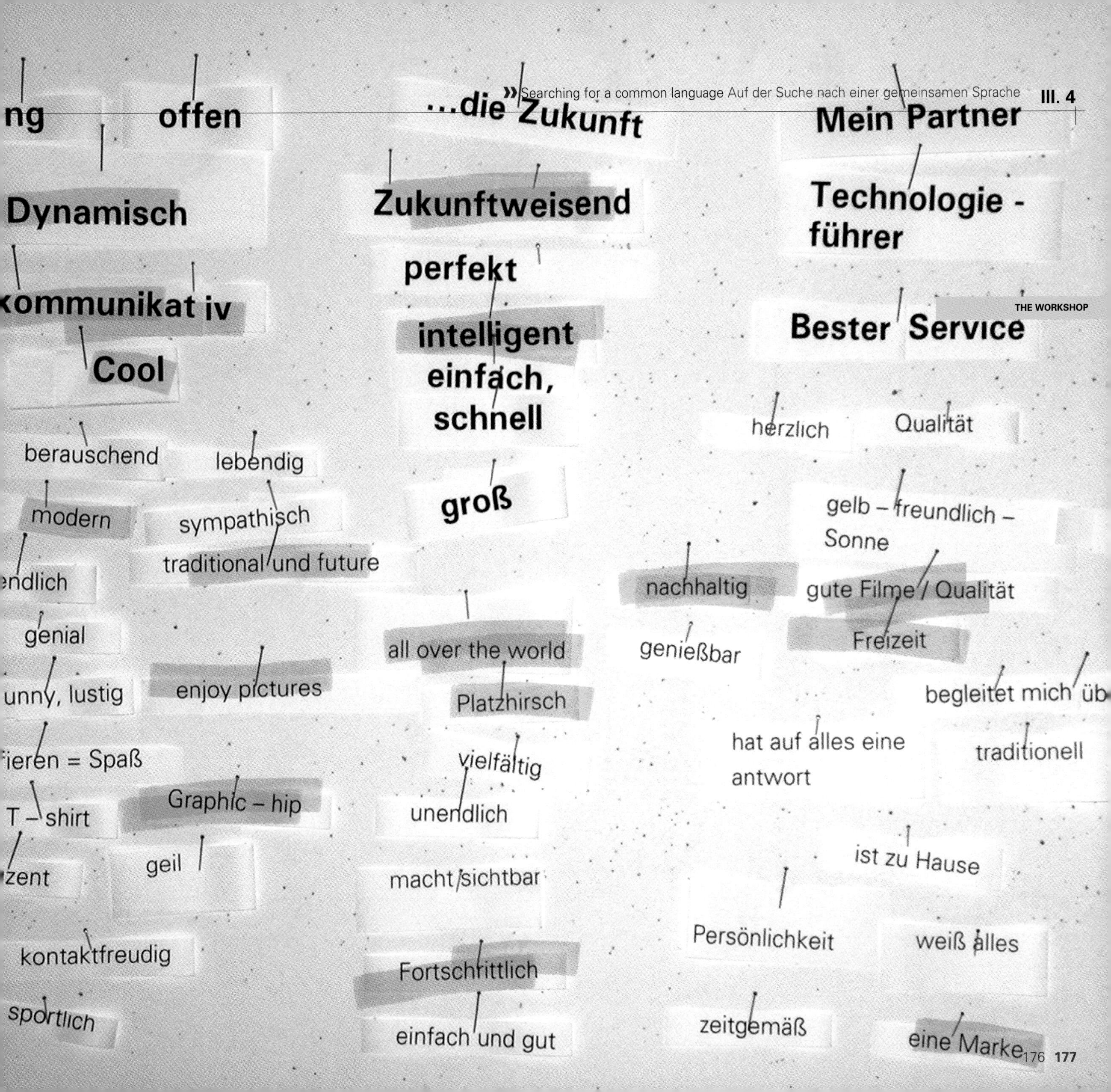

ng   offen   ...die Zukunft   Mein Partner

Dynamisch   **Zukunftweisend**   **Technologie - führer**

kommunikativ   **perfekt**

Cool   **intelligent einfach, schnell**   **Bester Service**

berauschend   lebendig   herzlich   Qualität

modern   sympathisch   **groß**   gelb – freundlich – Sonne

traditional und future   nachhaltig   gute Filme / Qualität

ndlich   genießbar   Freizeit

genial   all over the world

unny, lustig   enjoy pictures   begleitet mich üb

fieren = Spaß   Platzhirsch   hat auf alles eine antwort   traditionell

T – shirt   Graphic – hip   vielfältig

geil   unendlich   ist zu Hause

zent   macht sichtbar

kontaktfreudig   Persönlichkeit   weiß alles

sportlich   Fortschrittlich   zeitgemäß   eine Marke

einfach und gut

chapter **III. 5 RESET** NEUSTART

LEARNING FROM THE PAST
AUS ERFAHRUNG LERNEN

pages and links/Verweise
I. 38 – 39
II. 110 – 111

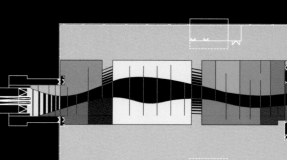

KODAK I

A well-functioning information system using color coding and corresponding product areas, images, and graphics. The paths and avenues between the buildings give visitors the chance to study the products undisturbed and away from the main traffic.

KODAK I

Gut funktionierendes Informationssystem durch Farbcodes und dazugehörige Produktareas, Bilder und Grafik. Die Wege und Straßen zwischen den Gebäuden geben den Besuchern die Möglichkeit, abseits des Hauptganges sich ungestört mit den Produkten zu beschäftigen.

KODAK II

Color coding gives a good orientation; zones are defined by portals and well-coordinated graphics and images. All products are present at the entrance and are thus easily accessible for all visitors. Sustained effect of the key take-away on the visitor and the press. Strong branding through use of yellow and red.

KODAK II

Gute Orientierung durch Farbcodes, das Bilden von Zonen durch Tore und einer gut abgestimmten Grafik- und Bildgestaltung. Alle Produkte sind am Hauptgang präsent und deshalb für jeden Besucher leicht zugänglich. Nachhaltige Wirkung des Key Take-Aways bei Besuchern und in der Presse. Starkes Branding durch Gelb und Rot.

»When you enter the hall you should see the whole stand and be overwhelmed by its size. *Wenn man in die Halle kommt, muss man den ganzen Stand im Blick haben und überwältigt von der Größe sein.«*

[FOM]

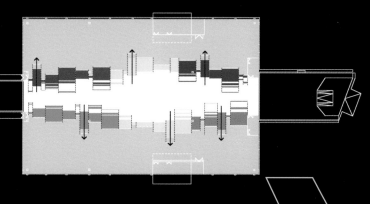

RESET

KODAK III

The positive elements of KODAK I and II should be carried over into the new world of KODAK. An extremely wide palette of products and services is offered – from image recording to finished picture. The fascination of printed pictures should be illustrated convincingly.

KODAK III

Die positiven Elemente von KODAK I und II übertragen in die neue Welt von KODAK. Geboten wird eine extrem breite Palette von Produkten und Dienstleistungen – von der Aufnahme bis zum fertigen Bild. Die Faszination von gedruckten Bildern soll überzeugend dargestellt werden.

»Where's the digital world got to?
Wo ist eigentlich die digitale Welt geblieben?«
[URB]

KODAK MUST BE PERCEIVED ANEW.

With KODAK II only the walkway (demonstration and display area) can be seen by visitors, and the size of the stand, over 8.500 m², cannot be appreciated. Many visitors confirmed this when questioned. When given a conducted tour of the complete stand they were surprised at the amount of space reserved for meeting rooms behind the high walls of the public area. To achieve a different impression we shall need to create transparency, and present an open overview of the whole hall. In summary: avoid high walls and use little material – fabrics, light, images.

KODAK MUSS NEU WAHRGENOMMEN WERDEN.

Bei KODAK II ist nur die Gangzone (Demo- und Displaybereich) vom Besucher einsehbar, dadurch kommt die wirkliche Größe des Standes mit über 8.500 m² gar nicht zur Wirkung. Diesen Eindurck bestätigten befragte Besucher. Sie waren bei Führungen über den Stand völlig überrascht, welche riesigen Flächen sich für Besprechungsbereiche hinter den hohen Wänden der Gangzone noch befinden. Eine andere Wahrnehmung zu erzeugen, heißt Transparenz schaffen. Offen, einsehbar, die ganze Halle auf einen Blick präsentieren. Fazit: keine hohen Wände und geringer Materialeinsatz – Stoff, Licht, Bilder.

THE NEW SCENOGRAPHIC CONCEPT: »OPEN AND TOUCHY«
DAS NEUE SZENOGRAPHIEKONZEPT: »OPEN AND TOUCHY«

pages and links/Verweise
I. 41 – 45
II. 118 – 121

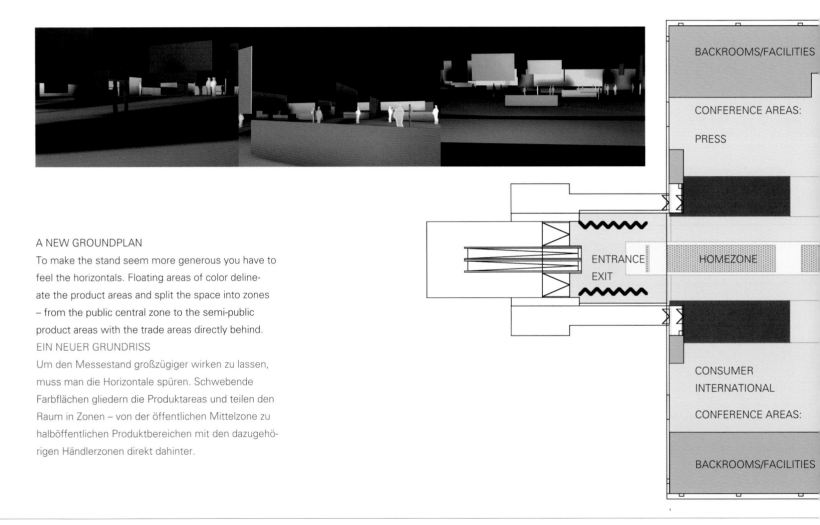

A NEW GROUNDPLAN
To make the stand seem more generous you have to feel the horizontals. Floating areas of color delineate the product areas and split the space into zones – from the public central zone to the semi-public product areas with the trade areas directly behind.
EIN NEUER GRUNDRISS
Um den Messestand großzügiger wirken zu lassen, muss man die Horizontale spüren. Schwebende Farbflächen gliedern die Produktareas und teilen den Raum in Zonen – von der öffentlichen Mittelzone zu halböffentlichen Produktbereichen mit den dazugehörigen Händlerzonen direkt dahinter.

»When you're building a private house, comply with the client's wishes, but so that you you'd like to live there yourself. Wenn du ein Einfamilienhaus planen sollst, dann mach das nach den Wünschen des Bauherren, und zwar so, dass du selbst gerne drin wohnen würdest.«
[**SAMPO WIEDMANN**, architect, to **URB**]

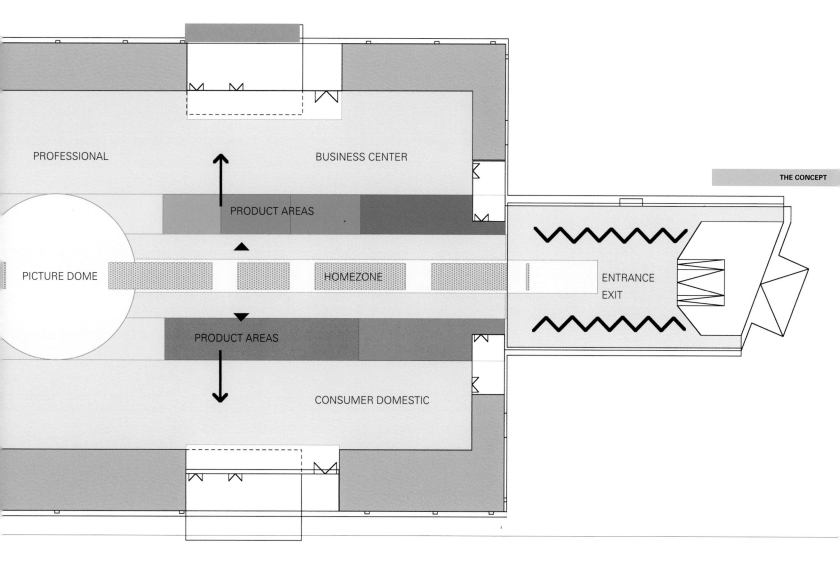

THE CONCEPT

PROFESSIONAL

BUSINESS CENTER

PRODUCT AREAS

PICTURE DOME

HOMEZONE

ENTRANCE

EXIT

PRODUCT AREAS

CONSUMER DOMESTIC

GUIDANCE WITH A PERSPECTIVE
WEGFÜHRUNG MIT DURCHBLICK

»The model looks good. I think it might work. Das
Modell sieht gut aus. Es könnte funktionieren.«
[FOM]

»When we get lighting in there it'll be even more impressive.
Wenn wir das dann noch zum Leuchten bringen, wird's noch
beeindruckender.«
[HV]

The established color coding defines product areas. Highly visible arrows give simple and precise guidance.
Der etablierte Farbcode definiert Produkt-areas. Gut sichtbare Pfeile erlauben eine einfache und präzise Orientierung.

THE CONCEPT

PIXELS ORGANIZE THEMSELVES IN SPACE
PIXEL ORDNEN SICH IM RAUM

pages and links/Verweise
I. 46 – 47
II. 122 – 129

Each model contributes to the client's understanding and imagination. The computer animation goes one step further and allows a virtual »walk through«. This virtual tour gives the viewer a feeling of security. It gives the impression that the exhibition is already finished and the trade fair can begin. The effort put into the presentation is well worth it; management is excited and has approved the concept.

Jedes Modell leistet einen wichtigen Beitrag zum besseren Verständnis und Vorstellungsvermögen des Auftraggebers. Die Computeranimation geht aber noch einen Schritt weiter. Sie ermöglicht einen virtuellen »walk through«. Dieser virtuelle Rundgang vermittelt dem Betrachter ein Gefühl von Sicherheit. Sie macht den Eindruck, alles sei bereits fertig, und die Messe könne beginnen. Der Aufwand einer solchen filmischen Aufbereitung lohnt sich. Das Management ist begeistert und hat das Konzept genehmigt.

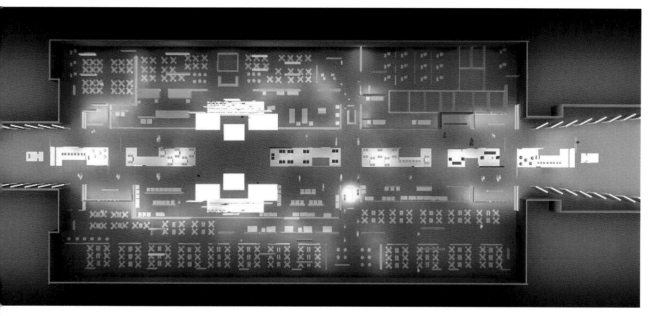

DESIGNERS DESIRE
GESTALTERS TRAUM

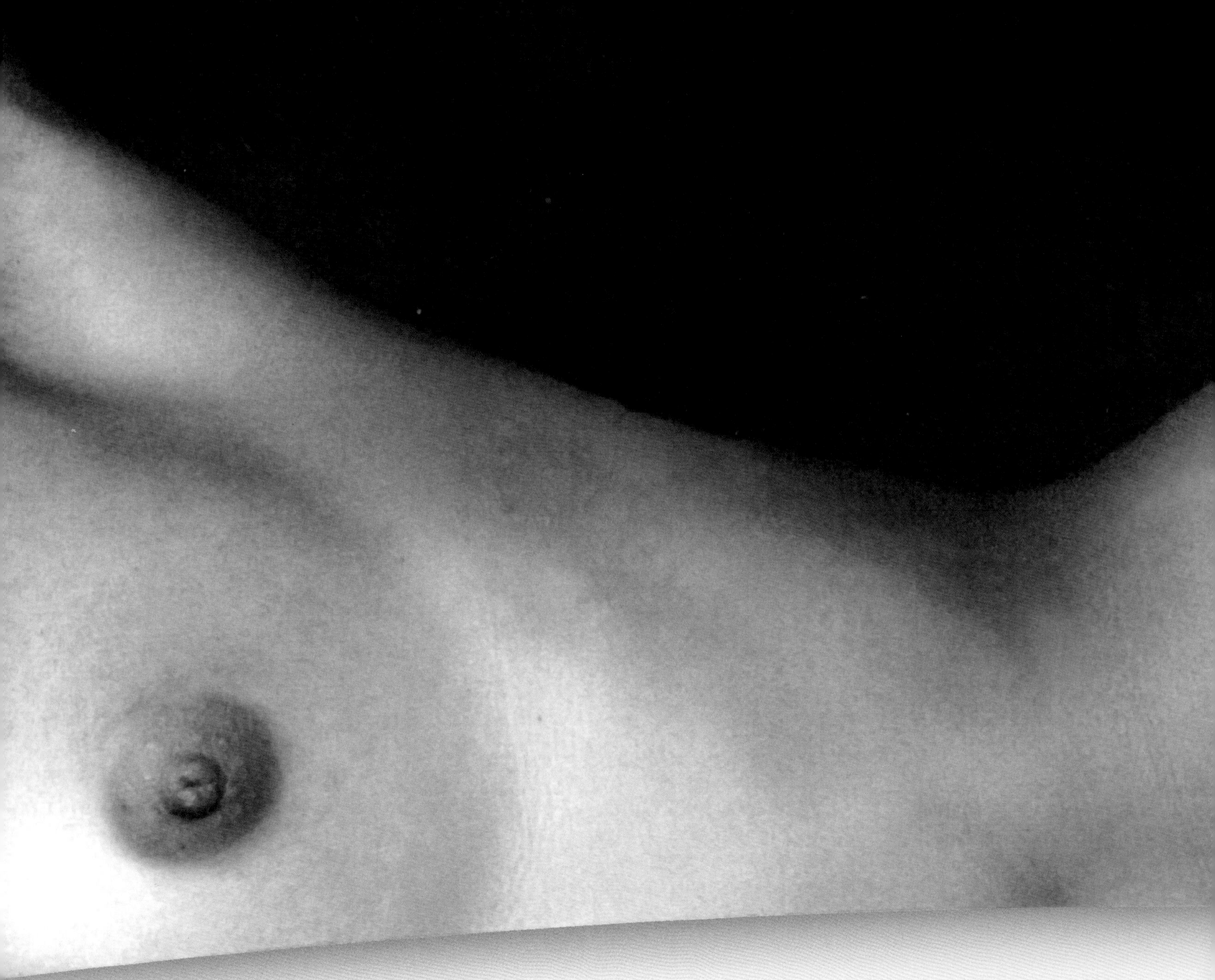

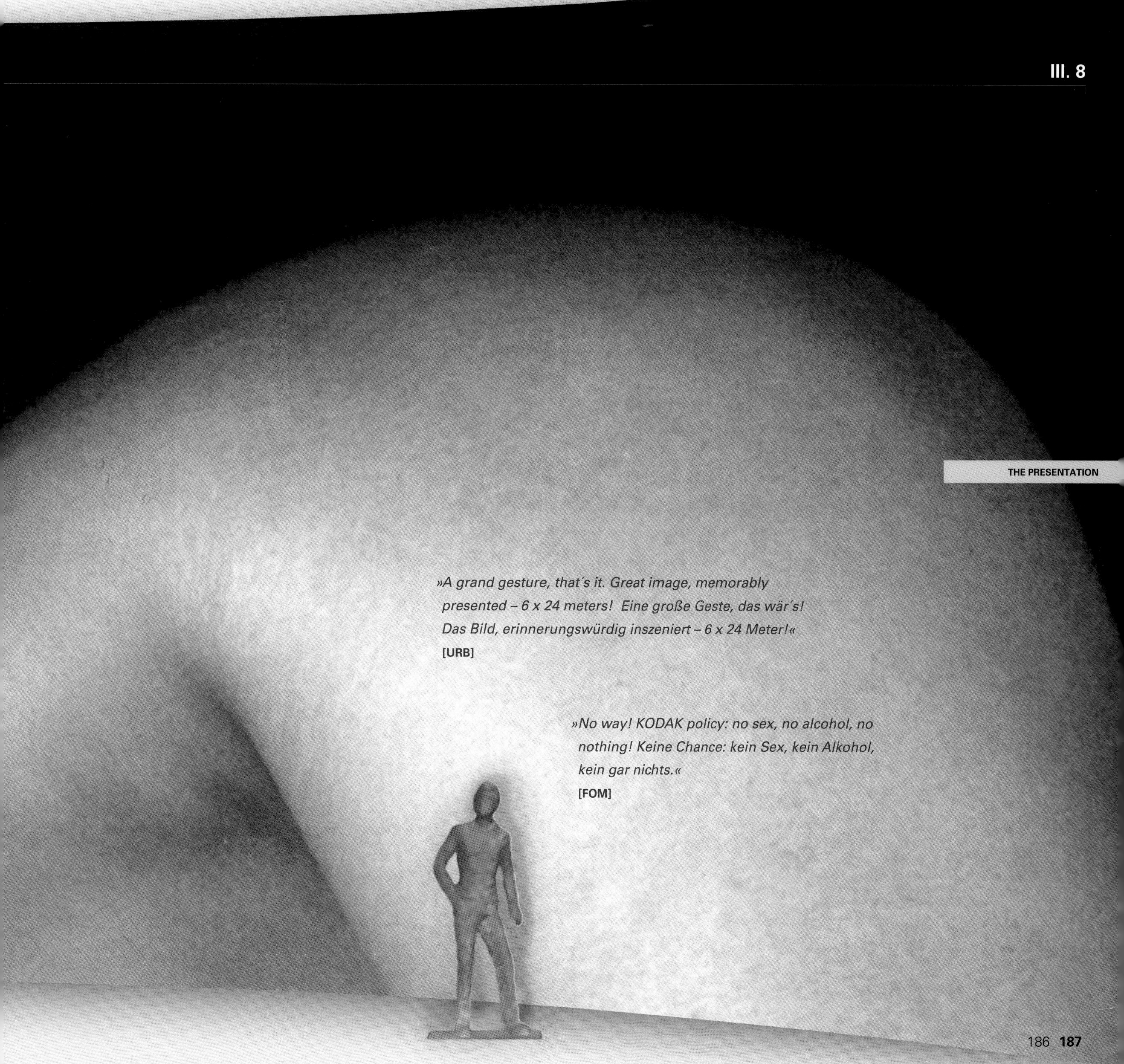

»A grand gesture, that´s it. Great image, memorably
presented – 6 x 24 meters! Eine große Geste, das wär´s!
Das Bild, erinnerungswürdig inszeniert – 6 x 24 Meter!«
[URB]

»No way! KODAK policy: no sex, no alcohol, no
nothing! Keine Chance: kein Sex, kein Alkohol,
kein gar nichts.«
[FOM]

THE FASCINATION OF THE PICTURE AS A GRAND GESTURE
DIE FASZINATION DES BILDES ALS GROSSE GESTE

pages and links/Verweise
I. 48 – 53
II. 130 –133

The grand gesture as an iconographic function, its iconographic potential, For the visitor trade fairs bring a visual over-stimulation through images, texts, media, and products. That makes is all the more important for the exhibitor to present himself uniquely and lastingly. It is like the flood of information and images that bombard us daily – we remember only those few of them that are extraordinary. The recipient must be able to understand the message clearly.

Often the visitor is confronted by too many messages; the one overwhelms the other and nothing is understood.

A sustainable design of a stand needs intensive, fast, directly effective gestures for communication and product placement. These must leave an explosive and unmistakable impression, and induce an associative and clear picture of the brand and products.

Die große Geste als ikonografische Funktion und ihr ikonografisches Potential. Messen sind für die Besucher eine visuelle Reizüberflutung von Bildern, Texten, Medien und Produkten. Umso wichtiger ist es für den Aussteller, sich eigenständig und nachhaltig darzustellen. Es ist wie mit den vielen Informationen und Bildern, die täglich auf uns einstürmen, nur wenige außergewöhnliche bleiben in unserem Kopf hängen. Der Empfänger muss die Botschaft eindeutig verstehen können. Häufig haben wir es mit zu vielen Botschaften zu tun, eine Message überlagert die andere, und nichts wird mehr vom Besucher verstanden. Eine nachhaltige Gestaltung von Messeauftritten braucht intensive, schnelle, direkte publikumswirksame und produktpositionierende Gesten. Diese müssen eine explosionsartige, unverwechselbare Wirkung auf den Kunden hinterlassen und ein assoziatives und schlüssiges Firmen-, Marken- und produktbezogenes Bild ergeben.

THE LETTERS

KODAK I

THE KISS

KODAK II

THE »WHAT«

KODAK III

We're looking for the unique and unmistakable »image space«. The so-called »key take-away«, which makes the impression and stays with you. The focus of communication is not on technology, pixels, and handling, but on a fascinating image as a lasting memory. The following pages show just a few of the ideas. Each example represents a design direction. Many were discussed and dismissed. Different designations like »center piece«, »shooting point«, or »picture dome« for the same thing make the rounds. The ideation phase becomes difficult for both parties and turns into a never ending story.

Der einzigartige und unverwechselbare »Bildraum« wird gesucht. Das so genannte Key Take-Away, das prägt und hängenbleibt. Nicht Technik, Pixel und das Handling stehen im Fokus der Kommunikation, sondern das faszinierende Bild als bleibende Erinnerung. Auf den folgenden Seiten ist nur ein kleiner Teil der vielen Ideen aufgeführt. Jedes Beispiel steht nur für eine Gestaltungsrichtung. Alle Ideen werden diskutiert und wieder verworfen. Unterschiedliche Bezeichnungen wie »Center Piece«, »Shooting Point«, »Picture Dome« für ein und die selbe Sache machen die Runde. Die Ideenfindungsphase gestaltet sich für beide Partner als schwierig und wird zur never ending story.

How can you leave visitors with a lasting impression and at the same time transmit messages? The concept should consider the following pairs of characteristics, and incorporate one, or better several, of these characteristics, because only in this way will the message be firmly planted in the target group's mind:
independent/adapted
new/familiar
unique/everyday
conforming with brand/brand challenging
unusual/normal
different from the others/mainstream
unexpected/predictable
larger than life/lost in detail
extravagant/plain
comfortable/offensive
This will make the exhibit individual, intelligible, and unforgettable.

THE KEY TAKE-AWAY

Wie kann man bei den Besuchern auf dem Messestand einen nachhaltigen Eindruck hinterlassen bei gleichzeitiger Vermittlung von Botschaften? Das Konzept sollte sich mit den nachfolgenden Eigenschaftspaaren auseinandersetzen und eine oder besser mehrere der Eigenschaften besitzen, denn nur so wird die Botschaft nachhaltig in den Köpfen der Zielgruppe verankert:
eigenständig/angepasst
neu/bekannt
unverwechselbar/irgendwie bekannt
markenkonform/extravagant
ungewöhnlich/normal
anders als die anderen/mainstream
überraschend/vorhersehbar
larger than life/detailverliebt
aufwändig/schlicht
angenehm/schrill
Ein Messeauftritt wird dadurch individuell, ei sam und unvergesslich.

THE GRAND GESTURE 1: THE PICTURE DOME
DIE GROSSE GESTE 1: DER PICTURE DOME

»What the hell is a Picture Dome? Was zum Teufel ist
ein Picture Dome?«
[MARIANNE SAMENKO, EKC]

»Fascinating portraits or skin-colored uniformity?
Faszination Portraits? Oder hautfarbener Einheitsbrei?«
[FOM]

THE KEY TAKE-AWAY

»If the image – whether analog as earlier or digital now – is to be at the center and at the same time it's the customer who plays the most important role for the company, then we need a center point of the center point. A picture dome of a thousand images arranged in a single scene where the whole functions as a background photographic image for the fascinated visitor. That'll bring product and customer into the same context.«

»Wenn das Bild – ob früher analog oder heute digital produziert – im Mittelpunkt stehen soll und gleichzeitig der Kunde für die Company die wichtigste Rolle spielt, braucht es einen Mittelpunkt aus dem Mittelpunkt. Ein Picture Dome aus tausenden Bildern, arrangiert zu einer Inszenierung, die im Ganzen wiederum ein Bild ergibt als fotografischer Hintergrund für den faszinierten Besucher. Das bringt Produkt und Kunde in einen Kontext!«
[URB]

THE GRAND GESTURE 2: KODAK GOES DIGITAL

DIE GROSSE GESTE 2: KODAK GOES DIGITAL

The center piece: a major visual attraction.

THE KEY TAKE-AWAY

»... of course the center piece will influence the whole design. We need a relationship between message and the impressive installation. ... natürlich wird das Highlight unseres Standes Einfluss auf das komplette Design haben. Deshalb brauchen wir eine Verbindung der Botschaft zu einer überzeugenden Bildinstallation.«

[URB]

THE GRAND GESTURE 3: THE BIG PICTURE

DIE GROSSE GESTE 3: DAS PANORAMABILD

> If the client needs illustrative storytelling motives with unavoidable productplacement we need a translation a sophiticated cypher in the installation beyond regular advertising banality. Wenn der Kunde illustrativ geschichtenerzählende Bilder wünscht mit einer unvermeidbaren Produktpräsenz, dann brauchen wir eine außergewöhnliche Umsetzung in die Realität, weit entfernt von herkömmlicher Werbung.

Working Model

THE KEY TAKE-AWAY

»This is KODAK. Any other questions?
Das ist KODAK. Noch Fragen?«
[URB]

»I think the photographic angle super, but how do we earn our money? With pictures of all sizes!
Die fotografische Auffassung finde ich super, aber womit verdienen wir unser Geld? Mit Bildern aller Formate!«
[FOM]

THE GRAND GESTURE 4: TULIPS LARGER THAN LIFE
DIE GROSSE GESTE 4: TULPEN GRÖSSER ALS DIE WIRKLICHKEIT

Associative motifs dissociated from the product work like codes;
their deciphering provokes a memorable experience of the brand.
Produktfremde, assoziative Motive wirken immer wie Codes, ihre
Entschlüsselung provoziert erinnerungswürdiges Erleben der Marke.

THE KEY TAKE-AWAY

»For this setting we need one of the world's best
photographers. That shouldn't be a problem for KODAK!
Für diese Inszenierung brauchen wir einen der weltbesten
Fotografen. Das dürfte doch bei KODAK kein Problem sein!«
[URB]

»Where's this leave our message? Where are our formats, fascinating pictures from
9 x 13 cm to large format? We not selling tulips!! Wo bleibt da die Botschaft, wo
bleiben unsere Formate, faszinierende Bilder vom 9 x 13 bis zum Großformat? Wir
verkaufen doch keine Tulpen.«
[FOM]

YET ANOTHER »YES, BUT...« MEETING
SCHON WIEDER EIN »JA, ABER ...«-MEETING

pages and links Verweise

I. 34 – 35

II. 130 – 131

The development and design of the ground plan are progressing well. The client accepts the layout of the different product areas, the paths of the visitors, the color concept, the orientation system and the placement of the supply spaces remarkably quickly.

But we're still searching for the actual highlight of the stand. Three different names for one and the same thing – the lasting impression, the real message, the individual and unmistakable, the grand gesture, as Uwe Brückner calls it – buzz around the atelier: Center Piece, Picture Dome, and the ever more popular Key-Takeaway. Perfect confusion. The creative crew must be restrained again. We put the famous question: what's the real message? The fascination of the printed picture, saving memories, that's the message. Pictures in your wallet and on the mantelpiece, pictures from 9 x 13 cm up to postcard size, that's the standard size, not mega-panoramas with clouds, forests, or body landscapes 6 x 25 meters long. But the big panorama picture helps us along. David Hockney's famous collages are an excellent example of how to arrange thousands of pictures in an arrangement that still forms a single image. The photographic background is fascinating and emotionalizes the message and the product in the mind of the visitor.

»This picture shows what we need, hundreds of pictures in album format. Dieses Bild zeigt, was wir brauchen. Viele Bilder im Albumformat.«

[URB]

»Again, where's our message, where are our formats, pictures from 9 x 13 to large format?
Wo bleibt da die Botschaft, wo bleiben unsere Formate, Bilder von 9 x 13 bis zum Großformat?«

[FOM]

What fulfills the desire for color, form, and esthetics best? Many ideas are discussed and dismissed. The tulip field, the designers' favorite, makes a comeback. The client concurs.

Die Entwicklung und Planung des Grundrisses kommt gut voran. Die Aufteilung der verschiedenen Produktbereiche, die Besucherführung, das Farbkonzept, das Orientierungssystem und die Anordnung der Versorgungsräume finden überraschend schnell die Zustimmung der Auftraggeber.

Nur das eigentliche Highlight des Messestandes wird immer noch gesucht. Drei verschiedene Namen, für ein und dieselbe Sache, schwirrten durch das Atelier – Center Piece, Picture Dome und das liebgewordene Key Take-Away. Die nachhaltige Botschaft, das was hängen bleibt. Das Eigenständige und Unverwechselbare, Die große Geste, wie Uwe Brückner das nennt. Die Verwirrung ist perfekt.

Die Kreativen müssen wieder einmal eingebremst werden. Die berühmte Frage wird gestellt: Um was geht es eigentlich? Die Faszination des gedruckten Bildes, Erinnerungen bewahren, das ist die Message, Bilder im Geldbeutel, im Album und auf dem Kaminsims, Bilder vom 9 x13 cm bis zur Postkarte, das sind gängige Formate und nicht Mega-Panoramas mit Wolken, Bäumen oder Körperlandschaften, 6 x 25 Meter lang. Das große Panoramabild hilft uns dennoch weiter. Die berühmten Bildcollagen von David Hockney zeigen hervoragend, wie man tausende von Bildern arrangiert zu einer Inszenierung, die im Ganzen wiederum ein Bild ergibt. Der fotografische Hintergrund fasziniert und emotionalisiert die Botschaft und das Produkt in der Besucherwahrnehmung.

Was erfüllt den Anspruch an Farbe, Form und Ästhetik am besten? Vieles wurde diskutiert, vieles verworfen. Das Tulpenfeld, die Lieblingsidee der Gestalter, kehrt zurück. Der Auftraggeber lenkt ein.

THE KEY TAKE-AWAY

BACK TO OUR FIRST LOVE, TULIPS
ZURÜCK ZUR ERSTEN LIEBE, TULPEN

pages and links Verweise

III. 196 – 197

In the design field increasingly comprehensive demands, symbolic to politically correct, are being placed on realistic motifs with representative functions. Discussions of this are always emotional, partial, and tiring.

An realistische Motive mit Stellvertreterfunktion werden in der Gestaltung immer umfangreiche Anforderungen gestellt, von symbolhaft über funktional bis hin zu politisch korrekt. Die Diskussionen darüber sind immer emotional, interessenorientiert und anstrengend.

The comeback of the tulip takes shape. Flowers are an option. Which flowers might we use? Roses are too laden with symbolism and are pompous. Gerbera are too simple and boring, sunflowers are too rustic and monotonous, carnations are too tired, callas have very little color. So it's tulips, but haven't we been there already? Tulips are value-free, and they come in all shapes and colors. They stand for spring and the fresh growth and fulfill the designers' esthetic demands. The fantastic pictures of flowers by Robert Mapplethorpe and Ernst Haas are both an example and an inspiration. The decision is made: we will use tulips as a leitmotif throughout our flow of communication.

Das Comeback der Tulpe nimmt Gestalt an. Blumen sind eine Option. Welche Blumen kommen in Frage? Rosen sind zu symbolträchtig und schwülstig, Gerbera sind zu bieder und langweilig, Sonnenblumen sind zu bäuerlich und eintönig, Nelken sind zu vorbelastet, Callas haben sehr wenig Farbe. Also Tulpen, das gab es doch schon einmal? Tulpen sind wertfrei, sie gibt es in allen Formen und Farben, sie stehen für Frühling und den Beginn von Wachstum und erfüllen am ehesten den Anspruch an Form und Design. Die fantastischen Bilder von Robert Mapplethorpe und Ernst Haas mit ihren Blumenbildern sind Vorbild und Ansporn zugleich. Die Entscheidung wird getroffen, Tulpen als durchgängiges Leitmotiv in unserem Kommunikationsflow zu verwenden.

THE KEY TAKE-AWAY

Commerci

»We had that already, but OK, tulips. I admit it. Their fascinating shapes and colors work best. Das hatten wir schon einmal: also doch Tulpen. Ich seh es ein. Die Faszination von Farbe und Motiv funktioniert am besten.«
[FOM]

FROM THE FIRST CONTACT TO LASTING MESSAGE
VOM ERSTEN KONTAKT ZUR NACHHALTIGEN BOTSCHAFT

	Level I	Level II	Level III	Level IV
	First contact	Develop contact Products	Business negotiations, business models	The lasting message
User/ dealer interests	Seeing, discovering, perceiving	Select, touch, activate… Cameras, films, printers, picture makers, Maker, mini-labs, large format printers, print systems, Photothandy service	Prices, conditions, delivery times, financing, contracts	Performance, results,
Architecture/ visitor guidance/ plan	Entrance and exit areas exit areas (open hall)	Home zone Central aisle	Controlled area, conference area, back rooms	The key-takeaway »The Grill Zone« The Center Piece
Communication	Stimulate interest	Inform, demonstrate, try out, options, possibilities, anytime, anywhere	Competence, security, trust	Visual fascination of hard copy

Integrative design systems create a credible perception of all effective parameters, from content through message, to design. With a central motif, a grand gesture, the ambitious brand appearance becomes a gesamtkunstwerk.

Integrative Gestaltungssysteme erzeugen eine glaubwürdige Wahrnehmung aller Wirkungsparameter ausgehend von Inhalt, Botschaft, bis hin zur Gestaltung. Mit einem zentralen Motiv, einer großen Geste, wird so der anspruchsvolle Markenauftritt zum Gesamtkunstwerk.

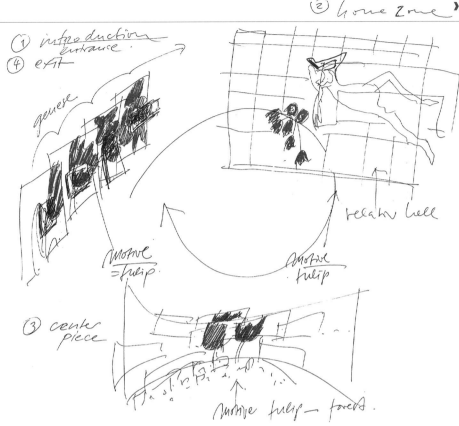

NEITHER MORE IS MORE,
NOR LESS IS MORE

Normally the transformation of such measures takes place with design elements created and used additively. This means that potential for technical product innovations, messages, customer service, and the standard architecture each use their own, often competing elements, and the result is a visual supermarket full of all known media. Total reduction, the so-called subtraction, also does not necessarily lead to better results, because beforehand, as afterwards, it is often necessary to indulge in costly and extensive explanations. Neither »more is more« nor »less is more« work in the long term; an integrative concept and design is needed.

Scenography offers an enormous potential for concepts developed from messages and using coding to reduce complex qualitative or voluminous contents to a reasonable volume. The self-explanatory deciphering of these codes using effectively remembered »icons« makes it easier to navigate and read the messages. The tulip motif has become an image and is effective not only in the central space but also functions as a recognition motif for the grand gesture to the detail. Even the large transparencies use the tulip motif as a symbol of the integrative ambitions of the KODAK company.

WEDER MEHR IST MEHR
NOCH WENIGER IST MEHR

Üblicherweise erfolgt die Umsetzung solcher Maßnahmen in Form von additiv erzeugten und benutzten Gestaltungselementen. Das heißt, produkttechnisches Innovationspotential, Botschaften, Kundenservice und die Standarchitektur bedienen sich eigener, oft konkurrierender Elemente mit dem Effekt eines visuellen Supermarktes aller bekannten Medien. Auch die totale Reduktion, die sogenannte Subtraktion, führt nicht zwangsweise zu besseren Ergebnissen, weil oft im Voraus – wie im Nachgang – erhöhter, kostspieliger Erklärungsaufwand notwendig wird. Weder »Mehr ist mehr« noch »Weniger ist mehr« funktionieren dauerhaft, sondern eher ein integratives Konzipieren und Gestalten.

THE COMMUNICATION CONCEPT

In der Szenographie liegt ein riesiges Potential für Konzepte, die aus Botschaften entwickelt werden, die mittels Codes komplexe qualitative oder üppige Inhalte auf ein justierbares Maß reduzieren. Die selbst erläuternde Dechiffrierung dieser Codes mittels erinnerungswirksamer »Icons« erleichtert die Orientierung und die Lesbarkeit der Botschaften. Das Tulpenmotiv als bildgewordener Code taucht nicht nur im Central Space als Hauptattraktion auf, sondern dient als Wiedererkennungsmotiv, von der großen Geste bis ins Detail. Selbst die Großdias übernehmen das Tulpenmotiv als Symbol für den integrativen Gesamtanspruch von KODAK.

FROM SINGLE PICTURE TO FASCINATING COLLAGE
VOM EINZELBILD ZUR FASZINIERENDEN BILDCOLLAGE

TULIPS FROM BARGFELD-STEGEN

It is April and the tulip season is ending. We have to act immediately. We have chosen
Christian von Alvensleben as the photographer. He is one of the few all-rounders who
is at home in all disciplines of photography. We need a large negative format for the
still life, beauty, and people pictures – at least 4 x 5 inches. That is a challenge for
shooting, because it's always a problem to make enlargements 2 x 3 meters in size
that are absolutely sharp. Experience shows that there is often a lack of data with large
format pictures, and this is the reason for the lack of image quality. More than 2.000
tulips are delivered to Barfeld-Stegen in Schleswig-Holstein, where Alvensleben's
studio is located. After three weeks the result is 150 extraordinary tulip pictures and 15
individual and unmistakable shots of tulips and people.

TULPEN AUS BARGFELD-STEGEN

Es ist April, und die Tulpenzeit geht zu Ende. Jetzt muss sofort gehandelt werden.
Die Wahl fällt auf den Fotografen Christian von Alvensleben. Er ist einer der wenigen
Allrounder, der alle Disziplinen der Fotografie beherrscht. Für die Still-Life-, Beauty- und
Peopleaufnahmen benötigten wir ein großes Aufnahmeformat – mindestens 4 x 5 inch.
Das ist eine Herausforderung für das Shooting, weil es immer Probleme bereitet,
Vergrößerungen von 2 x 3 Metern in absoluter Schärfe herzustellen. Die Erfahrung
zeigt, dass bei großformatigen Bildern immer wieder Schwierigkeiten mit zu geringen
Datenmengen auftreten und dies der Grund für eine schlechte Bildqualität ist. Über
2.000 Tulpen, in den unschiedlichsten Farben und Formen, werden im schleswig-hol-
steinischen Bargfeld-Stegen in Alvenslebens Studio angeliefert. Das Ergebnis nach drei
Wochen sind 150 außergewöhnliche Tulpenbilder und 15 eigenständige und unverwechselbare Tulpen-People-Shots.

»Unbelievable – each individual picture
is a work of art. Unglaublich, jedes einzelne Bild ist für sich ein Kunstwerk.«
[FOM]

»The next time we'll start like this right
away. Das nächste Mal fangen wir
gleich so an.«
[URB]

Christian von Alvensleben

Pictures are a part of the staging, and they simultaneously represent product and proof quality. Bilder sind sowohl Teil der Inszenierung als auch Produkt und Qualitätsbeweis. III. 11

POTENTIAL OF PHOTOGRAPHY

THE WHOLE IS MORE THAN THE SUM OF ITS PARTS
DAS GANZE IST MEHR ALS DIE SUMME ALLER TEILE

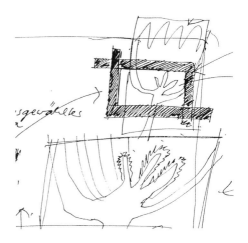

The most difficult task lay ahead.
We couldn't compose and assemble the individual pictures into a giant collage using the selection and production methods we were used to. It was just too much to try to put together 1.250 pictures and coordinate the color, form, and cropping while considering the different picture planes. The solution: a composition of two times 60 single pictures.

Die schwierigste Arbeit steht noch bevor. Das Komponieren und Zusammenstellen der einzelnen Bilder zu einer gigantischen Collage war mit den gelernten Auswahl- und Produktionsmethoden nicht zu schaffen. 1.250 Bilder in Farbe, Form und Ausschnitt unter Berücksichtigung der verschiedenen Bildebenen zusammenzustellen, das ist einfach zu viel. Die Lösung: ein Composing aus zwei mal 60 Einzelbildern.

LARGE AMOUNTS OF DATA

A picture installation of 5 x 25 meters (13'1'') in size requires huge amounts of data. Because of the high resolution 4 x 5 inch sheet film was chosen for the originals. With digital photographs this equates to at least 200 megabytes. When scanning in the originals, care must be taken to ensure a natural look in the enlargements and to avoid an exaggerated digital sharpness. Cropping out the tulips took a lot of effort, as the white reflections on the petals had to remain. Seventy five individual data packages had to be positioned on 28 picture planes, and this took an enormous amount of time because of the amounts of data and the necessity for safety copies. To correct the colors in the two picture installations we had to work over 155 individual data packages. That project was fun – I worked on it for four weeks!

GROSSE DATENMENGEN

Eine Bildinstallation von einer Größe von 5 x 25 m erfordert große Datenmengen. Als Aufnahmeformat werden wegen der hohen Auflösung Planfilme im Großformat von 4 x 5 inch verwendet. Das entspricht bei digitaler Aufnahmetechnik mindestens 200 Megabyte. Bereits beim Scannen der Dias musste darauf geachtet werden, dass bei diesen Megaformaten später eine naturgetreue Wiedergabe entsteht und nicht eine übertriebene Digitalschärfe erzeugt wird. Das Freistellen der Tulpen war sehr aufwändig, weil die weißen Reflexe auf den Blüten erhalten bleiben sollten. 75 Einzeldateien mussten auf 28 Bildebenen positioniert werden, was bei diesen Datenmengen und den nötigen Sicherheitskopien einen enormen Zeitaufwand bedeutet. Für die Farbkorrekturen der beiden Bildinstallationen müssen 155 Einzeldateien bearbeitet werden. Ein Projekt, das Spaß gemacht hat, vier Wochen habe ich daran gearbeitet.
Nicole Röckle, EBV Operator

FROM THE DATA BATTLEFIELD TO A SEA OF FLOWERS

After the photographer, the designer, and the client had developed the idea, the »mountain of tulips« landed at Heinze & Malzacher. We all thought that »all« that was needed was to go into production. The most difficult thing was to keep an overview. Hundreds of picture elements were to comprise a whole and the colors had to match. All elements were defined according to their dimensions, their sequence, their reproduction method, their mounting material, their attachment form, and their position, and were clearly prepared and carefully packed in groups. The result: an enormous battlefield of picture material, an unforgettable sea of flowers, an exquisite collage.

VON DER DATENSCHLACHT ZUM BLUMENMEER

Nachdem der Fotograf, die Gestalter und der Auftraggeber ihre Ideen entwickelt hatten, landete der »Tulpenberg« bei H&M. Alle waren der Meinung, dass jetzt »nur« noch produziert werden muss. Das Schwierigste war, die Übersicht zu behalten. Hunderte von Bildteilen sollten ein Ganzes ergeben, und die Farbanpassungen mussten stimmen. Alle Bildteile wurden definiert nach ihren Abmessungen, ihrem Bildseitenverhältnis, ihrer Umsetzungsart, ihrem Trägermaterial, ihrer Halterungsform und ihrer Position, sauber verarbeitet und penibel nach Gruppen zusammengepackt. Das Resultat: eine bildgewaltige Materialschlacht, ein unvergessliches Blumenmeer, eine Collage vom Feinsten.
[MV]

POTENTIAL OF PHOTOGRAPHY

SIMULATION PROVIDES A CONVINCING TOTAL IMPRESSION
DURCH SIMULATION ZUM ÜBERZEUGENDEN GESAMTEINDRUCK

Only when we build a 1:10 model can we show the complex collage of over 300 individual pictures. To get the optimum viewpoint for visitors the tulip collage is projected on to the white model. This »laboratory installation« enables us to get quite a precise idea of the overall impression and also showed the necessary image overlaps.

Erst mit einem Modell im Maßstab 1:10 gelingt es, die komplexe Collage aus über 300 Einzelbildern darzustellen. Um die optimale Perspektive für die Besucher zu finden, wird die Tulpencollage auf das Weißmodell projiziert. Diese »Laborinstallation« erlaubt eine ziemlich präzise Vorstellung vom Gesamteindruck und zeigte darüber hinaus auch die notwendigen Bildüberlappungen.

Model Scale 1:10

»I was immediately convinced. We're out of the
woods now. Ich war sofort überzeugt. Die Kuh war
vom Eis.«
[FOM]

FLOWERPOWER BY KODAK

FLOWERPOWER VON KODAK

ONE IMAGE WITH 362 PICTURES

EIN BILD AUS 362 BILDERN

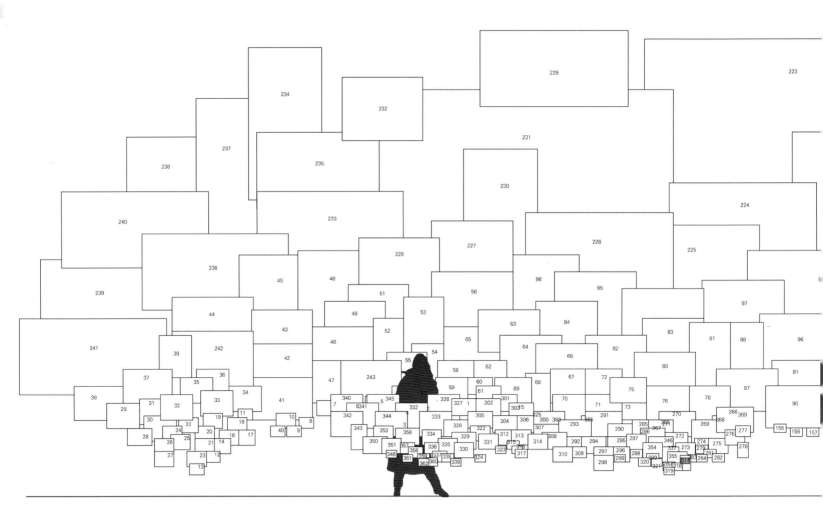

FROM 9 x 13 cm (3 1/2'' x 5 1/8'') TO 3 x 4 m (6'7 x 9'10'')

The pictures are printed on widely differing KODAK materials to give a convincing demonstration of quality. The more than 724 pictures in the flower installation give visitors an impressive visual experience and enable the KODAK papers to impress in detail and en masse.

VON 9 x 13 cm BIS 3 x 4 m

Die Bilder werden auf den unterschiedlichsten KODAK Materialien gedruckt und stellen so einen überzeugenden Qualitätsbeweis dar. Die über 724 Bilder in der Blumenbilderinstallation vermittelten dem Besucher ein eindrucksvolles Bilderlebnis und lassen die KODAK Papiere im Detail wie eine Gesamtinszenierung wirken.

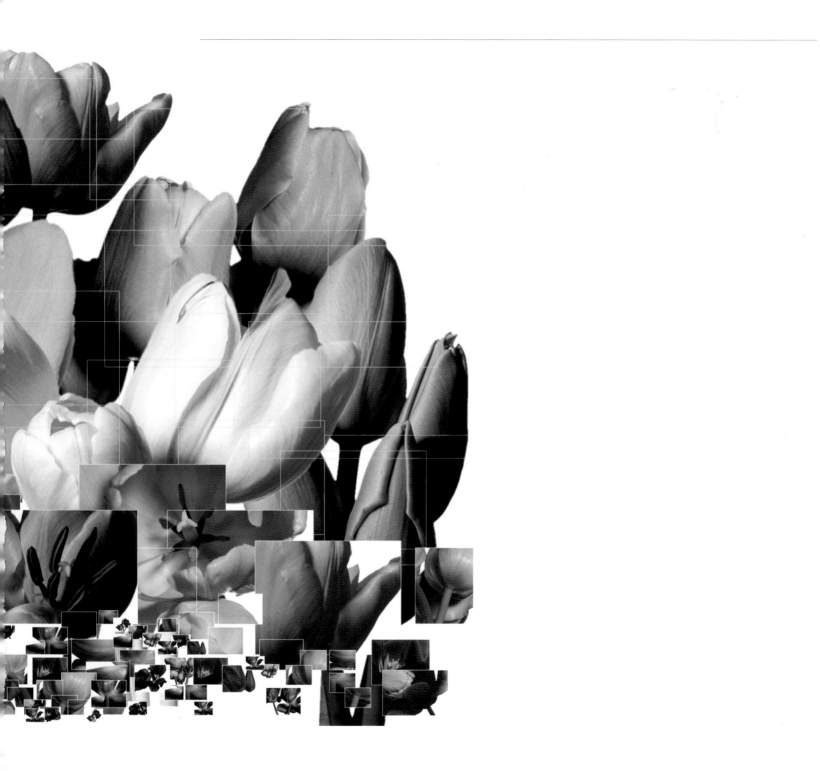

THE TULIP HAS BECOME A PICTURE CODE
DIE TULPE ALS BILDGEWORDENER CODE

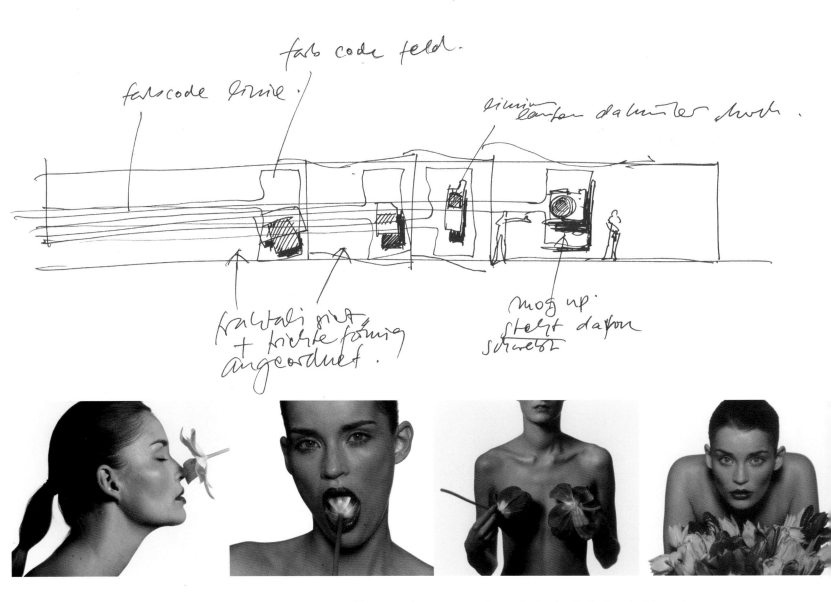

»Pictures on the screen, monitor, or in the viewfinder just don't have the
fascination of the printed picture. Das Bild auf dem Bildschirm, das Bild
im Sucher, das Bild auf dem Monitor haben nicht die Faszination eines
gedruckten Bildes.«
[FOM]

In the entrance areas pictures of people with tulips are shown on large plasma screens integrated in product cutouts. The images are on all screens change simultaneously. Visitors are drawn into the new world of KODAK emotionally eye-catching photos, and are at the same time prepared for the tulip installation. The message is: from screen to fascinating and touchable printed picture. The story, »You have the choice, we have the connectivity« is convincingly represented.

In den Eingangsbereichen werden auf großen Plasmabildschirmen, die in Produkt-Cutouts integriert sind, Menschen mit Tulpen gezeigt. Auf allen Bildschirmen wechselten die Motive gleichzeitig. Der Einstieg in die neue Welt von KODAK wird über emotionale Eyecatcher-Fotos erreicht. Die Besucher werden im Eingangsbereich auf die Tulpenbildinstallation vorsensibilisiert. Das Bild auf dem Bildschirm zum faszinierend gedruckten Bilderlebnis, brillant und erfahrbar ist die Botschaft. Die Story: »You have the choice, we have the connectivity« wird überzeugend dargestellt.

POTENTIAL OF PHOTOGRAPHY

Christian von Alvensleben

THE TAMING OF THE INSTANT
DIE DRESSUR DES AUGENBLICKS

pages and links/Verweise

III. 244 – 245

home-zone shooting

*Henneka — shooting
the protagonist
are doing the
"designer work"
— at home*

Dietmar Henneka's still lifes with people. The
Stuttgart photographer provides the key visuals for
the home zone. The brief is short and clear. The
leeway for the photographer is huge and he uses
it brilliantly.
People-Still-Lifes von Dietmar Henneka.
Die Key-Visuals für die Home-Zone fotografiert
der Stuttgarter Fotograf Dietmar Henneka. Das
Briefing ist kurz und knapp. Der Spielraum für den
Fotografen ist groß und wird in souveräner Weise
genutzt.

PHOTOGRAPHER'S BRIEF

Daring, cool, modern image. Unusual picture crop-ping. Identical viewing angles and eye heights for all all four motifs. Cool palette, crisp, clear colors. Motif quiet and graphically forceful. Area colors picked up in motifs. Motifs without floor in foreground. Material KODAK 8 x 18 inch film.

FOTOBRIEFING

Freches, cooles, modernes Erscheinungsbild.
Ungewöhnliche Bildausschnitte und Anschnitte.
Gleiche Blickwinkel/Augenhöhe für alle vier Motive,
eher kühle Farbigkeit, knackige, klare Farben.
Motive ruhig und grafisch aufgeteilt.
Die Area-Farbe im Motiv aufnehmen.
Motive ohne Boden im Vordergrund.
Aufnahmematerial: KODAK 8x18 inch Film

POTENTIAL OF PHOTOGRAPHY

KODAK pictures on TV
Modern living space

»Dietmar, have you time? Müller wants something
 unusual. Dietmar, hast du Zeit? Der Müller will
 was Außergewöhnliches.«
 [URB]

»Sure, but you're probably running late as usual.
 Ja, sicherlich bist du wieder verdammt spät dran.«
 [DIETMAR HENNEKA]

»Yes, but don't forget to get the tulips in ...
 Ja. Aber vergiss die Tulpen nicht ...«
 [URB]

STORYTELLING IN THE HOME ZONE
STORYTELLING IN DER HOMEZONE

pages and links/Verweise

III. 244 – 245

KODAK EasyShare System.
Shoot. Touch. Print.
Home Office Environment

»... the practical thing about Dietmar's studio in Stuttgart
being so close is that the wine for the discussion stays cool
on the way there. ... das Praktische an der kurzen Entfernung
zu Dietmars Atelier in Stuttgart ist, dass der Wein für die
Besprechung auf dem Weg dorthin kalt bleibt.«
[URB]

KODAK EasyShare System.
Shoot. Touch. Share.
Home Environment

KODAK Mobile Service.
Your pictures. Anytime. Anywhere.
Cool Lifestyletype

SEEING REDISCOVERED
DAS SEHEN NEU ENTDECKEN

Andrej Barov, Digital Art

For KODAK the work of Andrej Barov provides extraordinary and innovative examples of how analog and digital photography can be combined creatively. He favors themes dealing with the phenomena of seeing and their effects on psychological experiences. With the help of new digital technologies the photographic artist creates for us completely new perceptions and sensory experiences. KODAK presented the pictures at photokina as an esthetic and yet critical commentary on the »digital age«.

Für KODAK sind die Arbeiten von Andrej Barov außergewöhnliche und innovative Beispiele, wie analoge und digitale Fotografie eine kreative Verbindung eingehen können. Bevorzugte Themen sind dabei Phänomene des Sehens und deren Auswirkung auf das psychische Erleben. Mit Hilfe von neuer digitaler Technik verschafft uns der Fotokünstler völlig neue Wahrnehmungen und Sinneseindrücke. KODAK präsentierte die Bilder auf der photokina als einen ästhetischen, aber auch kritischen Kommentar zum »digitalen Zeitalter«.

THE COLOR MATRIX OF BRANDS

Vertical section for the simulated movement.
Vertikalschnitt für die simulierte Bewegung.

POTENTIAL OF PHOTOGRAPHY

COCA-COLA can

Reducing everyday objects to a color code is the idea of the series of pictures called »Thirst quenchers«. The artist was inspired by the barcodes on supermarket goods, which contain all relevant information about the product. In his pictures the artist plays with the conditioned perceptions that filter out key elements of objects that we no longer consciously perceive in our haste.

The powerful color codes are created by taking a vertical section of a digitized photograph of an object and moving it using 3-D animation to create a wide image.

COCA-COLA, Dose

Gegenstände des Alltags reduziert auf einen Farbcode. Das Ist die Idee der Bildserie »Durstlöscher«. Inspiriert wurde der Künstler vom Scanner-Code bei Produkten für Supermarktkassen, die alle relevanten Informationen über das Produkt enthalten. In seinen Bildern spielt der Künstler mit der konditionierten Wahrnehmung, bei denen Schlüsselreize von Dingen herausgefiltert werden, die wir im Vorübergehen gar nicht mehr bewusst wahrnehmen.

Die prägnanten Farbcodes entstehen durch einen vertikalen Schnitt digitalisierter Fotografien der Objekte, die am Computer mit einer 3D-Animation, durch simulierte Bewegung, zum Breitbild berechnet werden.

THE COLOR MATRIX OF BRANDS
DIE FARBCODES VON MARKEN

THE COLOR MATRIX OF CELEBRITIES

THE COLOR MATRIX OF FRAGRANCE

NAOMI CAMPBELL

CHRISTIAN DIOR: FAHRENHEIT

In the »Stardust« series portraits of stars are transformed into color sequences. An intellectual and esthetic play with the exploitation mechanisms and value systems of the consumer goods industry is applied to the omnipresent media superstars of our time. The digital transformation turns each portrait into a characteristic color sequence.
In der Bildserie »Stardust« werden Starportraits zu Farbverläufen. Intellektuell und ästhetisch ein Spiel mit den Verwertungsmechanismen und dem Wertesystem der Konsumgüterindustrie – angewendet auf die in den Medien allgegenwärtigen Superstars unserer Zeit. Durch die digitale Bearbeitung ergibt sich für jedes Starportrait ein charakteristischer Farbverlauf.

In the series »Colors of fragrance« photographer Andrej Barov attempted to visualize scents. What look at first like color runs are in fact images of world-famous perfume bottles. Taking a section of photographs of bottles, digitalizing them, and manipulating them by computer, the characteristics of a scent can now be experienced as a picture.
Das Bild eines Geruches sichtbar zu machen versuchte der Fotograf Andrej Barov mit seiner Serie »Colors of Fragrance«. Was auf den ersten Blick aussieht wie verschiedene Farbflächen, sind in Wirklichkeit Abbildungen weltberühmter Duft-Flakons.
Durch die fotografierten Flakons wurde ein Längsschnitt gezogen. Die digitalisierten Bilder wurden danach am Computer bearbeitet. Das Charakteristische eines Duftes ist dadurch als Bild erlebbar gemacht worden.

THE COLOR MATRIX OF MASTERPIECES

THE DIGITAL ALBUM

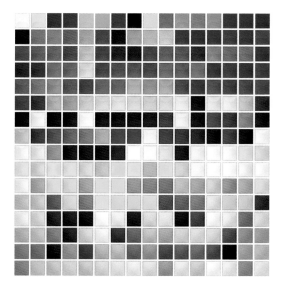

POTENTIAL OF PHOTOGRAPHY

ROY LICHTENSTEIN: GIRL WITH HAIR RIBBON

NEW YORK: STATUE OF LIBERTY

Behind the apparently randomly ordered color squares in Adrej Barov's »256« series are hidden paintings by world-famous artists. Barov digitizes photographs of the paintings and reduces each picture to 256 squares, retaining the placing and frequency of each color while freeing it from the concreteness of the original.

Scheinbar willkürlich sind die Farbquadrate in der Bildserie »256« von Andrej Barov angeordnet, doch dahinter verbergen sich Gemälde weltbekannter Künstler.

Die Fotografien von Gemälden werden digitalisiert und jedes Bild auf 256 Farben reduziert. Erhalten bleibt die Platzierung und Häufigkeit der Farbe im Bild, allerdings losgelöst von der Gegenständlichkeit im Bild.

Andrej Barov photographed a series of cityscapes, digitized them, and reproduced them as computer codes. He also extracted from a vertical section of the picture a representative sum of pixels, which he multiplied into a wide format.

Andrej Barov fotografiert eine Serie von Stadtansichten, die digitalisiert und als Computercode wiedergegeben werden. Zusätzlich extrahiert er aus einem vertikalen Schnitt im Bild eine repräsentative Summe an Pixeln, die ins Breitformat vervielfältigt werden.

chapter **III.12 GRAPHIC CONCEPT DAS GRAFIKKONZEPT**

PERCEIVING THROUGH COLORS AND SYMBOLS
WAHRNEHMEN ÜBER FARBEN UND SYMBOLE

pages and links Verweise
I. 58 – 63
II. 134 – 141

Color perception is not a question of taste, but an inborn feeling for harmony and wellbeing. The key lies in the reception of symmetrical tonal, spacial, and visual events. Colors possess the characteristic of stimulating sensory effects only in combination with other colors. It is important to realize that colors and color combinations have not only a single expression. Independent of symbols and codes, colors and color combinations contain coded messages that are learned through our individual and collective experiences. What is learned is affected largely by the sensory meaning of colors, but also by smells and tactile experiences. The choice and composition of colors should be checked against perceptions and effects, because the messages of colors embody a great potential for the successful staging of an exhibition stand.

Farbempfinden ist keine Frage des Geschmacks, es ist ein angeborener Reflex für Harmonie und Wohlbefinden. Der Schlüssel besteht in der Rezeption symmetrischer Klang-, Raum- und Sehereignisse. Farben haben die Eigenschaft, erst im Zusammenklang mit anderen Farben sinnhafte Wirkungen zu erzeugen. Das Kombinieren von Farben ist ein höchst ästhetischer, kritischer Prozess. Bedeutsam ist: Farben und Farbzusammenstellungen haben nicht nur eine Aussage allein. Unabhängig von Symbolen und Chiffren enthalten Farben und Farbkombinationen codierte Botschaften, die durch Eigenerfahrungen und Kollektiverfahrungen erlernt sind. Das Gelernte wird dabei weitgehend von den Sinnesbedeutungen von Farben, aber auch von Gerüchen und Haptiken geprägt. Die Auswahl und die Zusammenstellung von Farben sollte auf Empfindungen und Wirkungsweisen überprüft werden, denn in den Botschaften von Farben steckt ein weiteres Potential für die erfolgversprechende Inszenierung eines Messestandes.

Primärfarben

KODAK Gelb

KODAK Rot

Neutrale Anwendung

CMYK:17/12/12/0
Pantone 428 C

Typografie und Claim

CMYK:0/0/0/80
Pantone 425 C

Sekundärfarben

Professional Wide Format Printing
CMYK: 0/70/100/0
Pantone 166 C
Sendal: UN 102

Printing Services

CMYK: 30/0/50/0
Pantone: 577 C
Sendal: UN 144

Professional Imaging Solutioins
CMYK: 45/0/15/15
Pantone: 5493 C
Sendal: UN 111

Pictures on Site Prints in One Hour
CMYK: 60/20/0/0
Pantone: 284 C
Sendal: UN 108

THE GRAPHIC CONCEPT

Produkt & Service Information
CMYK: 0/70/35/0
Pantone 702 C
Sendal: UN 136

Pictures On Site Prints in Minutes
CMYK: 30/0/0/0
Pantone: 290 C
Sendal: UN 145

Press / Films, Papers, Media
CMYK: 0/8/50/0
Pantone: 1205 C
Sendal: UN 142

Professional Digital Capture & Output
CMYK: 0/42/10/0
Pantone: 494 C
Sendal: UN 137

The color concept is coordinated with the product groups and the graphics are consistently designed and explained in a comprehensive style guide. Never before has the graphic design for all the advertising media produced for photokina been adopted by almost all countries. The same look was designed and applied to power point presentations, invitations, advertisements, leaflets, press kits, and fair passes.

Das auf die Produktgruppen abgestimmte Farbkonzept und das Grafikdesign ist konsequent durchgestaltet und wird im Vorfeld mit einem umfangreichen Styleguide kommuniziert. Nie zuvor ist das entwickelte Grafikdesign für alle Werbemittel, die anlässlich der photokina produziert werden, von fast allen Ländern übernommen worden. Von der Powerpoint-Präsentation über Einladungen, Anzeigen, Prospekte, Pressekits bis zum Messeausweis, alles war in einem Look gestaltet.

2

3

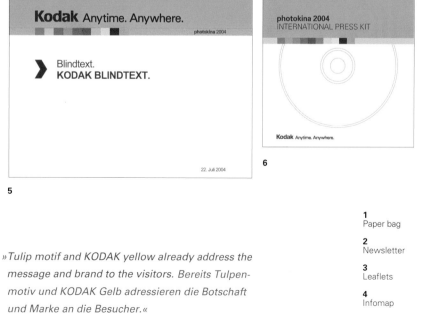

THE GRAPHIC CONCEPT

7

4

5

6

»Tulip motif and KODAK yellow already address the message and brand to the visitors. Bereits Tulpenmotiv und KODAK Gelb adressieren die Botschaft und Marke an die Besucher.«

[URB]

1
Paper bag

2
Newsletter

3
Leaflets

4
Infomap

5
Powerpoint design

6
Press Kit

7
Stuff identification badges

INTEGRATIVE SYSTEM AS DESIGN PRINCIPLE
INTEGRATIVES SYSTEM ALS GESTALTUNGSPRINZIP

Elevation of the public zone – KODAK Easyshare Cameras

Before the show product messages are already given their color coding. For example, invitations, leaflets, and photokina-News were coded so that they could be recognized and the desired products easily and quickly found on the stand. The public zone in the center is conceived as a home environment. Short and punchy statements work well in conjunction with individual and unmistakable picture compositions and the respective color coding. There's no busy small stuff here, but clear and structured messages.

Schon im Vorfeld der Messe werden Produktbotschaften mit Farbcodes versehen. Zum Beispiel werden Einladungen, Prospekte und die photokina-News farblich so gestaltet, dass die Wiedererkennung, das Auffinden der gewünschten Produkte, am Stand einfach und schnell funktioniert. Die Publikumszone im Mittelgang ist als Home Environment konzipiert. Kurze und einprägsame Aussagen in Verbindung mit eigenständigen und unverwechselbaren Bildkompositionen und der entsprechen Farbzuordnung funktionieren bestens. Kein vielteiliges Klein, Klein, sondern klare und einfach strukturierte Botschaften.

Innovation

THE GRAPHIC CONCEPT

8.500 SQ. METERS OF EXHIBITION BECOME A MEGAPIXEL SPACE
8.500 QUADRATMETER HALLE WERDEN ZUM MEGAPIXELSPACE

pages and links Verweise

I. 64 – 75

II. 142 – 145

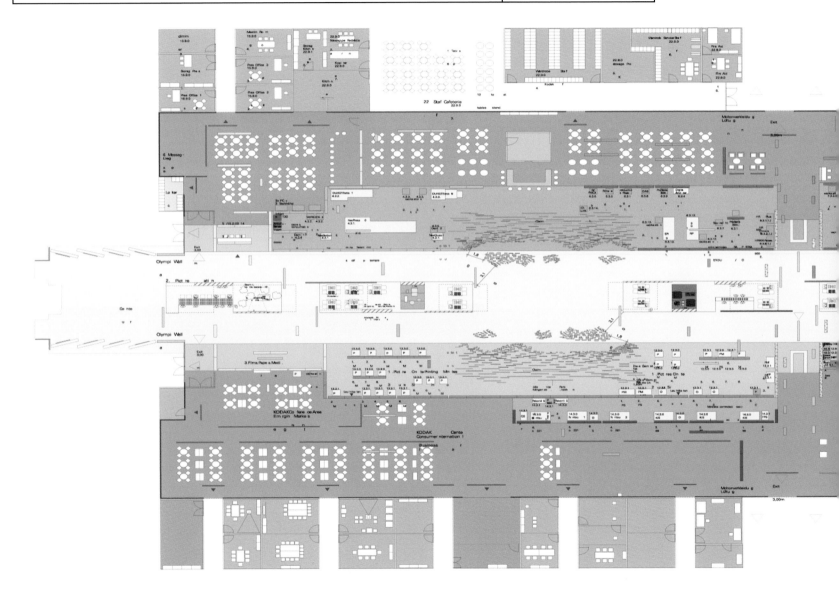

We have to orchestrate 8.500 m² (59.201 ft²) completely. The whole thing is bigger than a football field, and keeps everyone on the run. Some of the staff use scooters. Despite the open plan and lightweight structure enormous amounts of material must be moved into the hall. Just a few examples show what the logistics were like: 6.000 m² / 64.583 ft² of modular panels, 8.500 m² / 91.492 ft² of floor panels, 12.000 m² / 129.166 ft² of fabric in different colors, 2.000 m / 6.560 ft of cabling for all the connections, more than 300 floodlights, 2.000 fluorescent tubes for the back-lighted screen and suspended elements. 200 tables and 800 chairs are installed. Four kitchens and 160 personnel in the hall and a mobile kitchen unit outside guarantee service for 45.000 customers and 750 stand personnel. These numbers represent just a small part of the logistic package, and could be continued at length.

PLANNING AND PRODUCTION

8.500 m² gilt es komplett zu bespielen. Das Ganze ist größer als ein Fußballfeld, was alle Beteiligten, einige davon mit Rollern, in Bewegung hielt. Trotz der offenen und leichten Bauweise müssen Unmengen von Material in die Halle transportiert werden. Nur einige wenige Beispiele sollen zeigen, dass es sich hier um ein logistisches Megaprojekt handelte: 6.000 m² Verlegeplatten, 8.500 m² Bodenbeläge, 12.000 m² Stoff in verschiedenen Farben, 20.000 m Kabel für die benötigten Anschlüsse, über 300 Scheinwerfer, 2.000 Leuchtröhren für die hinterleuchteten Wand- und Hängeelemente. 200 Tische und 800 Stühle werden aufgestellt. Mit vier Küchen und 160 Serviceleuten im Stand und einer transportablen Küchen-einheit außerhalb der Halle wird die Versorgung von 45.000 Kunden und 750 Standmitarbeitern sichergestellt. Diese Aufzählung ist nur ein kleiner Teil aus einer gigantischen Logistik-Leistung und könnte beliebig fortgesetzt werden.

SECTIONS AND ELEVATIONS FOR THE XXL STAND
SCHNITTE UND ANSICHTEN FÜR DEN XXL-STAND

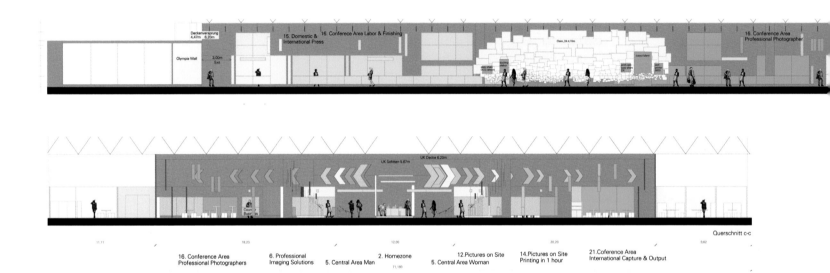

»Obviously the hall is smaller than the Cologne Trade Fair admits. Even the best plan can't survive the first contact with reality. Offensichtlich ist diese Halle kleiner, als die Kölnmesse zugibt. Kein noch so guter Plan überlebt die erste Begegnung mit der Realität.«
[MV]

Mini-sections and mini-elevations for a maxi-stand. After a comprehensive planning phase with models of different scales it is always surprising to see the real thing, full size. Everything seems bigger, despite years of experience.

Minischnitte und Miniansichten für Maxistand. Immer wieder ist es überraschend, nach einer umfangreichen Planungsphase mit Modellen in verschiedenen Maßstäben der Realität, den wirklichen Maßen, ins Auge zu sehen. Alles wirkt größer, trotz langjähriger Erfahrung.

17. Business Center   7. Professsional Wide Format Printing   2. Homezone   10. Professional Digital Capture & Output   19.Coference Area Domestic Capture & Output

PLANNING AND PRODUCTION

THE DIGITS – A SHINING EXAMPLE

DIE DIGITS – EIN LEUCHTENDES BEISPIEL

The idea of giving the colors more power and intensity was based on a consistent development of the successfully applied color concept. The real challenge was to light the wall and suspended elements without shadows and with the minimum of effort. The back-lighted fabric-covered color pixel panels represent an esthetic structure and create functional zoning in an area of 8.500 m² (59.201 ft²) and help make the perception of form, color, and message into an open, transparent, airy, and multi-layered color experience.

Der konsequenten Weiterentwicklung des erfolgreich praktizierten Farbkonzeptes lag die Idee zugrunde, den Farben mehr Strahlkraft und Intensität zu verleihen. Die eigentliche Herausforderung liegt darin, mit möglichst wenig Aufwand die Wand- und Hängeelemente schattenfrei auszuleuchten. Die textil hinterleuchteten Farbpixelwände bilden, auf einer Fläche von 8.500 m², die ästhetische Struktur und eine funktionale Zonierung, was die Wahrnehmung von Form, Farbe und Botschaft zu einem offenen, transparenten, luftigen und vielschichtigen Farberlebnis werden lässt.

Inside a light element

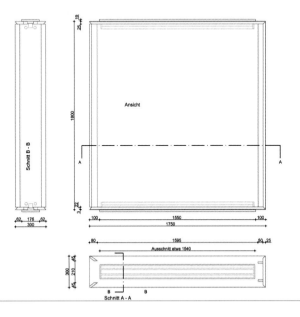

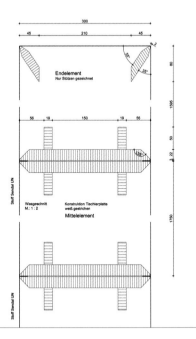

A trial installation shows that the
shadow-free illumination works.
Beim Probeaufbau zeigt es sich,
dass die schattenfreie Ausleuchtung
funktioniert.

»The result of the trial installation helped decide who got the
job. Das Ergebnis des Probeaufbaus war auch ein Kriterium,
wer den Job bekommt.«

[FOM]

CONCEPT TO CONCEPTION
VOM KONZEPT ZUR KONZEPTION

Concept to conception means that complex and ambitious projects need many individual and detailed concepts, for architecture, lighting, graphics, media, production, etc. These concepts must be coordinated and synchronized with one another, so that a coherent conception for a total work of art is generated from the sum of all the corresponding individual concepts. Vom Konzept zur Konzeption bedeutet, dass komplexe und anspruchsvolle Projekte viele Einzel- und Detailkonzepte brauchen; für Architektur, Licht, Grafik, Medien, Produktion, etc. ... Diese Konzepte sollten aufeinander abgestimmt sein, synchronisiert werden, um aus der Summe aller korrespondierenden Einzelkonzepte eine schlüssige Konzeption für dieses Gesamtkunstwerk zu generieren.

Hall 4 of the Cologne Fair is consciously left as a large open space in which visitors can see into almost all of the exhibition and meeting spaces. Visitors enter the hall space through a gallery of networked digital products.

Die Halle 4 der Kölnmesse ist bewusst als ein großer offener Raum belassen, in dem für den Besucher nahezu alle Ausstellungs- und Besprechungsbereiche einsehbar sind. Durch eine Galerie vernetzter digitaler Produkte gelangt der Besucher in den Hallenbereich.

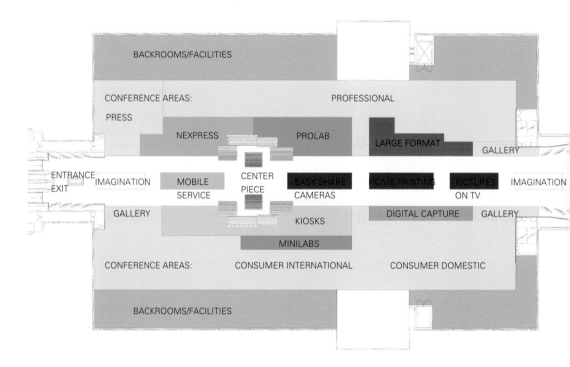

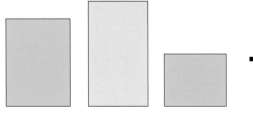

The back lighted wall, counter, and hanging elements

Shoot. Touch. Share.
KODAK EasyShare SYSTEM.

The suspended information elements

The back-lighted directional arrows

This huge open communication space is structured by a system of »digits« – fabric-covered, backlighted wall panels of different sizes and colors that separate product, presentation, and meeting areas. Three different heights create differentiated surfaces, areas, and spaces.

Dieser große offene Kommunikationsraum ist durch ein System einzelner »Digits« strukturiert – textile, hinterleuchtete Wandelemente –, die in unterschiedlichen Maßen und Farben Produkt-, Besprechungs- und Präsentationsbereiche voneinander trennen. Durch drei unterschiedliche Höhenmaße werden differenzierte Flächen, Bereiche und Räume ausgebildet.

In the center of the hall visitors reach two accessible image installations each 25 x 6 m (13'1'' x 18'20'') in size. On each side a three-dimensional picture composed of 750 individual images demonstrates the fascination of the printed picture. This accessible »picture space« is the favorite place for souvenir snapshots in the whole photokina.

In der Hallenmitte erwartete die Besucher auf einer Fläche von 2 mal 25 x 6 m eine begehbare Bildinstallation. Zwei gegenüberliegende dreidimensionale Großbilder, die sich aus 720 Einzelbildern zusammensetzen, demonstrieren bildhaft die Faszination des gedruckten Bilderlebnisses. Dieser begehbare »Bildraum« ist der meistgenutzte Hintergrund für Schnappschüsse auf der Photokina.

PLANNING AND PRODUCTION

The »Home zone« along the major path consists of single alternately standing and hanging wall panels that suggest private spaces and here KODAK products for private use are shown separately. In the open hall applications for public spaces and professional uses are presented.

Die »Homezone« entlang der Hauptwege besteht aus einzelnen Wandscheiben, die, im Wechsel stehend und hängend, private Räume andeuten. In der offenen Halle werden Anwendungen für die Nutzung im öffentlichen Raum und im Profibereich präsentiert, so sind es zum Beispiel in der »Homezone« (Mittelgang) KODAK Podukte für den privaten Gebrauch.

chapter   **III. 14 THE OPENING** DIE ERÖFFNUNG

THE SUSPENSE BETWEEN START AND FINISH

IM SPANNUNGSFELD ZWISCHEN BAUBEGINN UND FERTIGSTELLUNG

pages and links Verweise
I. 76 – 87
II. 146 – 155

The tension increases. Communication becomes simple and short. The most frequent questions are: How's the time going? Is it all going to plan? Is there anything to drink? Where can I connect my computer? Where can I lock my things away? Shortly before the opening the questions change: Are you satisfied? Can you still change this? Questions, questions: What's where? Where can I find this? Where can I find that? Die Spannung steigt. Die Kommunikation ist einfach und knapp. Die meistgestellten Fragen sind: Wie seid ihr in der Zeit? Läuft alles nach Plan? Gibt's hier was zu trinken? Wo kann ich meinen Computer anschließen? Wo kann ich meine Sachen einschließen? Kurz vor Messebeginn ändert sich der Fragenkatalog: Wie sind Sie zufrieden? Können Sie das noch ändern? Fragen über Fragen. Wo ist was? Wo finde ich dies? Wo finde ich das?

*»The texts for the entrance area are still missing. Can I remind you that the costs will increase significantly if by tomorrow noon we don't …
Uns fehlen nach wie vor die Texte für die Eingangsbereiche. Ich muss Sie darauf hinweisen, dass erhebliche Mehrkosten entstehen, wenn wir bis morgen Mittag nicht …«*
[KM]

The entrance area.

THE PUBLIC TOUCH AND FEEL ZONE
DIE PUBLIKUMSZONE FÜR TOUCH AND FEEL

»Scenography is a great profession where you can test the value of the idea and the abstract concept in reality.

Szenographieren ist ein herrlicher Beruf, ausprobieren zu können, was die Idee, das abstrakte Konzept, in der Realität wert ist.«

[URB]

Perspectives, insights, and orientation.

MEMORABLE ICONS
ERINNERUNGSWIRKSAME ICONS

pages and links Verweise
III. 218 – 221

THE OPENING

»Dietmar's changes of perspective create an amazing dialog between
the surreality in the picture and the staged reality in the public zone.
Dietmars Perspektivewechsel erzeugt einen verblüffenden Dialog
zwischen der surrealen Realität im Bild und der inszenierten Realität der
Publikumszone.«

[FOM]

»That's what I understand by creative corporate scenography.
Das verstehe ich unter creative corporate scenography.«

[URB]

THE SMELL OF SPRING WITH BIRDSONG INCLUDED

FRÜHLINGSDUFT UND VOGELGEZWITSCHER INKLUSIVE

»It's great moment when the installation starts to speak, or even to give off a scent.
Ein großartiger Moment, wenn eine Inszenierung anfängt zu sprechen oder gar zu duften.«
[URB]

THE OPENING

»Midnight is always the photographers' hour. Mitternacht ist immer die Stunde der Fotografen.« [FOM]

FURNITURE TO INFORM AND RELAX WITH

MÖBEL ZUM INFORMIEREN UND RELAXEN

»Among all the picture-mania at the fair, it's great to be
soothed by a little cool esthetics. In all dem Bilderwahn
einer Messe tranquilisiert ein wenig kühle Ästhetik ganz
angenehm.«
[URB]

ESTHETIC IN THE BUSINESS CENTER

ÄSTHETIK IM BUSINESSCENTER

Good bye
Auf Wiedersehen
Au revoir

THE OPENING

160.000 VISITORS IN FIVE DAYS
160.000 BESUCHER IN FÜNF TAGEN

750 pictures, printed on the most different materials and from 9 x 13 cm (3 1/2'' x 5 1/2'') up to 2 x 3 m (6'7 x 9'10'') in size, demonstrate impressively the emotional power that printed pictures still have. The concept, showing the way from products to printed emotional picture experience, has worked perfectly. From the entrance area with the connectivity story through the product presentation to various target groups to our visual highlight, the real key take-away, the fascination of the printed picture has convinced everyone.

Exhibition stands are an important experimental area for designers. The budgets are higher than for museum projects, the timescales are short, the risk of failure is lower, and the effects are immediately visible. Visitors' perceptions are mostly spontaneous and honest. Messestände sind ein wichtiges Experimentierfeld für Gestalter. Die Budgets sind vergleichsweise höher als für Museumsprojekte, die Laufzeiten kurz, die Gefahr des Scheiterns geringer und die Wirkung unmittelbar ablesbar. Die Wahrnehmungen der Rezipienten sind meist spontan und ehrlich.

THE OPENING

Mit 720 Bildern von 9 x 13 cm bis zu einer Größe von 2 x 3 m, auf den unterschiedlichsten Materialien, wird eindrucksvoll demonstriert, welche emotionale Kraft ausgedruckte Bilder noch immer haben. Das Konzept, vom Produkt zum gedruckten emotionalen Bilderlebnis, hat bestens funktioniert. Vom Eingangsbereich mit der Connectivity-Story über die Produktpräsentation für die verschiedenen Zielgruppen bis zu unserem visuellen Highlight, dem eigentlichen Key Take-Away, die Faszination des gedruckten Bildes überzeugt alle.

THE INVESTMENT PAID OFF
DAS INVESTMENT HAT SICH GELOHNT

pages and links Verweise

I. 88 – 89

II. 156 – 157

Der „Gelbe Riese" ist wieder im Rennen

Eastman Kodak hat den Anschluss an die Digitaltechnik schneller geschafft, als viele geglaubt hatten · Der Aktie hat das sichtlich gut getan

Von **Horst Fugger**

Als die Aktie von Eastman Kodak vor einigen Monaten aus dem Dow Jones Industrial Average flog, wurden in einigen Wirtschaftsmagazinen schon die Totenmessen über den „Gelben Riesen" aus Rochester gelesen. Die Kommission, die über die Zusammensetzung des Dow entscheidet, hatte sich nämlich in den vergangenen Jahren als sehr treffsicher erwiesen. Die in jüngerer Vergangen-

Financial Times Deutschland 25.09.2004

heit eliminierten Unternehmen, man denke etwa Goodyear Tire, Bethlehem Steel, Woolworth, Westinghouse oder AT&T, hatten zumeist eines gemeinsam: Es handelte sich um einstige Industriegiganten, die ihre besten Jahre eindeutig hinter sich hatten.

Als Eastman Kodak aus dem Index ausschied, in dem das Unternehmen ununterbrochen seit 74 Jahren repräsentiert gewesen war, schien auch dies nur folgerichtig zu sein: Eastman wies die mit Abstand

niedrigste Marktkapitalisierung aller Dow-Titel auf, hatte seit Jahren für negative Schlagzeilen und nach unten weisende Analystendaumen gesorgt. Der Weltmarktführer hatte die Entwicklung weg von der klassischen, hin zur digitalen Fotografie schlicht verschlafen.

Das führte zu sinkenden Umsätzen und Gewinnen. Außerdem traten neue Wettbewerber auf den Plan. Im Segment der klassischen Fotografie hatte es Eastman Kodak hauptsächlich mit Fuji und einigen kleineren Konkurrenten wie Agfa-Gevaert oder Konica zu tun. Bei Digitalkameras mussten die Amerikaner plötzlich gegen Riesen wie Sony antreten, die eigentlich aus der Unterhaltungselektronik stammen.

Eastman hat die Herausforderung angenommen und zur Verwunderung vieler Marktbeobachter beachtliche Erfolge erzielt. Das ging nicht ohne Schmerzen ab: auch die Aktionäre mussten leiden, weil ihnen neben den Kursverlusten der vergangenen Jahre auch noch die Streichung der traditionell üppigen Dividendenausschüttungen zugemutet wurde.

Aber jetzt scheint man auf dem richtigen Weg zu sein, Eastman hat

Eastman Kodak
Aktienkurs in $

in seinem zweiten Geschäftsquartal Umsatz und Gewinn gesteigert. Für das Gesamtjahr hob der Konzern am Mittwoch seine Gewinnprognose an. So rechnet das Unternehmen nun mit einem operativen Gewinn zwischen 2,39 und 2,69 $ je Aktie. Zuvor war Kodak noch von 2,15 bis 2,45 $ je Aktie ausgegangen. Wie Eastman Kodak weiter mitteilte, ist der Gewinn je Aktie im zweiten Jahresviertel von 0,39 $ im Vorjahr auf nunmehr 0,54 $ gestiegen.

Von den meisten Marktbeobachtern kaum bemerkt, hat sich der Aktienkurs seit seinem 12-Monats-Tief (20,50 $) um gut 36 Prozent erholt. Das liegt zum einen daran, dass Eastman im klinisch-diagnosti-

schen Bereich nach wie vor führend ist, und der Ergebnisbeitrag dieses Sektors von vielen Beobachtern wohl ebenso unterschätzt wurde wie das Wachstumspotenzial.

Zum anderen scheint die Umorientierung hin zur Digitaltechnik schneller vonstatten zu gehen, als viele Skeptiker geglaubt hatten. Zum Beginn der Photokina, der für die Branche bedeutendsten Messe, die bis zum 3. Oktober in Köln stattfindet, hat Eastman Überraschendes angekündigt. Zusammen mit japanischen Partnern wie Minolta, Konica oder Olympus will Eastman im kommenden Jahr einen neuen Standard für den Ausdruck von digitalen Aufnahmen ohne Einsatz eines PC auf den Markt bringen.

Damit wäre der Kreis geschlossen: Wenn schon klassische Kleinbildfilme – jahrzehntelang Eastmans Domäne – auf Dauer von einer völlig neuen Technologie verdrängt werden, dann bleibt noch eine weitere große Stärke: Der Ausdruck der Fotos und die Herstellung des weltweit besten Fotopapiers.

Die Aktie ist trotz des jüngsten Kursanstiegs nicht teuer und hat im Vergleich zu früheren Höchstkursen noch einiges Potenzial.

Ralf Banse, Shirin Brückner, Friedrich O. Müller and Ulf Aschenbrenner are delighted with the Adam-Award.

Over 50 publications in the most important influential newspapers and magazines in the lifestyle press reached more than 130 million readers. The most important TV stations ZDF, WDR, Deutsche Welle TV, Sat 1, RTL, NTV, and N24 report on the KODAK stand, resulting in millions more contacts. Five cover stories are placed in the professional press. Two awards for outstanding stand design rounded off the success story.

Über 50 Veröffentlichungen in den wichtigsten meinungsbildenden Zeitungen und Zeitschriften der Lifestyle-Presse und dadurch über 130 Millionen Leser werden erreicht. Die wichtigsten TV-Stationen wie ZDF, WDR, Deutsche Welle TV, Sat 1, RTL, n-tv und N24 berichten vom KODAK Messestand, was weitere Millionen Kontakte bringt. Fünf Coverstorys können in der Fachpresse platziert werden. Zwei Auszeichnungen für vorbildliches Messedesign machten die Erfolgsstory komplett.

PRAISE FROM ALL SIDES

The press is united: at photokina 2004 KODAK has again presented by far the most attractive and imposing stand. In Hall 4 KODAK has given an impressive demonstration of its new digital strategy. Rainer Dick, Managing Director of KODAK GmbH Germany, summed it up. »For us photokina 2004 was a trade show that showed the way. We were able to present KODAK as a modern enterprise, and as a leader in digital picture technology.«

LOB VON ALLEN SEITEN

Die Presse ist sich einig: KODAK bietet auf der photokina 2004 in Köln wieder den mit Abstand attraktivsten und imposantesten Stand.
KODAK präsentiert eindrucksvoll seine neue Digitalstrategie in Halle 4.
Rainer Dick, Geschäftsführer KODAK GmbH Deutschland, brachte es auf den Punkt. »Die photokina 2004 war für uns eine Messe mit richtungsweisendem Charakter. Es ist uns gelungen, KODAK als modernes Unternehmen zu präsentieren, das federführend in digitalen Bildtechnologien ist.«

SUMMARY: PHOTOKINA 2004 EVALUATION

The 2004 KODAK stand is much more attractive than at photokina 2002 according to visitors able to compare the two.

Almost half (49%) of those asked think that the current stand is much better or somewhat better than in 2002 The most positive opinions about the 2004 stand were from people under 30.

Almost all (91%) visitors liked something very much about the KODAK stand.

Spontaneous positive opinions were concentrated particularly on visual aspects, with design elements being cited most often. The flower picture installation was a special highlight: more than one in four visitors (28%) mentioned and described it specifically. Further "likes" were the comfortable quiet zones/seating areas/cushions, the friendly color scheme, clear layout and open display of the products, and the impressive overall size of the KODAK stand.

The flower picture installation was noticed by 90% of those asked and almost all (93%) of these said they liked it very much.

»*Designers are always dependent on the quantitative success of commercial projects. On the other hand the client's satisfaction, praise from colleagues, awards, or praise from other disciplines reflects quality. Gestalter sind immer abhängig von quantitativem Erfolg kommerzieller Projekte. Die Zufriedenheit des Klienten, Lob von den Kollegen, Auszeichnungen oder gar disziplinübergreifendes Lob reflektieren andererseits die Qualität.*«
[URB]

PRESS AND EVALUATION

RISK TAKING AND DECISION MAKING
ZWISCHEN RISIKOBEREITSCHAFT UND ENTSCHEIDUNGSFÄHIGKEIT

A POSITIVE CHEMISTRY IS THE FOUNDATION
OF AN EXCELLENT RESULT

Friedrich O. Müller is one of those fanatics who
fight for their ideas without compromise, a restless
workaholic who drove us to the limits every time.
But he's extremely fair and generous and, unusually
for a Swabian, with a disarming humor and gratitude
the moment the curtain has risen successfully on the
premiere.

EINE POSITIVE CHEMIE IST VORAUSSETZUNG FÜR
EIN EXZELLENTES ERGEBNIS

Friedrich O. Müller ist einer jener Überzeugungstäter,
die kompromisslos für ihre Einstellung kämpfen,
ein ruheloser Workaholic, der uns jedes Mal an die
Grenzen der Belastbarkeit brachte. Er ist aber immer
extrem fair und großzügig, und – selten genug für
einen geborenen Schwaben – mit einem entwaff-
nenden, versöhnlichen Humor und Dankbarkeit, so-
bald sich der Premierenvorhang erfolgreich geöffnet
hatte.

Values like courage, respect, understanding, fairness, and sympathy are still responsible for a positive and fruitful climate between client and designer. The competence and professional qualification of experienced professionals is finding less and less recognition. Instead every client knows better and can express an opinion. The result is that creative professionals spend more time impressing clients with their professionalism than putting all their energies into the actual project. The relationship between client and designer in many companies has undergone significant changes during the last 20 years. The collegiality, respect, and responsibility, an almost friendly relationship, which in the past formed the basis of a good working relationship has been replaced by a certain coolness based on the promotion of one's own career. Negotiations about price are used for sporting self-presentation. Short deadlines are set, without knowledge of the situation and without a thought for people and materials. Decisions are not made quickly and simply. Problems are simply circulated by e-mail and then a reaction is awaited. Recently, several organizations have established so-called steering committees, whose task it is to prepare decisions for the board. The young managers in these circles have become careful and risk shy, because the future path of their careers is being decided here. It is noticeable that young managers especially cling to traditional ideas and show less inclination for new ones. Constructive input and support for new ideas are seldom found nowadays. In their place we get unspecific critique – »I don't like it. We're looking for something with more pizzazz. We need more alternatives.« Increased costs due to unclear briefings and self-induced additional services are dismissed out of hand as a matter of course and invoice payments are deliberately delayed to improve the quarterly results. Contractor loyalty is no longer expected. Clients change their »creative contractors« like they change their shirts, believing that they can get better performance or terms or simply because it is chic to do so. Frequent changes of personnel at management level are another reason for faster changes of contractor, because potential clients often bring their advisers and idea producers with them. Continuity is no longer desired. Everything planned and built up with a long-term view is destroyed and replaced by something new and generally humdrum. Risk-avoidance at board level is on the increase. Creative space for the designer, for innovation, for the unusual and unique will shrink, despite the fact that it is the client's willingness to take risks, to experiment with new ideas, that provides the source from which designers draw inspiration.

Für ein fruchtbares positives Klima zwischen Auftraggeber und Auftragnehmer sind immer noch Werte wie Mut, Achtung, Verständnis, Fairness, aber auch Sympathie verantwortlich. Das Anerkennen von Kompetenz und fachlicher Qualifikation von bewährten Profis findet immer weniger statt, vielmehr glaubt jeder Auftraggeber alles besser und überall mitreden zu können. Das Ergebnis ist, dass Kreative sich mehr damit beschäftigen, sich gegenüber ihren Auftraggebern als kompetenten Gesprächspartner darzustellen, als ihre volle Energie dem eigentlichen Projekt zu widmen. Die Beziehung zwischen Auftraggeber und Auftragnehmer hat sich in vielen Unternehmen in den letzten 20 Jahren tiefgreifend verändert. Wo in der Vergangenheit Vertrauen, Kollegialität, Respekt und Verantwortung, ja fast freundschaftliche Verhältnisse die Grundlage für eine gute Zusammenarbeit waren, herrscht heute eine gewisse Coolness, die vom eigenen Karrieredenken geprägt wird. Preisverhandlungen benützt man zur Selbstdarstellung mit sportlichem Charakter. Kurze Termine werden gefordert, ohne Kenntnis der Sachlage und ohne Rücksicht auf Mensch und Material. Entscheidungen werden nicht mehr schnell und unkompliziert getroffen. Probleme werden ganz einfach per E-Mail breit distribuiert, und dann wartet man ab. In jüngster Zeit hat man in vielen Unternehmen sogenannte Steuerungskomitees etabliert, deren Aufgabe es ist, Entscheidungen für die Vorstände vorzubereiten. Die Jungmanager in diesen Zirkeln sind vorsichtig und risikoscheu geworden, weil es sich dort entscheidet, ob es für diese Herren auf der Karriereleiter nach oben oder nach unten geht.

Auffallend ist auch, dass gerade jüngere Manager mehr traditionellen Vorstellungen anhängen und wenig Risikobereitschaft für Neues zeigen. Konstruktiver Input und das Mittragen einer innovativen Idee ist nur noch selten zu erleben, vielmehr steht eine unspezifische Kritik, unter dem Motto, es gefällt mir nicht, wir suchen etwas mit »Pfiff«, und wir brauchen noch mehr Alternativen, im Mittelpunkt der Beziehungskommunikation. Mehrkosten für unklare Vorgaben und eigenverschuldete Zusatzleistungen werden mit einer Selbstverständlichkeit abgeschmettert und Zahlungsanweisungen für Rechnungen werden zur Verbesserung des Quartalsergebnisses bewusst verzögert. Lieferantentreue ist nicht mehr gefragt. Auftraggeber wechseln häufiger als früher ihre »kreativen Zulieferer«, weil sie glauben, noch bessere Leistungen und Konditionen zu bekommen, oder weil es einfach chic ist. Der häufige Personalwechsel im Managementbereich ist ein weiterer Grund für das schnellere Auswechseln von Lieferanten, weil die potentiellen Auftraggeber häufig ihre Berater und Ideengeber mitbringen. Kontinuität ist nicht mehr gefragt. Alles was langfristig angelegt und aufgebaut wurde, wird zerstört, um es durch Neues, meist Durchschnittliches zu ersetzen. Das Sicherheitsdenken in den Vorstandsetagen wird weiter zunehmen. Der kreative Spielraum für die Gestalter, für das Neue, Außergewöhnliche und Einzigartige wird abnehmen, wo doch gerade die Risikobereitschaft von Auftraggebern, das Experiment, Neues ausprobieren zu dürfen, die Quelle ist, aus der die Gestalter schöpfen.

FOUR YEARS OF SUCCESSFUL COOPERATION

Dear Herr Brückner,

After the exciting weeks full of stress and tension that now lie behind us, I would like today to take the opportunity of expressing my sincere thanks to you and your staff. The cooperation between our teams was not always characterized by harmony and the intensive discussions motivated both designers and client to deliver the highest performance. The effort was worth it for both sides. We can be proud of the results. We have had great praise from all sides, and I would like to pass this on to you here.

All three exhibition stands were accepted outstandingly well by customers, press, and KODAK staff from all over the World. The innovative character of all three designs completely fulfilled the demands of KODAK as market leader. The creativity of the architectural concepts, incorporating the specifications set out by KODAK, was extraordinary, and has made a lasting and positive impression on the KODAK brand. The logical, informative layout and the structure of the show appearance, which enabled visitors to find their way quickly and simply and to gain a comprehensive overview of KODAK products, worked extremely well. The representation of a world of experience offering enjoyment and fascination that encouraged spending time on the stand was uniquely and unmistakably achieved. The functional requirements for the spatial program, the open architecture, and the design and spatial qualities were worked out cooperatively by both teams and executed outstandingly. The economics of all three stands was unusually good, because the erection of a conventional structure on site was eschewed from the beginning. Fabrics were the primary material used to delineate space, and all components could be prefabricated in the shop ahead of time and erected simply and easily on site. The consistent show appearance of KODAK, which has demonstrated the highest standards of creativity over the years, was very worthwhile. The positive effect on the brand was noticeable and paid off for KODAK. In the best sense: celebrating the brand.

At the end of this year I shall be leaving KODAK and shall be looking for new challenges. Dear Herr Brückner, many thanks once again for the good and constructive cooperation over the last four years.

Yours sincerely,

Friedrich O. Müller

*The underlinings are by Uwe Brückner, who added his own handwritten expressions of assent and praise (see right) before passing the correspondence to his staff and sending a letter of gratitude to FOM.

[handwritten: ⊗ Uwe. → team-credits. + anhang]

Atelier Brückner
z.Hd. Herrn Uwe Brückner
Quellenstraße 9
70376 Stuttgart

Stuttgart, den 10.11. 2004

Vier Jahre erfolgreiche Zusammenarbeit

Sehr geehrter Herr Brückner,

nach den hinter uns liegenden aufregenden Wochen, die von Stress und Anspannung *[handwritten: allerdings!]* geprägt waren möchte ich heute die Gelegenheit nutzen Ihnen und Ihren Mitarbeitern meinen aufrichtigen Dank auszusprechen. Die Zusammenarbeit der Teams war nicht immer nur von Harmonie geprägt, die intensiv geführten Diskussionen haben sowohl die Gestalter als auch die Auftraggeber zu Höchstleistungen motiviert. Die Mühe hat sich für beide Seiten gelohnt. Die Ergebnisse konnten sich sehen lassen. Großes Lob von allen *[handwritten: / danke team !]* Seiten, das ich an dieser Stelle gerne an Sie weiter geben möchte. Alle drei Messestände wurden von den Kunden, der Presse und den Mitarbeitern aus aller Welt hervorragend angenommen. Der innovative Charakter aller drei Entwürfe wurde dem Anspruch von Kodak als Marktführer voll und ganz gerecht. Die Kreativität der architektonischen Konzepte, unter Einbeziehung der Vorgaben von Kodak, war herausragend und hat positiv und nachhaltig auf die Marke Kodak eingezahlt. Die logische und informative Gliederung sowie die Strukturierung des Messeauftrittes, die es dem Besucher ermöglichte sich schnell und unkompliziert zurechtzufinden, und sich einen umfassenden Überblick über die Produktpalette von Kodak zu verschaffen, hat bestens funktioniert. Das Darstellen einer Erlebniswelt mit Spaß und Faszination, die zum Verweilen einlädt, wurden eigenständig und unverwechselbar umgesetzt. Die funktionalen Anforderungen an das Raumprogramm, offene Architektur sowie an die gestalterische und räumliche Qualität wurden im Team gemeinsam erarbeitet und hervorragend umgesetzt. Die Wirtschaftlichkeit aller drei Stände war außergewöhnlich gut, weil von vorneherein auf eine konventionelle Bauweise Vorort verzichtet wurde. Vorwiegend wurde Stoff zur Raumbildung eingesetzt. Alle Teile konnten in der Werkstatt vorgefertigt werden und an Ort und Stelle leicht und einfach montiert werden. Der konsequente Messeauftritt von Kodak, über viele Jahre Kreativität auf höchstem Niveau zu bieten, hat sich gelohnt. Der positive Einfluss auf die Marke war spürbar und hat sich für Kodak ausgezahlt. Im besten Sinn, Celebrating the brand. *[handwritten: der Lotse geht von Bord …]*
Zum Jahresende werde ich die Firma Kodak verlassen und neue Herrausforderungen suchen. Sehr geehrter Herr Brückner nochmals vielen Dank für die gute und konstruktive Zusammenarbeit in den letzten vier Jahren.

[left margin handwritten: … wir shall overcome … am ende zählt doch das ergebnis /]

Mit freundlichen Grüßen

[signature]

Friedrich Müller
Kodak GmbH, Stuttgart
Director Communication
Event Manager European, African,
and Middle Eastern Region

*[handwritten right: … der erfolg gibt ihm recht ✓!
(… da geht eine epoche _Müller_ zu ende).]*

[handwritten bottom: ⊠. Danke im namen der teams. Almanach]

THE COMMON DENOMINATOR – THE CONSISTENT PRINCIPLE
DER GEMEINSAME NENNER – DAS DURCHGEHENDE PRINZIP

The layouts of all three KODAK photokina stands were based on the same design principle: Trade dress color for positioning the brand, good visitor orientation by means of colors and symbols, and a »key visual« – the so-called key take-away – that is eye-catching and that leaves a lasting impression.

Alle drei KODAK photokina Standentwürfe beruhen auf dem gleichen Gestaltungsprinzip: Farbe zur Positionierung der Marke, gute Besucherorientierung durch Farben und Symbole und ein Key Visual, das sogenannte Key Take-Away, das prägt und hängenbleibt.

»THE LETTER«

KODAK I photokina 2000 – KODAK The Universal Language

Well-functioning information system using color coding, images, and graphics. The paths and routes between the buildings allow visitors to venture from the main path and make discoveries.
Gut funktionierendes Informationssystem durch Farbcodes, Bilder und Grafik. Die Wege und Straßen zwischen den Gebäuden gaben den Besuchern die Möglichkeit, abseits des Hauptganges auf Entdeckungsreise zu gehen.

»THE KISS«

KODAK II photokina 2002 – KODAK Share Moments. Share Life.

Product slogans, zoning by portals, and well-tuned graphics and pictures garanted good orientation. Lasting effect of the key take-away on visitors and press. Strong branding through yellow and red.
Gute Orientierung durch Produktslogans, Zonierung durch Tore und einer gut abgestimmten Grafik- und Bildgestaltung. Nachhaltige Wirkung des Key Take-Aways bei Besuchern und in der Presse. Starkes Branding durch Gelb und Rot.

WHY MAKE COSTLY TRADE SHOW
APPEARANCES?

In times of digital manipulation and the noticeable
weariness caused by virtual over-stimulation an
authentic experience is beginning to play an increasingly important role. It is personal contact, visual and
tactile experience in an emotional communication
space, which cements the authenticity of a brand or
a product.

Only collective events with synchronous appearances by competitors enable comparative evaluation
of product potential and credibility.

For dealers and customers, trade shows are not
only an exchange market for information, but social
events. The more ambitious the stand design, the
better and more attractively the company can dif-
ferentiate itself from its competitors.

WARUM AUFWÄNDIGE MESSEAUFTRITTE?

In Zeiten der digitalen Manipulation und der regis-
trierbaren Müdigkeit einer virtuellen Reizüberflutung
spielt das authentische Erlebnis wieder eine zuneh-
mend wichtige Rolle. Die Authentizität einer Marke
oder eines Produktes wird erst durch den persönlichen Kontakt, durch visuelle und haptische Erfahrung im emotionalen Kommunikationsraum zu einem
nachhaltigen Erlebnis.

Nur kollektive Ereignisse synchroner Auftritte von
Wettbewerbern erlauben eine vergleichbare Evalu-
ierung von Produktpotentialen und deren eingehal-
tener Versprechen.

Für Händler und Kunden sind Messen nicht nur eine
Informations- und Austausch-
börse, sondern auch ein gesell-   THE RÉSUMÉ
schaftliches Event. Je ambitionierter ein Messestand
gestaltet wird, desto attraktiver können sie sich
gegenüber den individuellen Hausmessen ihrer Mitbewerber absetzen.

»THE TULIPS«

KODAK III photokina 2004 – KODAK Anytime. Anywhere.

KODAK presents itself to the public effectively with the central »Picture
Dome« as a memorable installation. The symbiosis of proven elements
such as the color coding of KODAK I and the clear zoning of KODAK II led to
a highly esthetic product presentation.

Mit dem zentralen »Picture Dome« als erinnerungswürdige Installation
setzt sich KODAK publikumswirksam in Szene. Die Symbiose bewährter
Elemente wie das Farbcode-System von KODAK I, die klare Zonierung von
KODAK II führten zu einer Ästhetisierung der Produktpräsentation.

IN THE BEGINNING THE WORD DOMINATES …

AM ANFANG DOMINIERT DAS WORT …

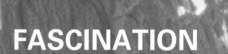

FASCINATION
SURPRISE

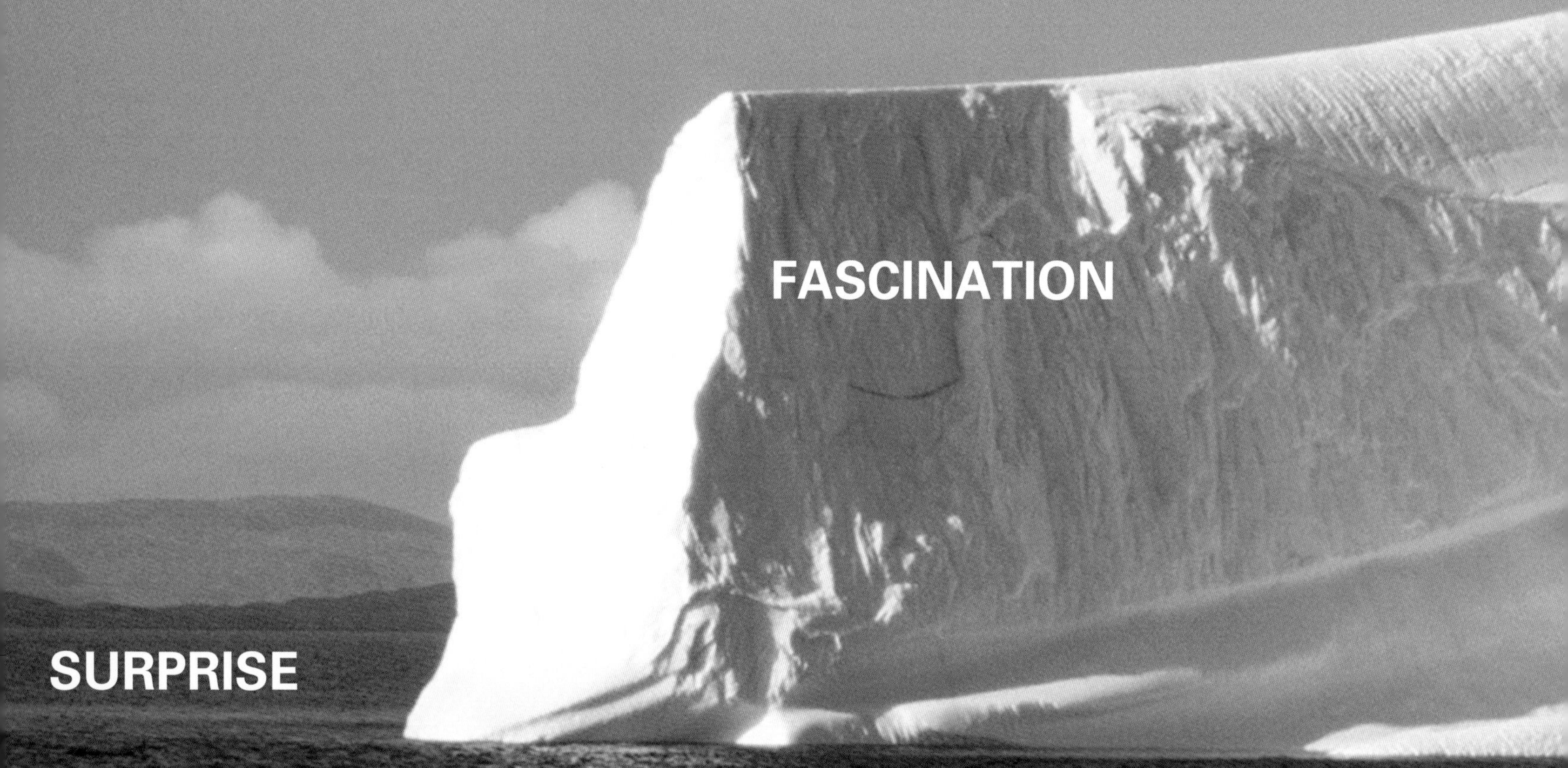

»If I now had to do KODAK IV, I still wouldn't know what I'd want. But I know what I don't want … Wenn ich jetzt KODAK IV machen sollte, würde ich wie immer nicht wissen, was ich will, aber was ich nicht will.«

[FOM]

»It's comforting to know that they'll always need us. Es ist beruhigend zu wissen, dass man uns immer wieder braucht.«

[URB]

AUTHENTICITY

MESSAGE

... IN THE END THERE'S ALWAYS
AN UNEXPECTED EXPERIENCE.
... UND AM ENDE STEHT EINE NEUE ERFAHRUNG.

THE RELATIONSHIP: CONTRACTOR OR PARTNER
DAS VERHÄLTNIS: LIEFERANT ODER PARTNER

THE BASIS IS EXPERIENCE, TRUST, DEDICATION

Everyone who has ever built a house knows the problems. Who is the right architect for me? Which builder fulfills my requirements? Who hasn't experienced the painful problem of inflated extra charges? Positive experiences with contractors are the basis for trusting cooperation. I'm always being asked why KODAK doesn't order everything from one source, turnkey fashion. My answer is always the same:» We have so many experienced employees with so much knowledge and photographic understanding that a full-service agency would need years to acquire this know how.«

 The decision on whether to use a full-service agency or partners depends on the quality of their employees and their organization structure. We have decided to use different partners and over the years have had good experience with that. The prerequisites are an experienced and competent in-house exhibition team, years of experience with and knowledge of the contractors, a cooperative purchasing team as partners, short decision paths within the team, and a good climate between client and contractor. The result is a pleasant and constructive cooperation, cost savings of up to 30%, and no unpleasant surprises.

Good projects can happen only when people with different skills come together, all are prepared to pursue a common goal, and in addition are prepared to dedicate themselves to extraordinary performance.

DIE BASIS IST ERFAHRUNG, VERTRAUEN, ENGAGEMENT.

Jeder, der schon mal ein Haus gebaut hat, kennt die Probleme. Wer ist der richtige Architekt für mich? Welche Baufirma erfüllt meine Qualitätsansprüche? Das leidige Thema mit den überhöhten Nachforderungen, wer kennt das nicht? Die positiven Erfahrungen mit Auftragnehmern sind die Basis für eine vertrauensvolle Zusammenarbeit. Immer wieder werde ich gefragt, warum KODAK nicht alles aus einer Hand einkaufe, also schlüsselfertig. Die Antwort ist immer dieselbe: »Wir haben so erfahrene Mitarbeiter mit so viel Kenntnis und fotografischem Sachverstand, dass eine Fullservice-Agentur Jahre bräuchte, um dieses Knowhow zu erreichen.«

Die Entscheidung, Fullservice-Agentur oder verschiedene Gewerke, ist abhängig von der Qualität der Mitarbeiter und der Organisationsstruktur. Wir haben uns für das Modell der verschiedenen Gewerke entschieden und sind über viele Jahre sehr gut damit gefahren. Die Voraussetzungen sind: ein erfahrenes und kompetentes Messeteam im eigenen Haus, eine langjährige Erfahrung und Kenntnis der Partnerunternehmen, und ein kooperatives Einkaufsteam als Partner. Kurze Entscheidungswege innerhalb der Teams und ein gutes Klima zwischen Auftraggeber und Auftragnehmer. Das Ergebnis: Eine angenehme und konstruktive Zusammenarbeit. Kosteneinsparungen bis zu 30%. Keine negativen Überraschungen.

Gute Projekte können nur dort entstehen, wo Menschen unterschiedlichen Könnens zusammentreffen und alle bereit sind, ein gemeinsames Ziel zu verfolgen und darüber hinaus Engagement mitzubringen, Außergewöhnliches zu leisten.

Friedrich O. Müller

THAT SPECIAL MOMENT

As an experienced professional stand builder I can safely state that the processes by which a stand is conceived, planned, erected, and then dismantled, always remain the same. That is the rule even at the highest level. There are, as always in life, exceptions. A special constellation is represented by the three related words: KODAK – photokina – Cologne. It is certainly not only the worldwide brand name which has a special feeling, not only the size of the stands, which were and are far bigger than average, not only the extremely short erection and dismantling times, or the materials, photos, or masses of chairs and tables used here – no, you'll find that more or less dramatically with other comparable brands. That is exciting, but not special. What's special is the approach, the creative process, the permanent questioning of everything, the untiring attempts to do things differently, and to discover them anew. Never to be satisfied with what's been achieved, never to give up, always thinking differently, always moving, questioning, trying, failing, laughing, talking – and then it's finished, and the people come, the stand's alive.

Tired and stressed, this was always a special moment for me. I am especially grateful for the trust and the experiences I have enjoyed over the last twelve years with KODAK.

DER BESONDERE MOMENT

Als erfahrener Messebauprofi könnte ich durchaus sagen, dass sich die Prozesse, wie ein Messestand entsteht, geplant, realisiert wird und wieder verschwindet, immer wieder gleichen. Das ist in der Regel auch so, auch auf hohem Niveau.

Es gibt aber, wie immer im Leben, auch Ausnahmen. Als besondere Konstellation nenne ich hier drei zusammengehörige Begriffe: KODAK – photokina – Köln.

Es ist sicher nicht die Weltmarke allein, die ihren besonderen Spirit hat, die Größe der Stände, die weit überdurchschnittlich waren und sind, auch nicht die extrem kurzen Auf- und Abbauzeiten oder die Materialien, Fotos und Unmengen an Stühlen und Tischen, die hier verarbeitet wurden – nein, das alles gibt es bei anderen vergleichbaren Marken auch mehr oder weniger dramatisch, das ist spannend, aber nicht das Besondere.

Es ist die besondere Herangehensweise, der Entstehungsprozess, das stetige Hinterfragen der Dinge, unaufhörliches Versuchen, die Dinge anders zu machen – neu zu entdecken, nie mit dem zufrieden sein, was man hat, nicht aufgeben, anders denken, sich immer wieder drehen, hinterfragen, versuchen, scheitern, lachen, reden – und dann ist es fertig, die Menschen kommen, der Stand lebt.

Müde und vom Stress gezeichnet, war dieser Moment für mich immer ein ganz besonderer.

Für das Vertrauen und die Erfahrungen, die ich mit KODAK in den letzten zwölf Jahren gemacht habe, möchte ich mich besonders bedanken.

Ralf Banse

TECHNICAL COORDINATOR

Ralf Banse

»Trade shows must always reinvent themselves;
without inventive entrepreneurship and the
courage to take risks everything remains
average. *Messen müssen sich immer wieder neu
erfinden,ohne Erfindergeist und Mut zum Risiko
bleibt alles nur Durchschnitt.*«
[RB]

»The idea, the whole concept, is only as good as
its execution. *Die Idee, das ganze Konzept ist nur
so gut wie seine Umsetzung.*«
[URB]

HEINZE & MALZACHER GMBH
PROFESSIONAL TRADE SHOW DISPLAY SERVICES

The staff of the firm Heinze & Malbacher of Stuttgart, Germany, provides designing, problem solving and liaison between planners, architects and clients. We have been assisting KODAK AG for more than 20 years.

Not only the proximity of our location and our fast and versatile services have made the execution of jobs with tight deadlines possible up to now – the personal contacts that developed over time fostered a trusting cooperation. The latter is absolutely essential, because we strive to provide cost-conscious, attractive and feasible solutions for all projects, especially the implementation of photokina plans.

Close contact with Friedrich Müller, manager of the KODAK photokina project, and his assistants Rainer Sahlberger and Detlev Gehrke was always a necessity, as it also was with the project managers from the Atelier Brückner, in order to implement their solutions as well as our own contributions.

We are familiar with the stand builders charged with constructing the KODAK stand, so that solutions for details can be worked out quickly and efficiently.

Our team consists of layout specialists, graphic designers, advertising specialists, decorators and stand builders, thus constituting the necessary bandwidth to accommodate every trade show task in its entirety. From high-grade digital printing or captioning of all kinds, all the way to decorations that complement the descriptions of the most diverse KODAK products, there are countless additional examples of tasks that have been entrusted to us.

Whether it involved suggested materials for creating displays or the application of new technologies – we were always able to achieve an attractive solution in a pleasant consensus with KODAK and designers. And, of course, for us as partners, suppliers and service providers it is much more exciting to implement unusual projects than handling profitable run-of-the-mill jobs.

Die Heinze & Malzacher GmbH mit Sitz in Stuttgart versteht sich als Gestalter, »Problemlöser« und Bindeglied zwischen Planer, Architekten und Kunden. Seit mehr als 20 Jahren arbeiten wir für das Haus KODAK. Nicht nur die räumliche Nähe und die schnelle sowie variable Umsetzungsvielfalt haben bislang kurzfristige Umsetzungen ermöglicht – sicher sind auch die inzwischen persönlichen Kontakte ausschlaggebend für eine vertrauensvolle Zusammenarbeit. Diese ist

»Longterm partnerships are valuable to us because the thought process does not have to be taught all over again. Langjährige Partnerschaften lohnen sich für uns, weil man nicht ständig das Mitdenken einfordern muss.«
[FOM]

absolut erforderlich, da bei allen Aufgaben, wie z.B. photokina-Umsetzungen, kostenbewusste, ansprechende und trotzdem »machbare« Lösungen von uns gefordert sind.

Ein enger Kontakt zwischen dem leitenden Ansprechpartner Herrn Friedrich Müller und seinen Mitarbeitern Herrn Rainer Sahlberger und Herrn Detlef Gehrke wie auch den Projektleitern vom Atelier Brückner war immer erforderlich, um eigene oder vorgegebene Lösungen umzusetzen. Die mit der Realisierung beauftragten Messebauunternehmen sind uns vertraut, so dass Detaillösungen auf dem »kurzen Dienstweg« machbar sind. Unser Team setzt sich aus Layoutern, Grafikern, Werbegestaltern, Dekorateuren und Messebauern zusammen und deckt dadurch die erforderliche Bandbreite aller Aufgabenstellungen komplett ab. Von hochwertigen Digitaldrucken oder Beschriftungen aller Art bis hin zu Dekorationen, die die unterschiedlichsten KODAK Produkte ergänzend erklären, gibt es unzählige weitere Beispiele der an uns gestellten Aufgaben. Ob Materialvorschläge bei Displayumsetzungen oder Lösungen mit neuen Techniken – immer haben wir uns mit KODAK und den Gestaltern auf eine attraktive Lösung einigen können. Und natürlich macht es als Partner, Zulieferer und Dienstleister mehr Spaß, ungewöhnliche Projekte umzusetzen, als nur profitablen »Mainstream« zu realisieren.

Alexander Heinze   Kai Malzacher

HEINZE & MALZACHER GMBH
FACHSERVICE EXPO-DISPLAY
Dornhaldenstraße 10/1
70199 Stuttgart

Fon: +49 (0) 711 – 60 17 18 62
Fax: +49 (0) 711 – 60 17 18 70

E-mail: k.malzacher@hm-expo.de
www.hm-expo.de

INTER CRIS

PROMOTIONS, SERVICE, CATERING – ALL FROM A SINGLE SOURCE

The Inter Cris Trade Show Agency and its specialized trade show staff offers an extensive program of expert services. We look after your projects or events from the initial analysis of your very special needs all the way to the final accounting of the services provided. Inter Cris has been a proven partner for numerous German companies for many years. The competent work performed by our staff is highly valued. We perform all the organizational and coordinating tasks ahead of the event, taking care of staffing and the logistics of catering. We maintain the flexibility, of course, to react to your wishes. An Inter Cris project manager oversees your event from the planning stage, through the organization phase, all the way through the actual show. In cases of large events, our project manager works right on site, so that you will always have an immediate and competent agency contact.

The women and men who are selected and trained by us are not only multi-lingual, having learned in school, college and practical training, they also have extensive experience in trade shows and functions, so that they perform absolutely professionally, conscientiously and self-sufficiently. We employ qualified male and female students who serve on exhibits and events with great frequency.

When you employ Inter Cris personnel, you can rest assured that our staff will represent your organization with consummate professionalism. To prepare them for optimal performance, all Inter Cris employees must complete an intensive trade show training course at the start of their careers. In addition, our hostesses and barkeepers are groomed especially for their specific tasks.

From extensive experience we are fully aware of the fact that the personal appearance as well as the outstanding customer care put forth by our staff create an image of your company. When our personnel is used for product presentations, we select extroverted and very experienced persons for such performances. As far as catering is concerned, we have a team of professionals ready to prepare the individual creations per your wishes – from a traditional buffet, snacks, finger food, all the way to extraordinary menus of the highest level. With our fine food capability and our professional service team we create exactly the right ambiance for every special occasion.

We have our own large kitchen and permanent cooks in Laatzen, in the immediate vicinity of the Hannover fairgrounds. We provide our own catering with food we prepare ourselves, so that we can assure you that our confections are of the highest quality and absolutely freshly prepared.

Die Inter Cris Messeagentur bietet ein umfangreiches Dienstleistungsprogramm im Zusammenhang mit dem Messepersonal an. Wir betreuen Ihre Projekte oder Events von der Ermittlung des ganz speziellen Bedarfs bis zur kompletten Abrechnung der Dienstleistung. Inter Cris ist für viele deutsche Unternehmen seit Jahren ein bewährter Partner. Die sehr gute Arbeitsleistung unseres erfahrenen Personals wird überaus geschätzt. Wir übernehmen im Vorfeld der Veranstaltung sämtlichen Organisations- und Koordinationsaufwand im Zusammenhang mit dem eingesetzten Personal und der Logistik des Caterings. Wir reagieren dabei selbstverständlich flexibel auf Ihre Wünsche. Eine Inter Cris Projektleiterin betreut Ihren Event von der Planung über die gesamte Organisation bis hin zur Durchführung. Bei Großveranstaltungen ist die Projektleiterin mit vor Ort, und Sie haben somit immer einen kompetenten Ansprechpartner unserer Agentur. Die von uns ausgesuchten und ausgebildeten Damen und Herren sind durchweg nicht nur mehrsprachig durch Schule, Studium und Praktikantenzeit, sondern haben auch umfangreiche Messe- und Veranstaltungserfahrung und arbeiten absolut professionell, verantwortungsbewusst und selbstständig. Wir arbeiten mit angestellten Studentinnen und Studenten, die mit einer großen Häufigkeit auf Messen und Veranstaltungen für uns tätig sind. Wenn Sie Inter Cris Mitarbeiter einsetzen, dann können Sie sicher sein, dass unser Personal Ihr Unternehmen bestmöglich repräsentiert. Zur optimalen

»I have the utmost respect for the company – everything must always be exactly right. Vor dem Betrieb habe ich ungeheuren Respekt – da muss immer alles auf den Punkt stimmen.«
[URB]

»I have complete faith in my staff.
Auf meine Jungs und Mädels ist halt Verlass.«
[RS]

Vorbereitung müssen alle von Inter Cris eingesetzten Mitarbeiter zu Beginn ihrer Tätigkeit an einem intensiven Messe-Training teilnehmen. Darüber hinaus werden unsere Hostessen und Barkeeper speziell für den Servicebereich zu Fachpersonal geschult. Durch umfangreiche Erfahrung wissen wir, dass sowohl das Erscheinungsbild des Personals als auch eine hervorragende Kundenbetreuung durch unser Personal ein Aushängeschild für Ihr Unternehmen ist. Bei einem Einsatz unserer Mitarbeiter im Bereich Produktpräsentation wählen wir für diese Tätigkeiten extrovertierte und sehr erfahrene Mitarbeiter aus.

Für das Catering steht ein Team von Profis für Sie bereit, um die von Ihnen individuell gewünschten Kreationen zuzubereiten – ob traditionelles Buffet, Snacks oder Fingerfood, bis hin zu außergewöhnlichen Menüs auf höchstem Niveau. Wir schaffen für jeden speziellen Anlass mit unseren Speisen und unserem professionellen Serviceteam das richtige Ambiente. Wir sind mit unserer eigenen Großküche und festangestellten Köchen in der unmittelbaren Nähe des Messegeländes in Hannover Laatzen ansässig. Wir bieten Ihnen unser Catering aus eigener Herstellung an und können Ihnen somit versichern, dass die angebotenen Speisen qualitativ hochwertig sind und absolut frisch zubereitet werden. Selbstverständlich ist es möglich, die Einrichtung einer Messeküche bzw. Getränke-Bar zu übernehmen, um z.B. die Speisen direkt am Stand vorzubereiten. In diesem Fall würden Köche aus unserer Brigade direkt an

Ihrem Messestand zum Einsatz kommen. In unserem Repertoire haben wir weiterhin eine große Auswahl an Leihequipment.

Als besonderes Extra verfügen wir über einen Lkw (7,5 t), der als »mobile Kücheneinheit« genutzt werden kann. Lediglich ein Wasser- und ein Stromanschluss werden vor Ort benötigt, um dieses komplett ausgestattete und HACCP-geprüfte und -abgenommene Fahrzeug zu nutzen.

Auf Wunsch erhalten unsere Mitarbeiter einheitliche Kleidung. Außerdem möchten wir noch betonen, dass unsere firmeneigene Garderobe eine gute Schnitt- und Passform hat und von sehr guter Stoffqualität ist (Dinomoda, Windsor oder Sonderanfertigung!).

INTER CRIS MESSEAGENTUR GMBH

Hildesheimer Straße 532
30880 Laatzen

Tel. 05102.93 84 -0
Fax 05102.93 84 -50

E-Mail: events@intercris.de
Internet: www.intercris.de

KLINGENBERG GMBH

DESIGNER CLASSICS FOR RENT – AND FOR SALE

Markets are becoming tighter, budgets ever smaller. If you want to be successful in this field, you need innovative ideas. And that is exactly what Uwe Klingenberg of Klingenberg GmbH in Hannover had. His company rents high-grade designer furniture with subsequent sales at unbeatable prices. He has been successful – not only in Hannover, but meanwhile also in Hamburg.

The idea of »rent – and subsequent sale as used« is ingeniously tailored to current marketing conditions. Because companies nowadays have to operate with significantly lower financial resources.

Add another perspective to that: »Why purchase when you can rent?« This enables a company always to avail itself of modern and refined interiors.

A responsible relationship with the client companies prevents much stress and avoids unpleasant recriminations if something goes wrong.

Designer classics available for international rentals, especially for trade shows, exhibitions, presentations and big events, have to be of high quality. In this context, it is worthwhile to cooperate with a furniture rental enterprise. But a large quantity of high-grade furniture classics for a high-class ambiance as required by the client – Klingenberg very likely is the only company in Germany that meets that standard. High-profile companies rely on Klingenberg. Today, practically no automobile manufacturer would do without the designer classics offered by this com-

pany in Hannover. Television studios are customers, as is the entertainment industry. Large exhibitions like the Berlin Broadcasting Exhibition, or international events such as Formula 1, or the Berlinale invite prominent personalities, guests and media representatives to receptions and conferences in a designer classics atmosphere.

DESIGNER FURNITURE CREATES AN AMBIANCE.

When important events are involved, the settings have to be appropriate. The image of outstanding designers is to be reflected by the events. In that sense, brands like Fritz Hansen, MOROSO, lapalma, Knoll International, Classicon, e15, THONET, USM, Vitra, and Wilkhahn assure an exclusive ambiance for events in Germany, Europe and overseas. The company that has the legendary Hansen chair in stock by the thousands, for instance, can furnish every event in every size to perfection. Commissions with the shortest delivery- and set-up times are not a problem for Klingenberg GmbH. Says Uwe Klingenberg: »Not only do we create a very special atmosphere, our meticulous service also ensures that this atmosphere is perfectly staged, precisely on time and completely self-sufficient. That makes us one of the outstanding enterprises in this market.«

After serving in rental, the designer classics are refurbished meticulously and placed on sale. The outlets in Hannover and Hamburg operate unpretentiously,

based on the concept »From the shelf into the basket«. They offer designer classics at absolutely attractive prices all year long.

Designer classics for rent and then for sale, available immediately at unbeatable prices – with this business idea, Klingenberg created an innovative entrepreneurial concept with great perspectives.

DESIGNKLASSIKER ZUM MIETEN – UND ZUM KAUFEN

Märkte werden enger, Budgets immer niedriger. Wer hier erfolgreich sein will, braucht innovative Ideen. Und genau die hatte Uwe Klingenberg von der Klingenberg GmbH aus Hannover. Das Unternehmen vermietet hochwertige Designmöbel mit anschließendem Verkauf zu unschlagbaren Preisen und hat damit Erfolg – inzwischen nicht nur in Hannover, sondern auch in Hamburg.

Die Idee des »Mieten – und danach gebraucht verkaufen« ist genial auf die derzeitigen Marktverhältnisse abgestimmt. Denn Unternehmen müssen heute mit erheblich weniger Finanzvolumen auskommen. Dazu kommt auch eine andere Perspektive, die heißt »Warum kaufen, wenn man mieten kann?« So kann das Unternehmen auf immer neues und gepflegtes Interieur zurückgreifen.

»A respectful relationship between the client and suppliers prevents much stress and avoids unpleasant recriminations when something goes wrong. Ein faires Verhältnis zu den Firmen erspart viel Stress und lästige Schuldzuweisungen, wenn mal was danebengeht.«
[URB]

DESIGN-KLASSIKER IN INTERNATIONALER VERMIETUNG

Insbesondere Messen, Ausstellungen, Präsentationen und große Veranstaltungen wollen hochwertig ausgestattet sein. Hier rentiert sich nur noch die Zusammenarbeit mit einem Mietmöbelunternehmen. Doch hochwertige Design-Klassiker für ein hochklassiges Ambiente in riesiger Stückzahl, so wie es der Kunde braucht, das kann Klingenberg in Deutschland wohl nur als einziges Unternehmen.

RENOMMIERTE UNTERNEHMEN BAUEN AUF KLINGENBERG

Kaum ein großes Automobilunternehmen mag heute auf die Design-Klassiker der hannoverschen Firma verzichten. Das Fernsehen ist ebenso Kunde wie die Unternehmen der Unterhaltungsindustrie. Große Ausstellungen wie die Berliner Funkausstellung oder internationale Veranstaltungen wie die Formel I oder die Berlinale bitten Prominente, Gäste und Medien-

vertreter in einer Design-Klassiker-Atmosphäre zum Empfang und zu Besprechungen.

DESIGNMÖBEL SCHAFFEN AMBIENTE

Bei renommierten Veranstaltungen muss der Rahmen stimmen. Das Image von Ausnahmedesignern soll sich auf die Veranstaltung übertragen. Und so sind Marken wie Fritz Hansen, MOROSO, lapalma, Knoll International, ClassiCon, e15, THONET, USM, vitra und Wilkhahn die Garanten für ein exklusives Ambiente auf Veranstaltungen in Deutschland, Europa und Übersee. Wer beispielsweise den legendären Hansen-Stuhl von Arne Jacobsen mehr als 2000-mal auf Lager hat, richtet jedes Ereignis in jeder Größe perfekt aus. Auch Aufträge mit kürzesten Liefer- und Aufbauzeiten sind für Klingenberg GmbH kein Problem. Uwe Klingenberg: »Wir schaffen nicht nur eine besondere Atmosphäre, wir sorgen mit unserem Service auch dafür, dass sie mit hochwertigster Dienstleistung perfekt, terminpräzise und völlig selbstständig in Szene gesetzt wird. Damit gehören wir zu den Ausnahmeunternehmen in unserem Markt.«

Nach der Vermietung gehen die Design-Klassiker perfekt aufgearbeitet in den Verkauf. Die Outlets in Hannover und Hamburg arbeiten unprätentiös nach dem Konzept »aus dem Regal in den Warenkorb«. Hier gibt es 365 Tage im Jahr Design-Klassiker zu absoluten Sonderpreisen.

Design-Klassiker für die Vermietung und dann im Verkauf, sofort verfügbar zu unschlagbaren Preisen – die Klingenberg GmbH hat mit dieser Geschäftsidee ein innovatives unternehmerisches Konzept mit großen Perspektiven geschaffen.

KLINGENBERG

KLINGENBERG GMGH

Göttinger Chaussee 76
30453 Hannover

Telefon +49 511.940858-0
Fax +49 511.940858-88

info@klingenberg.org
www.klingenberg.org

EXPOMOBIL – ACCESSORIES FOR TRADE SHOW PROFESSIONALS
EXPOMOBIL – ZUBEHÖR FÜR MESSEPROFIS

The core business of the Expomobil®-Messe-Zubehör-Vertriebs-GmbH (Expomobil® Trade Show Supplies Distribution Company), founded in 1983 by Hans Staeger of Octanorm, is dedicated to trade shows and events. Floor coverings and their competent installation are the company's principal specialty. Innovative products and international trade show activities brought rapid growth to this firm. In the year 1990, its range of services was expanded by the inclusion of furniture and accessories for use in trade shows, conventions and events.

Professional, customer-oriented trade show support services during the construction and operation of a stand, as well as market observation of products, materials and color trends are important factors in the cooperation with our clients. Advanced technologies and customer-specific solutions require intensive and direct discussions with the client. »Special services« are standard with us: Expomobil considers itself to be a service provider who participates in the development of concepts and who strives for innovative

solutions. Floor coverings made of wood or metal, tiles made with gel, artificial turf in white, high-grade materials in silver or gold – as well as sophisticated installation techniques are readily available.

That is why we also regard the many years of cooperation with KODAK and with the Atelier Brückner as especially interesting and constructive.

Numerous high-grade trade show stands have been created on or with our floor coverings. We congratulate you on this review of the many beautiful projects featured in this book and we thank you for the positive cooperation! We look forward to additional fascinating projects!

Die Expomobil® -Messezubehör-Vertriebs-GmbH – 1983 von Hans Staeger/Octanorm gegründet – ist im Kerngeschäft mit Messen und Veranstaltungen beschäftigt. Hauptunternehmensgegenstand sind die Bodenbeläge und der dazugehörige Verlegeservice. Mit innovativen Produkten und internationaler Messepräsenz ist das Unternehmen schnell gewachsen. Durch die Aufnahme von Möbeln und Zubehör für Messe, Kongress und Veranstaltungen hat sich das Spektrum 1990 erweitert.

Professionelle, kundenorientierte Messeunterstützung in der Auftragsabwicklung sowie Marktbeobachtung von Produkten, Materialien und Farbtrends sind wichtige Faktoren für die Zusammenarbeit mit unseren Kunden. Hochwertige Technologien und kundenspezifische Lösungen verlangen intensive und direkte Gespräche am Produkt. Das »Besondere« ist Programm: Expomobil versteht sich als ein Dienstleister, der Konzepte mitentwickelt und innovative Lösungen sucht. Bodenbeläge aus Holz oder Metall, Fliesen aus Gel, Kunstrasen in Weiß, hochwertigere Materialien in Silber oder Gold – auch mit aufwändigen Verlegetechniken …

So sehen wir auch die langjährige Zusammenarbeit mit der Firma KODAK und dem Atelier Brückner als besonders interessant und richtungsweisend an. Viele hochwertige Messestände sind auf bzw. mit unseren Böden entstanden. Wir gratulieren zu diesem Kompendium der vielen schönen Arbeiten, welche hier zu sehen sind, und bedanken uns für die positive Zusammenarbeit! Auf weitere spannende Projekte freuen wir uns!

EXPOMOBIL
Messezubehör-Vertriebs-GmbH

Raiffeisenstraße 39
70794 Filderstadt
Tel. 0711 7 78 91-0
Fax 0711 7 78 91 96
E-Mail: info@expomobil.de
www.expomobil.de

KODAK stand at photokina in Cologne

Webware with cobblestones

Installation experts

Transparent artificial turf backlit with LEDs

»We start at the bottom so that you'll look good at the top. Wir fangen unten an, damit Sie oben gut aussehen.«

[EXPOMOBIL]

GRIEGER
GRIEGER

KOMPETENZFELDER

Laserchrome® Großfotos
Laserchrome® Diapositive
Laserchrome® Serien-Fachvergrößerungen
Ultrachrome® Digitaldrucke
Jetposter® Tintenstrahldrucke
EBV
Aufzieharbeiten
Diasec®-Acrylglasverbindungen
Montagen-Fullservice
Werbedisplays

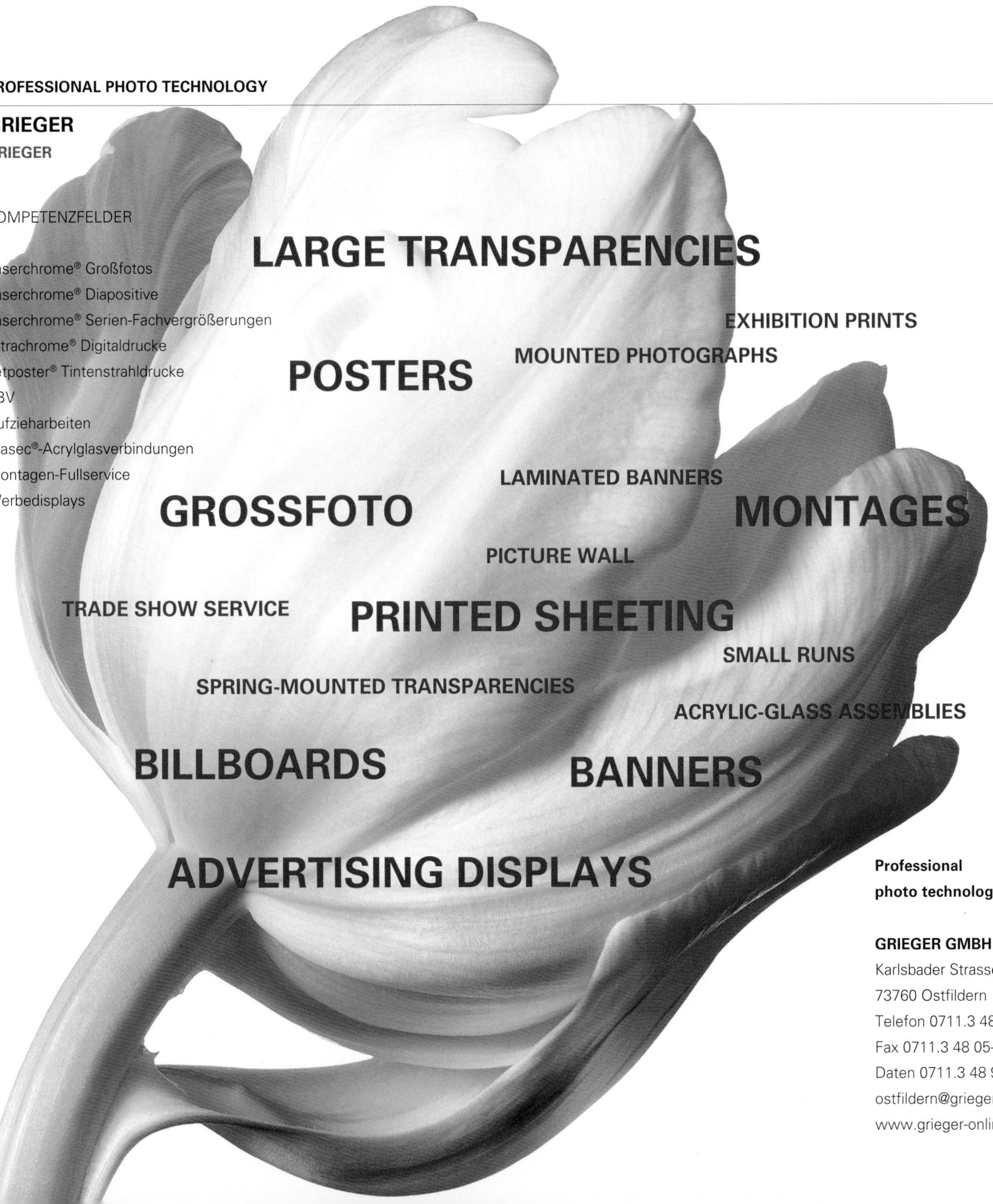

LARGE TRANSPARENCIES

EXHIBITION PRINTS

MOUNTED PHOTOGRAPHS

POSTERS

LAMINATED BANNERS

GROSSFOTO

MONTAGES

PICTURE WALL

TRADE SHOW SERVICE

PRINTED SHEETING

SMALL RUNS

SPRING-MOUNTED TRANSPARENCIES

ACRYLIC-GLASS ASSEMBLIES

BILLBOARDS

BANNERS

ADVERTISING DISPLAYS

Professional
photo technology

GRIEGER GMBH + CO.KG
Karlsbader Strasse 12
73760 Ostfildern
Telefon 0711.3 48 05-0
Fax 0711.3 48 05-11
Daten 0711.3 48 99-10
ostfildern@grieger-online.de
www.grieger-online.de

Grieger

G

FACTS AND FIGURES
DATEN UND FAKTEN

	KODAK I. photokina 2000	KODAK II. photokina 2002	KODAK III. photokina 2004
Client	KODAK GmbH, Stuttgart	KODAK GmbH, Stuttgart	KODAK GmbH, Stuttgart
Project Manager	Friedrich O. Müller	Friedrich O. Müller	Friedrich O. Müller
Worldwide Coordinator	Gunter Plapp	Gunter Plapp	Gunter Plapp
Fascilities Managment	Rainer Sahlberger	Rainer Sahlberger	Rainer Sahlberger
Product Planning / Installation	Detlef Gehrke	Detlef Gehrke	Detlef Gehrke
Photography / Displays	Ines Sahlfrank, Sandra Jirsch	Sandra Jirsch	Sandra Jirsch
Photography / Production	Waltraud Hüttl	Waltraud Hüttl	Waltraud Hüttl
Staff Planning	Renate Mühlberger	Sabine James	Sabine James
Telecommunication / Network	Kai-Uwe Kappich	Kai-Uwe Kappich	Kai-Uwe Kappich
Travel / Hotel Bookings	Hans Thalhofer	Hans Thalhofer	Hans Thalhofer
	Frank Tonne	Frank Tonne	Frank Tonne
Press Services	Gerd Böhm	Gerd Böhm	Gerd Böhm
Budgetcontrol	Annegret Rolph	Annegret Rolph	Annegret Rolph
Team Coordinator		Heide Talmon	Heide Talmon
Team Assistant	Holger Zeising	Holger Zeising	Holger Zeising
Architecture	Atelier Brückner, Stuttgart	Atelier Brückner, Stuttgart	Atelier Brückner, Stuttgart
Project Managers	Dominik Hegemann	Dominik Hegemann	Harry Vetter
	Britta Nagel	Britta Nagel	Juliane Herdfelder
Graphic design	Birgit Koelz, Stuttgart	Birgit Koelz, Stuttgart	Helmut Kirsten, Stuttgart
Lighting design	Delux, Rolf Derrer, Zürich	Biplan, Markus Tilman	V-Mann, Nürnberg
	Biplan, Markus Tilman		
Technical coordination	Ralf Banse	Ralf Banse	Ralf Banse
Stand construction	Zeissig Messebau, Springe	bluepool AG, Springe	Design Productions, Hannover
Graphic production	Heinze & Malzacher, Stuttgart	Heinze & Malzacher, Stuttgart	Heinze & Malzacher, Stuttgart
Lighting technology	Showtec, Cologne	Boelke, Berlin	V-Mann, Nürnberg
Media	Cancom / Stuttgart, ITC / Leonberg	Cancom / Stuttgart, ITC / Leonberg	Cancom / Stuttgart, V-Mann / Nürnber
Start of planning	1 Sept. 1999	1 Sept. 2001	1 Sept. 2003

	KODAK I. photokina 2000	KODAK II. photokina 2002	KODAK III. photokina 2004
Participating persons (planning & production)	170	150	160
Hall area	5.500 m² / 59.201 ft²	8.500 m² / 91.492 ft²	8.500 m² / 91.492 ft²
Stand area	4.400 m² / 47.360 ft²	4.000 m² / 43.055 ft²	4.200 m² / 45.208 ft²
Offices, incl. 2nd floor	2.150 m² / 23.142 ft²	3.300 m² / 35.521 ft²	3.300 m² / 35.521 ft²
Construction time (days)	13	12	13
Press day / public days	1 / 6	1 / 6	1 / 6
Number of visitors	172.000	165.000	160.000
Facade & wall sizes, Trevira CS	3.200 m² / 34.444 ft²	2.400 m² / 25.833 ft²	3.600 m² / 38.750 ft² in various colors
	850 m² / 9.149 ft² painted MDF	1.500 m² / 16.146 ft² painted MDF	5.200 m² / 55.972 ft² Molton
Total length, system walls	550 m / 1.804 ft	1.400 m / 4.592 ft	1.200 m / 3.936 ft
			200 m² / 21.528 ft² painted MDF
Large transparencies / prints	140 m² / 400 m²	120 m² / 220 m²	140 m² / 400 m²
Carpets / floor covering	3.000 m² / 32.291 ft² velours	7.800 m² / 83.958 ft² velours in various colors by Vorwerk	8.200 m² / 88.263 ft² embossed felt carpet
	1.900 m² / 20.451 ft² stripes		360 m² / 3.866 ft² Tartan flooring, white
	1.600 m² / 17.222 ft² PVC	700 m² / 7.535 ft² PVC	200 m² / 2.153 ft² PVC
Tables & chairs, Arne Jacobson	250 / 1.000	200 / 800	200 / 800
Sprinkler Installation	2 Tanks @ 5.000 l / 1.321 US Gallons	–	–
Cables (power, light, network)	14.000 m / 45.920 ft	16.000 m / 52.480 ft	18.000 m / 59.040 ft
Exhibited products	170	140	128
Paper bags / Give-aways	10.000 / 3.000	10.000 / 3.000	10.000 / 1.500
Stand staff incl. KODAK	1.200	800	700
Kitchens	5	5	6
Meals per day	500	700	800

Model shots, working collages, and documentation photos by Atelier Brückner

Sketches by Uwe Brückner

KODAK file photos	12, 13, 71, 72, 73, 74, 75, 76, 77, 80, 81, 82, 87, 89, 146, 147, 150, 151, 152, 153, 154, 253
Uwe Dietz	17
Werner Eisele	14, 90, 158
photocase.com	23, 262
Igor Panitz	55
Walter Fogel	56, 163, 186
Dieter Leistner	78, 79, 146, 147, 148, 155, 196, 241, 242, 243, 244, 245, 246, 260
Jan Michael	83
Christian von Alvensleben	121, 134, 135, 136, 137, 204, 216, 217, 226, 227, 219, 220, 221
jangled nerves	184, 185
Monika Studer, Christoph van den Berg	194
Dietmar Henneka	218, 219, 220, 221
Andrej Barov	220, 221, 222, 223
Udo Beier	248, 249, 250, 252

The copyrights of the photographs remain with the respective photographers.
Die Copyrights der Fotos liegen bei den jeweiligen Fotografen.